# KEEPERS

## OF

# THE STORY

# KEEPERS

## OF

# THE STORY

A Memoir

MICAH SPRINGER

VITAL

PLUME

Keepers of The Story is a true account. In order to protect people and places, the author has fabricated the names of both.

For information about this title, contact the publisher:
Vital Plume
3955 Tennyson Street
Denver, CO 80212

ISBN 978-0-9987277-1-4 (paperback)
ISBN 978-0-9987277-0-7 (e-book)
ISBN 978-0-9987277-6-9 (casebound-Limited Edition)
Library of Congress Control Number: 2017947419

Printed by Thomson Shore in the United States
100% Post-Consumer Recycled Paper

Cover Art by: Jolie Springer
Cover Graphics by: Awdience Design

Senegal

gambia

Mali

Ivory
Coast Ghana

Nigeria

Cameroon

Democratic
Republic
of
Congo

Uganda Kenya

Tanzania

♡
Mitch

For you, the mystery, may you always be.

# BOOK I MIND

# BOOK II BODY

# BOOK III SPIRIT

SOME DAYS *HE* walks with me, but you will never see him. He points out fallen feathers, foxes, the smell of cedar and suspended smoke, which reminds me of sitting with him by her fire, listening to them speak a wordless language.

Today is the beginning of spring, but the unsure light and the way my breath hangs in the brisk air feel like the beginning of fall. An equinox. Equal day and night. Everything, including the light, teeters in the balance, the in-between—trees budding but the buds not yet broken open, not yet green, not yet certain on which side of life or death they belong.

Life is a love story that keeps telling itself—an unbroken prayer that invokes both the living and the dead. For they are not dead to me; he is not dead to me. He is here with us now. Do not be afraid. It is how we play. He is everywhere I ask him to be—what you would wish of an unbound, timeless lover. I am form, physical incarnate, but I feel sometimes as free as he, floating, not really here, not really there.

I know there is a story told by our senses, like seasons, cycling yet linear, winter, spring: the time on the face of a clock, chasing each moment. I smell, I see, I hear, and within that story there is another told by the mystery, the scenes looping and spiraling, breaking through the veil, far beyond senses. The truer version.

Let me keep that story. Let me tell it to you.

# BOOK I MIND

"Sell your cleverness and buy bewilderment."
—*Rumi*

# ONE | WESTERN BRAIN

*Dakar, Senegal, West Africa, 1993. Midnight.*

LEGALLY WE WERE not allowed to drink alcohol, but we could fly thousands of miles from home without a chaperone or inkling of a plan. In 1993, the only international communication happened via slow post or rotary phones, the latter found exclusively in fancy African hotels and government agencies. We avoided fancy hotels due to our budget. And who visited a government agency to call home? Kas and I intended to spend one entire year in Africa on eight dollars per day and our wits, with a phone call to our folks every three months or so. Our parents trusted us. They cherished us. Our first view of the continent gave no indication all would be well.

From the sky, Africa appeared abandoned, nobody home.

I gripped the narrow armrest, peering over my best friend Kasia's window seat, trying to ready myself for landing. How long was a year, truly? How long when you knew no one on a continent, including yourself?

I asked Kas where the "real" airport was—the one where planes from Paris usually landed. Lights flickered weakly ahead, as though electricity had just been introduced to the city of Dakar. I wanted it to hurry up and work so there would be something familiar to catch us. Adequate light did not seem too much to ask. But that may have been because I was American, about to land on what Europeans still called the Dark Continent.

"Ready?" I sighed to myself. Kas' black hair pressed the grease-streaked window. Without taking her eyes from the ground, she said, "I don't know yet." Others began preparing for the descent, which normally excited me. People hid money in more secure pockets, traded European-style clothing for bright, full-length gowns and matching head wraps,—men put on traditional Islamic caps; women applied perfume and lipstick. We just sat, hugging our small packs on the floor between our legs. Come to think of it, my calves cramped from clutching so hard.

Kas and I had nothing left to prepare. We either possessed what we needed for this adventure, or we didn't. Soon even the security of the plane would abandon us and dump us on the continent of shoddy electricity.

We lumbered down the ramp onto dewy dirt, the air so warm it slicked my skin. A fingernail arc of moon waned in the black sky, mocked by brilliance. So many stars hung above us I had to stop, upright at last, standing on African soil. *Stelliferous.* Turned out weak lighting had its benefits. My excitement did an end run around the tarmac, despite my unsure heartbeat. Kas bumped my arm and we took in a deep breath, bolstering ourselves for the leap.

To taste Africa's wildness and follow that wildness to our own unbound essence, to test our mettle against a myriad of frightening unknowns, racism, sexism, eaten by animals, who knew? With a whole year stretched out before us, we proceeded to the terminal, more than a bit wary.

Inside, water stains streaked the walls, and ceiling tiles sagged. My shoes stuck to matted carpet. I wanted so much to like it, but the rotting smell messed with my sensibilities. Kas and I stood, smiling rigidly in the immigration queue—the only white people, the only self-conscious people apparently obsessed with cleanliness. Kas merely looked ill at ease; at least her dark eyes and hair blended in, color-wise. My raggedy waves of chestnut curls capped my blue eyes and freckled nose.

I felt like a searchlight, short but unmistakable. The Senegalese rang out with sounds of reunion. French and tribal dialects bounced alive amongst them, the flash of white teeth, lipstick, excited embraces and animated eyes.

With the ink still glistening, we tucked our passports into our money belts, lugged everything outside, and reviewed *The Lonely Planet*. Kas got her headlamp out and pointed to rule number one: Beware dishonest cabbies who charge a fortune for trips into Dakar.

Something rammed the back of my legs. A man, mid-twenties, snatched my backpack—and began running. *Shit*, I thought, *we're being robbed—already!*

Kas grabbed the small backpack that I tossed at her feet and gave a vigilant nod that said, *Go get him.* I took off in my sage-green Converse, kicking up the hem of the floral dress I had worn to please the Islamic Senegalese.

*The elders grow silent when I ask* Apaya *to tell us about the beginning.* Apaya *smiles and lifts his beaded walking stick, drawing circles in the dirt, as he speaks. I move from squatting to sitting on the Earth and fall in love with the stars as the sun gives way and one by one they reveal themselves.* He *translates, waiting for his father to form the words, though his sexy grin tells me he has heard this many times.*

Apaya *says,* N'kai *created everything—the rocks, the sky, the sun and mountains, all animals. But after much time, he grew lonely. He thought to himself, let me make something I can speak through, and created three humans, all with black skin due to the fire from being made.*

*I feel the elders' eyes on me, making sure I understand.*

Apaya *continues,* N'kai *then instructed the humans to bathe and gave them a small amount of water. The first black human went to the water when it was plentiful and clear. He bathed and became white. The second man's water was a little dirty because he was not first and he became brown. The third met the water when it was very dark and almost finished. He remained black, except for his palms and soles of his feet where he tried digging for more water.*

*The elders bust out in laughter, turning their hands over to one another. One asks, as he takes a pinch of snuff from the ivory canister hanging from his neck, Which color human was the first woman?*

*Apaya ignores them and urges his son to keep translating. As he does I watch the light in his eyes compete with the glowing night sky: My father says, We are one creation and he will care for you like his own daughter, his white one, the one who went to water first. We call that* Niborr. *The first at water, where I met you.*

·

The muscled thief looked over his shoulder at my one hundred and ten pound, five-foot-three frame. *Sonofabitch!*

My heart boomed in my ears. Sweat came instantly, and desperation spun my legs. I was gaining on him but we both knew he could outrun me. The thought dropped like a rock—so where was I following him? To a gang of thieves? Some hidden alley? My year depended on that pack, and I hurtled into the unknown to save it, in the face of fear and jet-lagged disbelief.

Then I realized I was running, in Africa, running in dirt, running from modernity, and my inner athlete roared—*Goodbye, white, stifled world! I am running with the African wind in my hair.* I ran harder, not so much for the pack but from all I had just left behind. I might as well have been nude, I felt so free. Until he glanced back once more and stopped abruptly—

At a car. I caught up and wrestled the pack off him. He let go so easily, the full weight nearly toppled me and my Jane in the jungle dream.

*"Je suis le taxi. Vous allez où?"* he gasped, putting his hands in the air, claiming his innocence.

I doubled over to breathe and reconnect to my lower half, the pack now leaning between me and the trunk. A taxi? Were all African cabbies this aggressive, this innovative? I laughed, hands on my knees. Kas ran toward us, rumbling along with her large backpack and the two smaller ones, confusion on her face.

"He's a cab driver!" I said. I thought Kas would melt into the dust.

"Oh man!" She rolled her eyes, amazed at his brazen tactic. "I thought we'd been robbed. Day one. Nice run, friend."

"Thanks, but he was loping, just fast enough to keep me coming." I pushed my mop of hair back and said, "Let's negotiate a price."

I'd hoped we could settle right in on our first night, recover from the 30-hour travel day. Adventure had blindsided us. If this taxi mix-up was indicative of the year ahead, it was gonna kick my butt.

For months, we had researched in Kas' parents' basement, tracing our fingers over African map lines. We scattered books and backpacking equipment about on the hunt—then tidied the loot, hiding everything, guarding our wonderful secret, until we invited our parents to join us out for Thai food.

"Kas and I have something to tell you. We've prepared for almost a year," I began, twirling the curried noodles on my fork. I used my other hand to high-five Kas, my best friend since high school. She was nineteen, and I had just turned twenty—too young to wander Africa for a year, but old enough to master manipulation. We impressed them with details. Kas had memorized stats; I spread out a map. It was impossibly difficult for either of our parents to prohibit our well-researched dream, and so they agreed and somehow felt good about it.

After, my mom said, "I'm not sure whether to fear your fiery confidence or trust it." Kas and I rode the momentum, like cowgirls at a rodeo, while Jolie, my Spanish-eyed mother, and Duane, my charming, now sober dad, took time to figure it out.

Our thief-cabbie gave us a fair price into Dakar but chose an expensive hotel. Said he did so for our safety. The hotel cost sixty dollars; the taxi, twenty. Our budget was eight dollars per day, per person. We could have delayed the trip to Africa and saved more, but we'd agreed if we forced ourselves to travel on a shoestring, Africa would ask more of us. The hubris of youth.

Too tired to argue, we let the stubborn cabbie pick the pricy hotel, and bemoaned our budget while he drove. The only aspect of this journey we thought we could control had unraveled the first evening. Now we each had less than eight dollars a day.

Mosquitoes stung my sweaty neck and chest as the sleepy attendant greeted us. The lobby, badly deteriorated save for the marble flooring, was an enduring remnant of the former French occupation. I slapped at bugs. He rubbed his eyes, took our money, and then showed us to our room, passing an elevator which was either inoperable or only for a caliber of guest who warranted its use. Instead we climbed a narrow staircase to the third floor, jostling our backpacks between walls like pinballs between flippers. My legs were already killing me.

Kas whispered, "It's not that nice, not sixty dollars nice."

When we banged from the tight hallway into the room, a dozen spiders fled to their corners. Mosquitoes stirred into sight. Thank God for the knotted netting over our beds. We hulked our backpacks onto the foam to test whether years of humidity and use had rotted them too deeply to bear weight. I thanked Kas for bringing the makeshift sleeping sheets and pretended to unpack, desperate to lie down but unable to touch the mattress. I shuffled into the bathroom and busied myself while my mind negotiated disillusionment.

Student tourists in a developing country. Decreased daily allowance after a mere hour on our year-long trip. Lots of insects. Too many odors. Mold-speckled bedding. A rusted showerhead that no longer worked, or the water pressure lacked force to run the pipe. The hotel supplied used soap wrapped in warped tissue paper. Another faucet halfway up jutted out, supporting a bucket with a plastic cup inside. *Oh! Bucket shower.* Cockroaches did not mind that the room smelled of running sewage. I, however, felt deeply reluctant to turn on the tap.

Kas and I could laugh at most things, but we did not laugh now.

She unpacked her bag and lay clothing over her sleep sheet, smoothing it over with her hands. I watched her face spasm with a silent pep talk. No matter how she smoothed, she struggled as I did to "move in" to Senegal.

"We really did it this time, didn't we?" I left the bathroom and settled for a seat at the edge of my bed.

She raised her eyebrows and swallowed hard.

A faint sensation of panic rattled my chest. I went to bed with it. *What will our daily budget give us if ten days' worth brings this squalor?* I rifled through my pack to touch our open-ended airline tickets. We could fly home in the morning, which is all I really thought about, swaddled in scratchy mosquito netting listening to taps run and doors slam, until I heard the rat.

Lariam prevents malaria. Lariam also prevents deep sleep. We'd been taking the drug for three weeks in preparation for our trip. Kas managed, that night, to sleep through my rat attack. I managed to shake the unwelcome rodent out of the netting and onto the floor without screaming.

At four thirty a.m., the haunting call of the mosque awakened her. The first *adhan*, an Islamic call to prayer, came long before sunrise, reminding Muslims that worship of Allah was better than sleep. I felt gratitude for the company. Morning crept in, the sun's first light spreading over the floor. It brought with it a calm, a realization that we too moved like morning—day carried us, urged us on.

"Are you sure it was a rat and not a mouse? How do you think it got into your net?" Kas asked, looking well rested.

Surety was a luxury I'd surrendered mid-Atlantic. "Maybe African mice have tails as long and thick as electrical cord. I don't know, but the net came undone in the night," I said as I braided my hair. "Kas, it was heavy. It ran across my neck with its scrabbly feet. That reminds me, I should wash my neck."

Washing did little to revive me. With jet lag, under Lariam's influence, I began the day nauseated, with a muted sensation like I was living inside a down pillow. I had yet to experience malaria, and I already preferred it. No point drifting through a year in Africa wrapped in a muslin bag.

"Maybe we should donate our Lariam stash to the Red Cross or somewhere in Dakar," I said.

"Yeah, it's bad. I can't wake up. I swear if I'd heard you say there were rats, I would have tried to help. That must have been awful!" Compassion pooled in her big, dark eyes. She rolled up her sleep sheet, her undaunted momentum pacing us both.

"Okay then, I guess we aren't going home quite yet," I said and smiled.

Just like in the States, a gentle determination flexed her athletic body. I often led in our adventures, Kas a ready accomplice. But now, her endurance for leaping into the unknown made me marvel.

Our first act of defiance that morning: we ditched the expensive year's-worth of pills in the trash, which somehow seemed kinder than leaving Lariam for other travelers or locals who might drug themselves into vapid stupidity by chance.

Our hotel window framed Senegal like a moving painting. We kept the lights off and spied down into a private compound. Five tall women dressed in colorful silks and matching head wraps gathered around a large wooden vessel. They took turns striking the contents with a vertical mallet that dropped heavily—an oversized mortar and pestle. Their hands gripped the end with elbows bent, lifted the mallet toward their foreheads, and let the weighted end barrel down, crushing the contents into powder which dispersed like mist. Barefooted children dirt-danced to the rhythms of Mosque and roosters, singing together. I felt calm watching them.

Kas quietly opened the window.

The air heaved with moisture and the scent of burning charcoal and something doughy frying, which conjured our appetites. Time to search Dakar for breakfast. Before stepping from the security of the lobby, I looked at Kas. She seemed strange, dressed liked me in a long flowing dress she would never normally wear—Laura Ashley with white doily collar—and that giant black Nikon strapped across her chest.

The unpaved road in front of the hotel slept, but one block further a cacophony of vendors alarmed us with early-morning hustle. We walked, and as the distance between us and the hotel grew, so did my nervous belly. Children stopped, watched us with a blend of curiosity and amusement. Kas readied her camera, and I took off my sunglasses. The smaller boy, wearing only an oversized tank top, pointed at my blue eyes and ran crying.

I posed for a photo and Kas clicked the shutter. The older child smiled, but as Kas zoomed in, a vendor stood and began yelling. This full-force woman stormed toward us. The whole market erupted, on high alert, and came to collect payment for the photo. I had one hand on my sunglasses and one eye on escape routes. Kas started to search her pocket for change. Then a boisterous young man in torn khakis asked for his photo to be taken, right in our faces, and Kas and I clammed up tight. No money for anyone. No photos, no thanks. Still smarting from the hotel fee, Kas put the Nikon back in her pack.

But the daring guy was not through with us. He pushed his wares—sponges, baby clothing, and socks—into our chests while shouting something. I smiled, not easily, but like my face had cracked apart. The personal space we were accustomed to as Americans, even dependent upon, gave way, first psychologically, then physically. The crowd was just that, crowding us with intent. I did some fast talking, in hobbled French, convinced everyone Kas had not taken a photo. They seemed appeased. The vendors, however, taking a cue from Khaki Lad, swarmed in our direction, demanding we, the white tourists, buy something, or pose for a photo with them.

I spotted a pyramid of ripened mangoes shining like happiness. That was my beeline from trouble to breakfast. Kas and I, unwilling to draw more attention to ourselves, tiptoed fast to the fruit stand. We squeezed between women with babies snugged by cloth to their backs and men eating breakfast. All convivial chatting ceased. Someone nudged us roughly into the mango table. The seller stood up, exposing ashen, filthy trousers with holes. His impoverished state shocked me. I thought, *Too soon to be rescuing—just buy his mangoes.*

Minnie, a Senegalese exchange student in Boulder, had given us a few hundred Central African Francs (CFA). Kas opened her money belt, and we bought our first mango. Mangoes need no translation: deep orange patches, streaked by shades of green, luscious flesh within. We paid four times the price we would have back home, but the mango would feed two and the droves around us seemed a little more jovial. Some bridge had been crossed.

Kas did not speak French, the colonial language. Obviously neither of us spoke Fulani, and most Americans sucked at bargaining. I had tried bargaining in Mexico but never mastered it; I either dug in my heels, undermining a desperate salesperson, and later felt ashamed, or I paid the inflated price and everyone walked away happier. With our ridiculous budget, and because I spoke French, each potential exchange in West Africa would burden me.

I glanced around—not another white person, same as the airport.

My eyes again beheld black everywhere—muscled bodies carrying crates, tall women in silk, men with embroidered hats, children playing. The whole street pulsed with activity. Old women rested their backs on hard, broken chairs. Laughter, loudness, living. It felt too alive for me. Even me.

The neighboring stall lured us over with a packet of roasted peanuts in a newspaper cone. The mob let up a little and gave us space. I pointed and asked, *"Ça coute combien?"* The old woman, gray hair poking out from beneath her headscarf, mumbled. I held out my palm and she took a few coins. I tried the peanuts in front of everyone. They crunched, broke open, and salted my mouth better than Planters. "Kas, get another—those are really good."

Two children giggled, seeing we liked their food and did not know their money. Exhilaration moved between us. A real sharing, even if a little tense. Our first person-to-person contact. We were all so new to one another, like new sneakers trying not to get scuffed.

Two street-market ordeals behind us, we hurried to the room, where I collapsed on my filthy bed in joy. Kas spread the newspaper, dumped the peanuts, and peeled the mango. I salivated, feeling strangely proud.

"I am exhausted," Kas said, which made me glad.

"You and your lens put us straight into the fray. You're gonna have to be quick. Or pay off a lotta people. I really wanted a photo of those kids and the market, though. Can you believe how they watched us? It's just breakfast, everyone!" I licked the mango slice and ate a peanut. Could my blue-gray eyes attract any more attention? Could my introverted nature handle being a daily spectacle? "How much of Africa do you think we can see through windows?" I asked, plinking ours closed.

"Hey, everyone, we just got off the plane—" Kas lifted her long hem and feigned a plié, "I've come from America to steal your souls."

"The Amish take Senegal, with a camera and floral prints," I said, winking, adoring my friend, my adventure-hungry, photo-snapping companion. "I feel sufficiently self-conscious after all that. Maybe we should stick with take-out."

In school, I compulsively researched slavery. I was not certain I believed in reincarnation or having multiple lives, but if I had had others, I must have either been a slave, a capturer, or an owner. Some compulsions you cannot trace to a single lifetime. Sometimes, in order to know a particular quality like freedom, you have to start with its opposite. Kas and I toured the infamous Ile de Gorée, a slave port. Not all who went to Dakar visited this site, but as students of African history, we had to. According to *The Monde Diplomatique*, from the sixteenth to nineteenth century, an estimated nine-to-twelve million slaves arrived on the North and South American continents from West Africa, including those from Ile de Gorée.

The island, three kilometers from Dakar, looked like most, though no idyllic palms stretched their heads above white sand beaches. Gorée was hot, not far from the encroaching Sahara. The shore broke, throwing cold Atlantic sea against steaming rocks; the dominant landscape of Gorée dropped along steep ragged cliffs.

Kas and I wound through the labyrinth of underground holding cells in the coral-colored Maison des Esclaves. Coral was such a vibrant color—too joyous, too healthy.

The "caves" had held people until they were transported. Slaves were not allowed to stand; they'd been bound supine, backs to dirt, to one another, peeing, defecating, eating only enough to exist. I kicked the rusted shackles still staked in red Earth, the actual chains that had held people—not museum props, not make-believe. Shackles for ankles, wrists, and necks, empty of bodies now but full of frightening impressions. Not enough space between the shackles for a small human, let alone a full-grown adult. People lined in rows, head to feet and parallel. When someone became sick and died—surely the result of being broken in spirit as well as body—the rotting body remained tethered to the line, touching people on either side, unless the captors had a new human to restrain. From cave to ship, the hopelessness grew. The end-to-end body formation worsened in the ship's hull, people now stacked on top as well as side to side.

I know other tourists walked with us, but I cannot remember them. Just the hint of restriction in this underground cave summoned a primal impulse to flee, to run. Fear and anger overwhelmed me.

Gorée was home to ghosts. Distressed voices echoed—mothers,

children, men. I could hear terrified breathing in the cave air. Bodies resisting, pulling, until their fight gave in, some people to death and some to an incomprehensible journey worse than death. Centuries later, I still felt them. One human life filled with grace or despair, either way, forced a ripple through us all, for always, it seemed. This place could never come clean.

*I will miss our village, I tell him.*

*We make love once more in the squalid Nairobi hotel but even that is painful. I do not know how to be this tender and still breathe, my nerves exposed to a fever that threatens to burn them numb. I try to be strong. I sing to him with my shaky voice, all our songs. Each time I believe I am really leaving Africa, I touch our necklace, and it tethers me back.*

*He says every forest has its sound, try to remember those sounds, those birds and special wind. He smiles, Or the way I speak with my mother in the early morning.*

*I break. How did he know that one image meant so much—a ritual, him with his back to me, an exposed shoulder, so sturdy and valiant, the first touch of morning light, and his mother making chai at the banked fire. I thought I'd been so stealthy, loving that image, their indescribable rhythm, in private.*

*At the airport, he stands next to me, beaded strands running across his naked chest, his red half-sheet exposing his knees. He holds a wooden bludgeon, his* rungu, *in his left hand. From the threat of lions, yes, but his* rungu *offers scant protection for what awaits us. Leather bands wrap his biceps like gifts to be opened. I know those gifts. The gap in his bottom teeth, I push my index finger into it tenderly and push downward, hoping to feel connected, to feel it stick. He taps my finger, removes it from his mouth and draws me near.*

*I weep and weep and he holds me.*

*His hands coil in the chained trusses of my African-sunned hair. What a strange and otherworldly sight we are, me in my straight-seamed clothing, him in his nomadic grit.*

*Remember Micah, every forest has its sound. You're going back to yours.*

*If I lean in to smell his neck, I smell the village. It lives on his skin, no matter how many showers he takes or soaps he uses. I breathe deeply and try to lock his scent into some vault within, somewhere it can never escape. Keep it safe, this reason to live. Keep it safe, this feeling that obliterates all ugliness and human depravity.*

*I don't know how but I pull my body away, free his hands from my hair, and turn from the face, the body I sense as well as my own. Magnetic, dense draw back. I look at least ten stinging times.*

*Then it is finished. The long airport corridor. That last image, him standing in the most inappropriate setting of modernity, the noise and straight lines, the false light—everything he is not.*
*A strange whimper escapes my throat.*
*The woman in stark blue with red neckerchief takes my ticket.*
*I stifle my panic. I already miss our village—*

Kas and I said nothing on Gorée. During the minutes we strayed from the sun, my bare arms prickled with chill and my bones shook with the worst of my humanness. I wanted to believe I could never have done it, but somehow that no longer mattered. Kas and I looked at each other. We were crying.

I touched the cold cave walls. Enslavement made its way in me.

Our veins and arteries enslave us—tightening like knots in twine, our careful skins an impassable barricade. I breathed into that coral darkness and knew I was bound first, as we all are, by this physical body of bone and sinew. And second, by convention. Training and schooling and ideas shackled me, not iron. Extreme self-consciousness restricted me, not cuffs—a world of ought and should, a learned social conditioning. The second enslavement governed in such gentle nuance, we rarely acknowledged it. We acquiesced. We even believed we were free. But we were all held—strangled from the inside out, and I had come to Africa to loosen that grip.

On the ferry back to Dakar, our moods could have sunk the boat with solemnity. The passengers tried, as I did, to leave shame on the Gorée shore. I watched the horizon, serene and predictable, and considered freedom, agony, repression and culpability. I was a free-country national, American-born, from the land of opportunity. The land slaves had delivered to riches. Could I be any freer? But ethereal layers of ghost slave bodies lay stacked on Gorée.

I did not and could not feel free.

I knew every human being desired freedom. I knew I needed it like air, like sun and love and food. Did they desire it as much as I? I burned with longing and felt suddenly afraid of this passionate need.

The wake of waves riding out from the ferry crested white and then dissolved.

How to love this life and not let it break your heart irreparably? Did we have to wait for death to feel truly free?

Spirits. Spirits no longer suffered; spirits no longer felt the brokenness, nor the restriction. They were free. But even to the most faithful believer, spirit was thinner than smoke. From this dense skin bag of intestines and brain, how could I ever feel that free?

I wanted *that*.

I held the hurt. I counted waves.

An agonizing distance lay between me and freedom. My complaint did not belong in the same universe with the Gorée slaves' suffering, but there it was, and me on that noisy, weighted ferry, wriggling from inherited chains of relative privilege. To belong to this world, it seemed, we traded true freedom for being.

# Two | CULTURE SHOCKED

OKAY, WE KNEW of *one* family on the entire African continent. Minnie, the exchange student from Senegal who gave us local money, had insisted on introducing us to this family. They lived in the Gambia, which shared a border with Senegal. That was all we knew. Our one and only plan was to visit this random Minnie-endorsed family.

"*Toubab!*"

Kas and I waited with others for the ferry to Banjul, Gambia, standing midway down a concrete pier line, where we first heard children scream, "*Toubab!*" They repeated it. We then heard it everywhere—this word for *white person*—in Wolof. People mumbled *toubab* this and *toubab* that. It was strange to be talked about as if we were not there—too green to engage in either language or culture. Kas and I stood close in the ambling crowd like art exhibits: observed, commented on, but incapable of contact, of intimacy. We relied on smiling until our cheeks hurt and our teeth dried. People smiled back, but they still said, "*Toubab.*" Standing with our bulging backpacks and long shapeless dresses, we seemed like such a big deal— wilting, white daisies coming to terms with the fact they'd sacrificed their pots and didn't yet have a replacement. Would we ever matter to Africans?

In Banjul, Gambia's capital, we phoned Pa Sinyani to request directions. He said to take a taxi—it was not far, about ten minutes. We did not spend *Dalasi* on a taxi. We walked through the potholed streets that were so narrow our wide packs tilted to dodge swerving vehicles. Diesel fuel spurted tufts of black that hung in the air and filled our lungs. Cars honked. It took an hour to finally round the dirt road into the family compound.

Dirt and diesel and foot travel delivered me to my mom's pet name for my sister and me—"ragamuffins." I felt ragamuffin all over when we arrived. Black dust covered our hands and feet and stuffed our nostrils. Filth in Eden. The Sinyani's gardens held so much color and beauty they stunned us: flowering bougainvillea draped the white stucco walls, mango and magnolia trees shaded the clean driveway, smelling sweet. Blossoms sprinkled the ground.

Pa's wife greeted us. She was tall, her height exaggerated by her blue head wrap and matching dupioni silk gown. "Oh, you are exhausted," she said as she looked disagreeably over our bodies and turned to call for help, moving like a runway model with her shining complexion, large lips, and sheet-white teeth. Two older children came quickly from play and grabbed the packs.

Pa's wife showed us to the bathroom first—two clean, narrow adjacent rooms just wide enough to stand in. Both were tiled in white from floor to ceiling without a single decoration—one for showering, the other a toilet. Our room had two beds with mosquito netting hanging like a canopy, and a couple of windows spilled sunlight that reflected the polished concrete flooring. A watercolor painting of hibiscus flowers and palm trees hung next to one. I parted the islet curtain to peek out. Three goats tied to a post wriggled and bleated.

Kas towel-dried her hair and whispered, "This place is amazing. I hope we can stay for a week. That warm bucket shower was great."

"Yeah, I wonder if it's always like this. Busy place. There are people everywhere—" I peeked again. A group of ten adolescents tossed the ball. "They have a lot of kids."

Someone tapped lightly on the door. "Yes, come in," I said, not sure if it was the ball outside I heard. The door did not budge. Kas opened it, and a timid boy said, "Please come and meet the family," then turned and ran down the hall.

The games and chaos! Children played near their nannies. Adults hogged printed velour sofas. Grandfathers and grandmothers, mothers and fathers, aunts and uncles and friends of the family chatted. And us. Thirty or more people fit easily into the large house. Africans do not wash their hands as obsessively as we do, and I have a clean-hand fetish. My hand soon shone with the grease of multiple introductions. This was the first time I had been around Muslim people. I wanted to make a good impression of me and my country.

I asked one of the women, "Is this common that the family spends time together? This is a big family!"

She said in heavily accented English, "Yes, we are celebrating the Tabaski."

The Tabaski—"Feast of Sacrifice" in Wolof—marked the end of Ramadan with the offering of goats (hence the three plump goats tied to a post) and a colossal feast known elsewhere as Eid-al-Adha. In West Africa every family, even the most penurious, saved for a goat.

The Sinyanis' jubilation sharpened the dread that Kas and I felt; eventually we would have to explain our strict vegetarian diet. Of course, we'd landed on the continent just in time for the mass slaughter.

Growing up in the mountains, my sister Desi and I had twelve Barred Rock chickens. My mom thought we should have responsibilities—chores, as we called them in rural Colorado.

"Micah, we keep the chickens for their eggs, but eventually the chickens will be food for us. Try not to get attached. I know you love animals," she cautioned while washing dishes.

I was eight and attached to all animals, domestic and wild. Each day we gathered the eggs from underneath the brooding hens, braving their pecks to our small hands. I befriended one. I coaxed her, sang to her, held her on my lap, and petted her triangle head as she looked up sideways. Desi and I took turns. The others we ignored as our mom advised, but Henrietta was our friend and came when called.

My mom's husband—who was not our father—told us that while my mom was working, he was going to butcher a chicken for dinner. I wanted to be strong. I agreed but told him not to kill Henrietta. Adults doubt children when they say they know one chicken from another. This man, oblivious to subtleties, was no different. He said, "Of course."

Desi and I put on our wool sweaters and mud boots and climbed the big hill that overlooked the property. We could not watch, but we could not continue playing either, torn between curiosity and fear. It was the first time we had ever killed anything as a family. He entered the henhouse, came out within minutes, and put a docile chicken on the round stump.

Without a head, it is true, they run. We screamed from the top of the hill, "No! No! No!" The hen stopped running. He scrambled to grab her headless body.

"Desi, don't worry. It's not Henrietta. He promised us." I consoled my little sister who buried her tearful face into my side. She cried so much the wool smelled like wet dog.

He left the chicken yard. Desi and I ran down. We searched for our friend. Stunned still—we could not find her. I searched around the hay bales, in the coop, everywhere. Desi's body began to tremble with little-girl rage. Henrietta was no more.

That day, Desi and I swore off eating people's pets.

When my mom returned from work, she did her best to reassure us. "We will never kill our chickens again. I promise." She glared red at her husband.

Scarred by betrayal, it was too late for me. I could no longer risk it, knowing the chickens' faces, watching their heads tilt, marveling at their unique feather patterns. I stopped singing special songs to the Barred Rocks; they just laid eggs now.

Henrietta's frozen, unfeathered body remained in our freezer for years, our family too guilty to eat her or waste what we had taken.

*The sun is hot, the dry grass breaks under our lightest step. Somewhere nearby lions are sleeping and young boys water and graze the livestock. The life of a herder so silently still, so full of the present's indescribable voice and rhythm. This life of solitude fascinates me. We can only share so many stories with those we have known all our lives, but our lives in silence together, those open to eternity. This truly is not my sky.*

*I never wear sunscreen anymore, my skin brown from all the exposure, Black Irish/Spanish genes capable of tanning—more golden than red. Africa would be a miserable journey otherwise, especially the village. No trees but one. So little time indoors.*

*Ploote with his afro halo walks behind with Kas, describing Lokop life and herding. I walk just in front of my lover, considering his life. The village demands he serve it, elders come to the hut asking for gifts, blessings, sometimes advice, women come for his counsel, or for his assistance with their children. He is reliable and wise. I treasure this about him, come to depend upon it, and am selfishly envious when he is not focused on me.*

*A thigh-high boulder blocks our path. I put my foot on it and lift my* shuka—*the Swahili printed-cotton skirt many African women wear— arching my back. I show him my bare butt and giggle when he grabs my waist from behind and kisses the back of my neck. His other hand moves over my breast. I taught him all of this, the kissing and the flirtation. He presses into my exposed skin holding the ends of my* shuka *in one hand and pulls my body tightly to him. His skin is so soft, the perfect temperature—a little cool in this sharp heat.*

Nanyorai, *are you teasing with me? He asks with a low, quiet voice.*

*I turn to kiss him instead of answering. His mouth tastes clean and sweet. I cannot imagine him ever being ill. He embodies health—a robust chemistry, the constitution of the most perfect stars. I like the smell of sweat when it's right. His smell is like charred cedar and fat. I want that smell on me.*

*We catch up to Kas and Ploote and he tells us the plan. The warriors need to eat so we will kill a goat and cook the meat in the bush. But we must not tell the village that we have eaten together. This is taboo.*

*I get the impression the warriors have cheated before. When we are alone again, I interrupt the silence with my unease.*

*I say, I'm nervous about watching the goat die. Can you help me to feel better?*

*He does not respond immediately which leads me to wonder.*

*The breeze threads through my hair and brushes my cheek, so aware, like breath. I think it is preparing to take back one of its own, all our breath belongs to the breeze.*

*Finally, he says, It is normal for you to feel this way. It is not your way* of living. *And it is normal for me to eat meat. I would have nothing to eat if I did not. How would I know you and care for you if I was too thin, like a boy?* I smile and nod in agreement, wringing my hands on my shuka, my stomach tight. I look at my hands. They so rarely know water here, always dirty, always touching grass, animals, ash, his hands.

*Micah, we do not fear death in Lokop. Our goats do not fear death. I will kill that goat knowing that it allows me to live longer. This is the most respect I can give to it. Just as I have used my life to make sure that goat lives longer, I protect it until I need it. If you don't want to watch I won't be angry. We have to know how to stay comfortable, you and me—then we are good together.*

He calls to his two young brothers, the shepherds in the bush. They come quickly hearing his voice, wiping their eyes of nap sleep, having found a place to rest in a nearby thicket. They have not yet heard the news of his homecoming nor that he brought company. They meander through the traditional greeting. Neither looks at Kas nor me. Two strange white girls wandering their land, entirely out of place, and they do not react at all. They look only at their brother and wait for formal introduction. Their eyes have ingrained patience, respect for right timing. Shepherd rhythm. Shepherd wisdom. It must be this. When they are finally invited they greet us.

Sopila is older, Liwan has the same round face as my lover. They help him choose the goat, a beautiful brown and white quilt-patch male. Four warriors come from the bush to slaughter it. I am saying little worried prayers; I don't frequent churches, but for animals I have always been able to pray.

He says, *Micah are you ready? Maybe you need to take a break with Kas behind those trees.*

I shake my head timidly and say, *No it's okay. Kas looks ready.* She has her camera. I step back but stay near enough to watch.

Warriors pile fresh boughs and leaves which they gather from the surrounding bush. My lover flips the goat on its side on the mounded foliage, then kneels on its lungs as he holds its muzzle in his hand and suffocates its breath. There is a brief struggle, a shaking resistance of the body and then stillness, and then breeze. He fixes his gaze on the goat's face, the living and the dead together in a continuous cycle, a oneness. The goat surrenders his final exhalation into my lover's hands.

He makes sure the goat is dead, checking for a pulse. Then he slits open *the goat's throat. The blood pools from the jugular into a trapping bowl made from the pulled skin. My lover kneels, puts his mouth to the bowl and slurps the warm blood. He stands and looks at me with deep red coloring outside the natural lines of his lips. The others follow and take turns drinking until all the blood is finished.*

*We wait for some moments in silence. No one speaks, though they are moving about, preparing the fire. Kas looks white, like me. The light of the sun streams in through tree leaves flashing its traces on our bodies and the goat's body. There is little trauma. No violence. I imagine allowing my lover to take my last breath, to kneel on my lungs and stare at me with his devotion. Why is this love I feel so closely related to death? It feels important like watching a birth.*

*I consider trying the meat but I have no hunger.*

*The warriors sit on boulders and eat goat. He keeps his commitment to his father and drinks only blood. They make us laugh with their light-hearted humor. They are jovial and joking in the spirit of celebration. We are jovial too. The goat's body—the center of us.*

The Sinyanis' goats bleated outside our window, devouring a feast of greens and grasses. Kas and I wandered the compound, not certain what to do with our clean selves. Kas' bright complexion finally gleamed, the grime now banished to the diesel-riddled road. People went about their business of play or preparation and left us to amusement. Walking in the garden, we neared the entrance of the house. Three elegantly dressed women sat on tree stumps in a stuccoed courtyard, their clothing too rich for such rough chairs. Their slender black fingers picked stones from jasmine rice and flicked them to the ground. I admired the tightly-woven plates they held on their laps, so well-used, still colorful. They tossed the rice into the air, softly blew the hulls, and re-caught the rice. The rhythm repeated. The bright silks flowed, like easy conversation.

"Kas, don't you think they're beautiful, the way they sit together and do things? They always dress so nicely," I said without taking my eyes from the scene.

One woman set down her plate and called for us to join. She gave

Kas her stump and disappeared in search of another. We each received a pile of rice. They showed me how to distinguish between rice and stones and use my fingernail to scoop out debris. They taught Kas to blow hulls using a steady stream of breath, not too forceful. We worked and felt useful, eavesdropping on the mix of heavily-accented English and Wolof. My printed cotton skirt hung next to the peacock blue silk of a young woman whose laugh reminded me of waterfalls. The women's eyes flashed with friendship.

Kas and I had time to venture from country to country, sample myriad African cultures. It appealed less to me suddenly. I felt and wanted to feel part of something. I wanted to sort the stones in jasmine rice, world without end.


Two bowls sat on the table while Kas and I sat down to our first meal. The Sinyanis had prepared slimy fish soup with the rice we had cleaned. Neither one of us had eaten fish for years, but it was better than goat. People passed by, glancing in to see if we enjoyed the meal.

I tried the rice. Kas sipped the broth. Her grimace said it all.

"We'll have the talk and tell them we don't eat fish either, I guess." I shrugged my shoulders, shame riding them. I had no desire to seem ungrateful to our hosts. And I knew that "we" meant I would do the talking, even though the Gambia was English-speaking.

I stuffed myself with three cups of rice while I squished a quarter of the oblong body, swimming it around the bowl, decimating the fish against the sides. The skin, slime, and eyes glistened—reflecting my regret in their sheen. When we had sat for long enough, we excused ourselves for bed.


The morning broadcast woke us via speakers mounted on the side of the mosque. Men walked outside the compound, appearing half asleep, the devotion to Allah greater than mine to any God.

Kas said excitedly, "Let's see what's for breakfast."

We crept down the hallway into the dining/living area. Someone stirred. Lights cast faint sunrays from the kitchen. On the table were two place settings and a vase of flowers waiting like hospitality defined. The tiny hardworking woman who helped clean and cook had already prepared our breakfast. She saw us and drew open curtains to the growing light.

Black tea steeped in a clay pot. A box of Weetabix cereal waited in the center next to a sweating pitcher of cold milk and one of rose-colored juice. We wolfed down the cereal and guava juice and were about to say thank you, when the woman, who was thin enough to be a child but as industrious as an adult, brought out a large steamer full of rice. What would we eat with rice for breakfast? She set another bowl in front of me. Before I removed the lid, I smelled it—the remaining three-quarters of my fish. My belly turned away. Kas' fish arrived.

We forced down a couple of bites but not before pulverizing the chum with our forks. I drank my body weight in guava juice to kill the taste, but the taste lingered. Our parents had taught us to be conscientious guests—we had, since being at the Sinyanis', offered to help clean, tidied up our rooms, preserved the family's routine. Good guests or no, visiting our first African-Islamic family or not, the rest of this fish was not going down.

"I can't do it. I'm gagging." Kas pushed her plate away.

We left for the beach with fish and guilt mingling in our mouths.


"I wonder if they miss us?" Kas said as she rubbed the sole of one sandy foot against the other. "We'll have to wait at least another month before any news from home."

"I think time is moving slower for us. We've been gone a little over a week, but it feels like months."

"Yeah. A lot has happened already … and nothing!" We giggled at doing nothing. No one from America was supposed to do nothing for a year. Not at any age.

An overcast sky filled in the gray Atlantic shoreline, blurring sky and shore into each other. Nearly time for lunch. Time to return to the Sinyanis' and reluctantly admit we were *strict* vegetarian. I readied myself trying to find the simplest, kindest way to refuse to eat more chum.

Near the compound, we passed a row of one-room businesses, the garage-style doors rolled back so we could see in. Most appeared to be tailors. We stopped at an older man easing a pair of pants under the needle on a push-pedal machine.

"Hey, let's get clothing made. African fabric. I'm tired of switching between this dress and the other one," Kas said determinedly.

The tin-box sewing room brightened with our patronage. The tailor told us to fetch fabric, which we could buy a few blocks down, and reminded us it was a good time for new garments with the Tabaski and all. Just like that, we were not "doing nothing" anymore. We made arrangements to pick up our skirts the following day.

No one had introduced us to Pa. I saw him from the window—short, with a round face, no eyebrows, which ironically exaggerated his lack of expression. He was an upstanding member of the community, of far-reaching consequence.

"Excuse me, Pa?" I said. I approached him. He sat peering over his glasses at me, reading a journal, dressed in pleated trousers and a plain, but high-quality Islamic button-down shirt. He flashed his eyes up, but did not open his mouth.

"We didn't realize we would be arriving for the Tabaski, or we would have waited to visit. It must be difficult having guests when there is a celebration?"

I paused for his reply, but he gave none.

"Kas and I don't eat meat or fish. We're, uh, vegetarian. We really only eat vegetables—oh, and your rice is delicious." Nothing from Pa. I slapped my hands against the Laura Ashley fading flower print. "Thank you for inviting us." My intonation rose a little like a plea.

His face stiffened. When I turned to walk back to our room, he stayed silent.

"How'd it go?" Kas asked, looking up from her book.

"I don't know. He didn't say anything. I used my best charm. Maybe I offended him by speaking to him? I'm not sure. I'll tell someone that we're staying in—that we're tired."

She halfway smiled. The fish, the waiting goats had taken their toll.

"I'm sure Pa can't wait for our next enthralling conversation."

More than fifty people gathered at Pa's home. Inside, outside, laughing and singing. The traditional tinny-sounding music started to pulse. I avoided going out for fear of seeing the slaughter, well, for fear of interaction, which pained me after my blissful hour sorting rice.

Outside our window, people floated in silk that shimmered from the light of the festive lanterns hung about the compound. Through the eyelet lace curtains, I watched our first African celebration, which was so loud we never heard the cry of Abraham's sacrificial goats. Everyone seemed so comfortable, so ripe with participation, so unlike me.

I once took a personality test and came out an ambivert: 50/50 introvert-extrovert. I considered this, as I settled into my canopied cocoon. *I'll spend more time with people tomorrow. Tonight I'm tired and need the rest*, I thought, gritting my soul's hard little teeth. My desire to connect could bring me all the way to Gambia but not beyond the walls of my room. *Truth is, I don't know how to belong.* Or maybe I wasn't yet desperate enough, still too close to my own culture in time and memory.

The following morning, we tried to make amends but for what exactly we were not sure. Pa's household man washed the goat's blood from the driveway with buckets of water while Pa stared into the distance, savoring the detritus of festival—paper lanterns, colorful confetti littering the ground, and the quietness. Kas came with me this time.

"Pa, thank you and your family for this beautiful opportunity. Kas and I have never been to Africa, nor experienced anything like the Tabaski."

As I tried to move into his line of sight, he rotated and shifted his gaze. I lost ground with each footing, so I settled on looking at what he looked at, which seemed reasonable, and certainly grounded. I wanted to convince Pa that we were good people interested in his culture. This was true, but we'd failed a giant test. No party, no shared holiday celebration, no sacred meat. I stood next to Kas, wrestling this moment with its awkward emotions, staring at our feet.

"Yes, okay. You must tell your parents you are safe," Pa said coldly. This was all he needed—for us to assure our parents that he had done his job. Kas and I stepped back, dismissed. Now we really were on our own (party shirkers!) with no other contacts, and the continent seemed suddenly enormous.

At the end of the fourth day we said farewell to the Sinyani household. We left them with gifts, took the ferry from Banjul back to Senegal, and found an expensive hotel in Dakar with much-needed privacy. We did, however, pick up our outfits from the tailor before leaving, and now we had African-style clothes. The colorful wax fabric sparkled, tropical birds and flowers lit in the sun. I even had a head wrap made but still felt too self-conscious to wear it.

On the ferry back, I sought Kas' take on things. "That whole thing was weird, wasn't it?" I asked. "I'm not sure what to think yet."

"Yeah. Culture shock—"

"Ours or theirs?"

"Theirs. Our culture shocked theirs."

I laughed. "I'm sorry, Kas. I fucked up the only relationship we had on the entire continent, chasing Pa around his driveway."

We bent over laughing, holding the ferry railing and our bellies.

"No more fish soup!" Kas said.

"No more slaughter party!" I countered. We might never be invited to see the inside of another family's home.

"How American! How un-Islamic!" Kas' anthropology degree shook its finger at us, while surprise blackened her already thick eyebrows.

I touched where they wrinkled, right between her eyes. "Maybe Pa had eyebrow envy?"

She laughed, a mighty dose of spirited glee, and we released the rift we'd caused with the Sinyani household. We tucked our African-style dresses between our knees in the hot wind. I watched the out-ward-fanning waves of the ferry's engine.

I later asked a kind Islamic man how I had gone wrong with Pa. He said, "As a sign of respect, women avoid eye contact with men. Even their own husbands. They never begin a conversation. They wait, sometimes forever." He smiled thinly.

I thought of Henrietta, my Barred Rock chicken. I don't know why. Henrietta before the chopping block—the innocence with which she came when called.

# THREE | NOMADIC FREEDOM

SOAKED COLD, KAS and I navigated puddles left by unexpected rains and purchased two second-class train tickets from Dakar to Bamako, Mali. Mali's sands shimmered with Saharan heat in the guidebook photos. Kas' backpack ballooned larger under the rain tarp cover, which made her seem small, shrinking before the overcast background. But I knew better. I suddenly felt proud of us. We were actually doing this. About one month into our African experience, two single Boulder, Colorado, college sophomores were headed to Mali without a plan and with no one to guide us.

"I have everything we'll need as far as basic first aid," Kas said, pointing to the pile on the carpet, her jet-black hair fanning her shoulder. She turned toward the ace bandages, braces, medications, and ointments. Her father was a doctor, so disease and injury were her departments. My mom wanted consistent communication, so I arranged post-restante in all countries we would visit, which was a system by which the postal service would hold mail for travelers expected to arrive. I charted a route across the continent of countries. We would visit about thirteen in all.

Before leaving America, we'd severed our intimate relationships.

Kas and I wanted to be available for any sorts of adventure. If our intentions were otherwise—say, of the missionary order—we might have left the heavy, cold wax, for removing hair from our legs, under-arms, and bikini lines, at home.

Kas' father insisted we get *all* inoculations. Fifteen vaccines assumedly prepared us for fevers, worms, parasites, and life-threatening water- and airborne diseases. For tsetse flies, mosquitoes, and their respective bites, we brought long-sleeved shirts and planned to take tablets. No guarantees. There were strange rules, like we could only ever swim in salt water. The salt killed bilharzia, a freshwater parasite that crawled into the opening of your penis or vagina to lay eggs in your liver, gradually killing you. I don't know why, but I liked the effect this particular parasite had on people I told.

I had known Kas since boarding school. We attended the presti-gious though rugged Colorado Rocky Mountain School (CRMS) in Carbondale. I met her on orientation day our sophomore year, jumping on a dorm- mate's bed, laughing wildly, hair flying across her pretty face. I watched her bouncing, zigzagging body and had this sense I needed to let go. Our friendship was the first key to my freedom.

The professors encouraged us, even needled us, to claim full citi-zenship on the planet. I will never forget my philosophy teacher, Mark Clark, saying, as he leaned across the table with glacial-blue eyes, "I want your brains to hurt from critical thinking." Our geopolitical teacher, A. O. Forbes, opened life in African villages to us right along with the harmful effects of colonialism. Dove-tailed provocation for African adventure travel, no?

Kas and I created mischief, played soccer, liked nature and physical labor, drank lavish amounts of hot chocolate, and covered for each other. I was a day student, but the intense curriculum helped justify sleeping in Kas' dorm. Her futon couch-by-day was often my bed-by-night. I placed a pair of shoes outside to convince the dorm head I was asleep, but mostly I was dashing commando-style across the soccer field in my other shoes, heading to my boyfriend's room.

"Kas," I said while lying on her futon, "let's go to Africa, backpack-ing." She was a little taller than me but had the same athletic build. Her fair, perfect skin and large, dark eyes with elephant lashes made girls envious and boys crazy. CRMS taught us how to travel light, be independent, and remain curious—to be good citizens.

Kas said, "Why not?" This quick *yes* was more her modus operandi than a response to anything in particular. I loved it. Our quest for adventure was equal, the only difference being I longed to run to Africa, and Kas ran away from anything dull. We waited until college to go, but the seeds sowed themselves into our fertile minds at CRMS.

We both had a fierce work ethic—another gift of that school—a love of language and culture, which our political science and anthropology degrees fostered. I spoke French. We had good health. Besides the obvious concerns we had about Africa—safety, disease and distance—Kas was Jewish, and we were heading deep into Islam. I admit that added texture to my dreams. It added a dangerous slippage, a slippery slope to we knew not what.

*Fear step aside,* her quick *yes* said.

And here we were, three years later, packing the largest first-aid kit on the continent. This go-for-it attitude was my mask for something far more authentic. I had no words, but the sensation lived in me. A desire to experience freedom fueled my travel to Africa—freedom from parents, religion, white-world institutions, social conditioning, expectations of myself. I had to know sustaining freedom—not the fleeting kind that drugs, sex, or exercise could provide. I already had that. I wanted the enduring knowledge of self that was as expansive as I imagined that continent to be. I wanted wild, awakened Africa. I wanted God—to make sure God was free. How do you explain that, when you are twenty, to anyone?

I hoped to dump the light-skinned, bearded man who judged our every move. And he was a man, a God-man. He who was handed to me sideways despite my parents' liberal take on spirit. Though I wasn't raised with significant religious tethers, my interpretation of God still hung on the cross, replaying those dry hymns I heard only once. He seeped in. But I was too young to understand that to experience existential freedom, something or someone had to unfasten the stricture of my cultural/religious/gender-biased conditioning. And this was gonna hurt.

*He says, Micah, you ready to meet my father and other village elders? Kas the Lokop council want to meet you. Are you ready Kas?*

*I think to myself, We have to get this over with. The whole village is abuzz with our visit. The elders will feel slighted not to be introduced. Their job is to welcome anyone staying for more than a few nights, formally, especially white girls.*

*But I have a thing with fathers. With my own father. We are still finding our way, rekindled after time apart. The man used his sense of responsibility to pull strangers out of snowbanks in a rusted old Jeep but left his own daughters waiting for him at the Greyhound bus station at Christmas—in velvet dresses and patent leather shoes, unwrinkled and unscuffed, even after hours on the bus ride to see him. My big-hearted, alcoholic dad affected both of us plenty without even knowing he could. I disowned him when I was twelve and he came back to us sober when I was sixteen. It still hurts to say but it felt easier being out of relationship to him than in. Twelve-year-old Lokop girls do not disown their fathers no matter how much the men drink. I have never been one for reining in temperament. Is it me or them I distrust?*

*Yes, let's go. Of course I will meet your father, I say.*

*Old hurt. Apprehension. Insincere response. Every relationship with men, especially fathers, asks me to heal, to keep healing until I am whole. Salt in the old wound stinging.*

*We walk together, Kas and I trailing him. Just beyond the* manyatta— *the Lokop word for village—a clearing of dirt worn down. The elders convene here, tell stories, settle disputes, sleep and play under the shade of a nearby acacia tree.*

*They are squatting in a circle with an opening, pulling us in. Some have white, coarse stubble on their chins and heads, the hair hardened by years of shaving with a knife. Some wear tattered felt and straw hats, all have single wool blankets diagonally draped like cloaks. Their ear lobes stretch, amber beads dangle from metal loops. These elders are still decorated with one strand of necklace, relics from their youthful warrior days. They sit on wooden stools, which by night or even noon, become pillows.*

*We hover at the edge of the circle. A tall man with high cheekbones wearing a green felt hat calls to us.* Ditai.

*The others chuckle. I think we are being ridiculed and swallow hard.*

*My lover tries to assuage me, sensing my defensiveness. He says, My father has greeted you in the traditional Lokop manner. He has called you his daughters.*

*I soften, still wary of this circle of men despite my best intentions.*

*How do we respond when he calls to us like that? I ask.*

*It is obvious the elders are waiting.*

*Call him* Apaya, *he says. It means father.*

*My love urges me to trust. Both Kas and I say back in unison,* Apaya. *Again laughter.*

*His father speaks to him. I feel stiff, afraid, standing with a wound, so exposed.*

*Say it like a small girl, not a woman, he instructs.*

*I see the sincerity of his desire. They all wait for us to relinquish the defensive, distrusting American woman voice. I cannot comprehend at first. How can you know clearly your own face without a mirror?*

*Seeing my confusion, he helps. He lovingly mimics a young girl's voice with high-pitched intonation.* Apaya?

*The greeting is more than a greeting. I begin to understand. It is a plea. Will you love me, protect me, see me? The biology echoes like a spiral among us, between us. The elders nod earnestly in approval and encouragement. No laughter this time, our turn.*

*Kas and I sing out like young girls, suspending years of justified fears and sadness.*

Apaya?

*Their low, resonant bellow immediately follows. In unison, they call as if from the sky,* Ditai!

*I feel my body tremble, an emotional earthquake. I begin to fall, my legs suddenly weak, unevenly weighted, not under me. He catches me. An unconscious desire to surrender my body's weight to the ground presses deep. Surrender. What an overwhelming gift when this relationship is intact. Where had my father been? How could we each have let go? No one to catch the other.*

*I feel so small, aware, now, not by thought, but by weight. The elders seem like giants towering over Kas and me with protection and guidance, though they remain seated.*

*I have to try it again. Make sure it is still real.*

*Apaya! I sing out to the group and as dependable as sunrise they respond.
Ditai!*

*I lift my heels and sway a little with joy. Their response beckons through
my doubts, disappointments, and even invisibility—like hollers in a canyon
bouncing off generations of unrequited yearning. The essential relationship,
daughter and father, is for me so much truer, so suddenly true.*

*From this day forward I practice wherever I can, calling out to all
village Apayas. Your daughter is here. Here I am. I am called into your
circle to forgive.*

*Forgive me Fathers.*
*Forgive me Papa.*
*Simple, sacred forgiveness.*

The train was an iron-rusted relic running from another, borrowed
time. People shoved and crowded around the cars' narrow entrance.
No courtesy, no gender chivalry—we all pushed.

"That's it, Kas. Dig in a little deeper. We can do this," I said beside
her as she nuzzled her elbow into a fat woman's ribs. In the less expensive, fewer vacancies, second-class line, weight mattered. The woman
wriggled her large body past us. Our politeness would be left at the
station, as well as our bodies, if we did not learn this game. People
carried food, boxes, chickens, many holding their children's hands, a
distinct advantage for blocking our entry. It wasn't personal.

Kas scrambled for a seat—one rigid vinyl-clad bench with no
partitions, discolored foam poking through in places. She put her
backpack on a steel rack above and turned for mine. We stood in the
aisle thinking we had time to get situated when a man slid past us
and stole the window bench. I sat down in a hurry next to him and
said, "Kas, you better get in here." A young, chubby guy filled the aisle,
eyeing Kas' seat. She jumped in.

I cramped my inner thighs to keep from touching "Window
Stealer's" leg. He turned toward the view. I smiled at the younger
man, trying to assure him his size was not a problem—there would
be plenty of space for him—somewhere else. He took my smile as

an invitation and slid in next to Kas, squishing the breath out of any remaining space. *Four* to a seat? Across the desert?

When I quit bitching inwardly about our lack of room, I lifted my head to black eyes fixed on me from across the aisle, steadily penetrating. He pinned me in place; was I an exotic butterfly or a frog sprawled on a cork board? Was his intensity attraction or disdain?

He would not look away. I saw him from my periphery—or, rather, felt him. I shifted my weight and crossed the opposite leg, turning my body as much as the tight quarters would allow. Sooner or later I would have to turn back. Dark, navy layers of robe fell around his slender frame, the head covering draped, collaring his throat, concealing the base of his chin, completely different from any other dress we had seen. I looked down at my hands, my skin standing out like a moon—calling the attention of many, but none so intensely as this nomad. His face was shaven and shining with natural oils, young skin pulled gently over apple cheekbones. His obsidian eyes baited mine, round and even. His lips closed with a tension at the upper corner that seemed pulled that way by mockery or intelligence. Faded tattoos decorated the back of his hands. Another turbaned man sat directly across from him, his frame smaller, shoulders more rounded, less proud. I could not see his face, but the backs of his hands were leathery with age. I could have easily mistaken them for strangers to one another. They did not interact.

His was a dangerous sort of sexy, but I kept returning his gaze. I remembered his look from the people pasted on my walls. He was Tuareg. His home: the Sahara Desert, the world's great, inhospitable sea of sand. His stillness reminded me of a cat's seconds before it pounced on a bird—not of repose but of calculation, readiness. Even my thoughts seemed like his prey.

I shifted in my seat, seeking to busy my self-conscious hands, my mouth. I acted for his sole audience. My eyes darted back to him more than I wanted. I carried on a lighthearted conversation with Kas, feigned laughter—all attempts to alleviate pressure. He remained unchanged when I smiled long and sweetly. Even flirtation failed. His eyes gripped without moving, as if he fed on nervousness.

The train jostled my body. Sweat dampened the man's pants next to me and streaked the dirt on my face like painted snakes on canvas. The heat melted what would not yield, and eventually it melted my resistance.

A friend said he once knew someone who'd visited the Sahara. The man wore a coin medallion and bent over to tie his shoes. The medallion freed itself from his body, suspended for moments. When he stood, it singed a circle on his chest. Were such tales desert legend? They did not seem so as I sucked in one hot breath after another.

Tuareg people were infamous for kidnapping tourists; they did not own much, but they did own this heat. His face was not sweaty, despite the hot desert air blowing in through the train windows. His people established trade routes connecting the Arabian north with Sub-Saharan Africa, exchanged spices and gold, fragrances, and sometimes people. What was he doing in Dakar, so far from home? Where did he stay when he visited the large city? I scanned him for luggage, indications of his journey. Nothing, save a knotted-up end of his robe concealing something not round but edgy—about the size of a movie ticket. He needed no other possessions.

The train slowed, and women and children ran alongside with baskets of fruit, roasted nuts, baguettes, and warm orange Fanta atop their heads. The passengers scrambled to the paneless windows, exchanging coins for food across hands. Heat, dust, flies, and mosquitoes flew in at night. The Tuareg sat, unmoved. I never saw him eat, blink his eyes, or open his mouth.

Sitting opposite the indigo-clad nomad, I felt vulnerable—somehow inexperienced and unwise. We might have been of similar age; I had no idea. Kas and I would return home to the comforts of life at a renowned university in an affluent town; he would ride camels into the swallowing desert, away from water, electricity, permanent building structure, even agriculture. His stamp-like face remained unmoving as I coaxed an imagined story from the black pupils he so readily offered.

When I was young, I cut out pictures from *National Geographic* that featured often partly-naked, dark-skinned indigenous people. I taped the images around my room: painted women carrying clay pots on their heads, men wearing headdresses and masks. My friends might have had posters of John Stamos, or Rob Lowe leaning against a car with wind-tossed hair, exposed tanned and toned belly. But those celebrity heartthrobs were too even, too un-storied for my gallery.

My mother was the postmaster in our small town and introduced me to stamps. I collected them as a means of mental journeying—her way of cultivating expansion, despite all the narrowness of the towns-people's minds. The stamp artwork of strange flora, fauna, maps, and symbols motivated me to dream. *Why did women cover their heads and seem distant? Why did men wear strange clothing or tattoo their bodies and faces and build round houses of straw?* An entire global culture lived in the shoebox under my bed. I transported myself into their lives for hours. I was a small-town girl with no justification for my interest in people who bore little resemblance to me. Who can say why passions snag us so early?

*I smell him before I consider anything. Before I think about the way he looks, or talks, my physical body wants him. His smell is not the sweat of man but rather a woody candle-wax smell that is both sweet and of the flesh, telluric not chemical; he is too raw for chemicals, too wild. As if he has lain down in Lokop land and absorbed the scents into his porous skin—cedar, sandalwood, dirt, smoke, black tea, baked and sealed with the heat.*

*He leads me by the hand into the dimly lit room with a single metal frame and a damp, mildewed mattress. The sheets are crisp and smell clean like Ono—African laundry detergent. I do not want to drop his hand. His skin is hot, and his fingers keep mine curled at the knuckles. There is no longer a valid reason to hold on, so I reluctantly release him. He turns to watch my hand falling, then looks at my face, aware of the thrilling nervy friction.*

*I'm tired now, but I'm happy to have met you, I say. I think we will share many things. I change my English to match his with some awkwardness. I am not tired but should be.*

*He lets me know he understands my coded message and says, I would like to hear your stories tomorrow, but tonight we'll sleep.*

*I cup water from the tap into my hand and drink, then lie on the side of the bed against the dingy wall. He takes his* rungu—*the heavy wooden bludgeon he carries everywhere, with large steel nuts fastened to one* end—and slips it under the bed along with his knife. He pulls out a small stick tucked into his red cloth where it meets his waist, presses the stick firmly against his teeth and moves it rigorously up and down while he looks at me.

Mswaki, *he says.*

*Toothbrush. Do you have another?*

I sit up. He hands me part of his, breaking it in two, snapping off the end. It's rough and sharp, not frayed and soft as his is. I rub it against my teeth until it resembles a toothbrush head. It tastes like tea tree oil. His teeth are white as porcelain. His lips show the fullness of his mouth, small rolling waves.

I watch the gap in his bottom jaw where his two middle teeth were pulled. This prepared him for the pain he would experience with adult circumcision. All Lokop boys and girls have the gap—a trademark of the tribe. It is used to administer medicine when tetanus locks the jaw. I see the gap only when he laughs, so it represents his happiness to me, and not sadness, sickness, or the intensity of initiation rites.

Before he lies down, he recites something in his native language and whoops victoriously at the end.

*I sit up. What are you saying? Is everything okay?*

He tells me he is praying to N'kai so he will sleep; he has never lain next to a woman with whom he is not intimate.

*Say that again. Say your prayer again, but for us both, please, I entreat.*

I watch his mouth move around unfamiliar words that I crave. His voice—low, quiet, pleading with the invisibility. Then he turns off the fluorescent light, lies next to me on his back, and teaches me how to say good night in Kiswahili.

La-la salama, *Micah, he whispers.*

I know this phrase, but it sounds sweeter under his tutelage, an honorable attempt to control his desire for me and bid me good night. That phrase moves between us without words for an hour. I turn this way and that. Heat emanates from him. Heat builds like wildfire. I ask him to turn to me. I know he is awake, but he waits to respond as if considering something. He lies still, eyes blinking only sparingly. After some time, he rolls to his side and asks if he can touch me. I nod.

I lead his hand around my body and my face. He caresses the features that distinguish his people from mine. It is how we see each other that first *dark night. We take turns touching. Bellies. Arms. Leather bracelets. Hands. Fingers. Throats. Beaded necklaces. Mouths.*

*I put my index finger in the gap between his bottom teeth.*

*When the energy rises and heaves, I hesitate.*

*I am afraid to go further because of AIDS, I say.*

*I am not infected, he says.*

*But you have been with many women? I ask, assuming that because he wants me, a foreigner, he has.*

*I have only made love to one girl in the village, and I was the first man she had been with. I have never desired a tourist before now, he says. My mind scans the twenty-plus years he has lived before meeting me.*

*Then I am the bigger risk, I say.*

*His eyes glitter in the darkness. I don't have this belief in my heart. This is the right way.*

*Without speaking I follow the right way, skim my hands over his chest and abdomen, his skin electric under my fingers. I feel him twitch. His heartbeat quickens.*

*I tap my fingers over a series of keloid scars rising from his skin in perfect symmetry along his solar plexus in a half-moon arc. Reading braille. Reading him. Asking why and where.*

*Those were given to honor me in a ceremony when I was a boy. I killed a male lion in the bush to protect my cows.*

*Please tell me more, I say.*

*I was very young, maybe nine or ten. I was serious about being a good shepherd but we do have to take breaks, to run home and drink milk when we are young. He had left the company of his brothers when he realized their best calf had strayed. He found the calf's remains—next to a lion, sleeping with its full belly facing the sky.*

*When it heard him coming, it woke and rose. It shook its mane and opened its mouth.*

*I knew that lion would kill me and that someone would find my remains with my calf. I knew I would die trying to kill that lion, he says. And yet, he did not run.*

*He waited until the lion came very close. Close enough that he could throw his red cloth over the lion's head, blinding it temporarily. Then my brazen, serious lover reached for his knife and stabbed several times until both he and the lion collapsed.*

*The words stuck in my chest, gripped in awe and shock. As a boy?*

*Back in the village, his father said, You killed a lion, but where's your calf? You can have ceremony, but these scars will remind you that you are both brave and heartbroken. The clan's knife-wielder cut his chest, then filled the wounds with hot ash to cleanse them and raise scars.*

*I touch them lightly one by one.*

*We cannot lose our animals, he said. They are our life, and they are also the lion's life. But the lion will not take them if we keep them protected.*

*I shiver. His hairless skin etches a smooth silhouette in the early gray light. Gratitude pools in my eyes. I have known him only a few hours, this courageous boy now man whom I desire, but I thank this life for sparing him.*

*We do not kiss. A Lokop warrior never kisses. Most snuff tobacco and their grins boast stained teeth. He does not like tobacco or snuff. His breath is clean, smells sweet to me. I savor the secret possibility of kissing him someday. As if the future guarantees it, I relish the knowing.*

*Only now, he smooths his hand along my belly under my* shuka. *He pulls gently until my underwear slide down to my inner thighs. Just enough room for his slim torso. My breath suspends with his dense weight pressing me into the bed, the Ono soap, the lion's rough black mane, my mane, the savanna and his lion-killing hands. Loneliness is there, too. Loneliness pulls me closer in. He pushes inside, pulsing and breathing ecstatically. Every separate thing dissolves into his eyes, their shining intensity. He looks through me, he looks at me, oblivion and my body beneath him. I hear myself say* Yes *as his whole being hardens, and though I want to go with him fear enters—a mother's voice, a whole chorus of sound advice.*

*I lift his pelvis. I break the perfect rhythm. We have discussed AIDS but not babies!*

*With that sharp physical* No, *he begins to shake. A seizure tightens his muscles. His eyes roll back. I panic. I have seen the warriors dance at Moloi, seen* Imurran *enter ecstatic convulsions after extreme emotion and fall into the arms of other warriors. Still I fear what I have done.*

*I am the one to catch him.*

*I am sorry. I'm so sorry. Can I hold you?*

*He pants through parted lips, this warrior, this dancer, his body quaking. I hold him tighter. Does pleasure or pain seize his body in spasm? I rock him, and soon he shakes less. His eyes close, his breath calms, and his limbs stretch out.*

*I pull him right to me, interlacing our fingers, resting my mouth on his shoulder. He grows still, makes no sound, in a sort of quelling meditation, where my thoughts race:*

*He is educated.*

*Well spoken.*

*Living in two worlds.*

*Yet he belongs to the raw and wild, like his smell. I hold his lithe body and grow sad, scanning my own inadequacy, my numbness, my blunted vitality. I am alive, yes, but buried in cumbersome thought. And I keep touching an awareness that I don't yet know who I am.*

*I press in closer, bringing my lips to rest at the hollow in his throat. I feel his heartbeat tapping my mouth. The tap of blood. The tap of fresh union. The tap of warrior.*

We disembarked twice while on the thirty-six-hour train journey through the Malian Sahara, to stretch our legs and buy a few provisions.

"You speak French. Find us something to eat. I'll stay with the luggage," Kas said, and urged me to jockey out with the others.

Some people remained on board, as did the Tuareg. Was it a relief or disappointment I felt, him not coming along?

The small village with earth-brick homes and thatched roofs held wood-fired clay ovens smoking in readiness for the arrival of the train. A line of people queued in front of an oven outside, swatting flies, holding children. I wished Kas could see, but our seats were on the other side. This was it—the storybook village we'd hoped to find by coming to Africa.

A teenage boy in a worn pink Western T-shirt asked me how many baguettes I wanted. He extended his hand for the coin. Darkened baker's racks teemed with hot, steamy bread inside that oven. I wanted ten but asked for two. On board, we had an avocado and two warm Fantas waiting. I smiled. Desert train fare was a lot like camping food.

The whistle blew. Air pressure hissed as the brakes released and heavy wheels turned. No one in line looked alarmed, but Africans lived with less urgency in general, surrendered to the now. The mass of iron and steel rolled with increased celerity; my car would pass me soon.

I stayed for bread and watched my train car fade, the distinction between the cars disappearing into a serpentine mirage, whipping through sand.

Kas had to have been panicking. Left behind in this village without a name, someone might take care of me, but I would lose Kas. I would lose our unplanned plan, our untold adventure. The boy handed me two baguettes wrapped in brown paper. I turned to sprint, shouting, "*Merci beaucoup,*" as I ran. Everyone ran. The loaves in my hands sweated. I squeezed both baguettes under one arm and used my free hand to hoist up onto the step. Panting, I clambered over tied goats, children who had crawled into the aisle to sleep, women feeding their babies, men eating stews and bread. About eight cars later I found ours, the baguettes misshapen, their tender insides compressed.

Kas leaned out the other side, searching, frantic.

"Sorry, they took their time," I said, handing her a deformed loaf as consolation.

"God, that would have been terrible," she said. "I don't even know the name of that place or if it has one. I can imagine telling your mom, 'I lost Micah in some village in Mali, or Senegal—I'm not even sure which.'" She thanked the people whose seat she'd crowded into and crossed back to ours.

"At least I would have been in a *village,*" I joked.

Her steady shoulder leaned into mine. I got it. I assured her that we would not ever risk losing each other again.

I sat before the Tuareg's gaze and next to Window Stealer's leg and held my bread. I told Kas about the village, the adobe-like ovens, the red-rich dirt, the whole scene fertile.

He watched.

When I broke open the golden outer layer of baguette, a wisp of steam wafted up. Heaven. I have since teased my French friends, saying the most delicious baguette I ever ate was in Africa, off a train somewhere in a village. This always pisses them off. The truth hurts. I wished, with my first bite, I had bought more. Everyone ate heartily, except for the Tuareg, who was too dignified for the need.

Night sauntered by—we took turns sleeping; the one awake would read by flashlight and try to keep at least one sleepy eye on our packs which were hard to access, buried under others' luggage, thus difficult to steal. I admit when it was my turn to keep watch, I drifted; the lulling motion of the train, the soft murmurs of distant conversations, and the starry sky made for wonderful sleep.

But then overhead lights blared. The train slowed and came to a stop. People sorted through their personal baggage. I asked the man next to me for the time. Perhaps it was morning and we had reached Bamako? Having just woken from sleep, I asked in English, forgetting.

*"Est-ce que vous avez l'heure?"* I corrected myself. He looked at the cheap Timex knock-off and flicked the glass face. Pleased by my attempt at French, he smiled and told me the watch was broken. I had the feeling he meant long ago. I asked if we were in Bamako. He answered not yet.

We herded into the night, into a one-room station off the side of the tracks. Someone said, *"Douaniere"*—customs. The Senegal-Mali border. We grabbed our small backpacks, clutching our American passports, their eagle engraving a symbol for freedom the world over. People sought a glimpse of that icon as though it would lift from the cover and take flight before their eyes. We held them tightly, our citizenship never so valuable or vulnerable.

Two agents at a schoolroom desk sat with a stamp pad. Stacks of faded papers and pens with chewed caps surrounded them. We handed over our passports and felt the pressure of the line lean in. They scanned our faces, then looked back at the photos—mine taken a few years earlier, cleaner face, fuller with youth. Veritably they stamped us into Mali, no less than seven *whumps*, soon to be added to the forgotten stacks.

Posturing policemen strutted through the train, selecting luggage to search.

*"Votres passports, s'il vous plait."*

They were young, in their late twenties, clad in army green, guns hanging from their shoulders and crescent-shaped sweat stains concealed in the caverns of their underarms. They asked if we had anything to declare. We told them no. They needed to search our bags. People left their seats for a better view. I stood on the back of ours and loaded the packs down to Kas.

"Center of attention, no matter what," I said to Kas as I climbed down.

With amusement, they rifled every corner, emptied each bivouac sack, and commented. Each item told them something, like opening the curtains of a previously shut home. We emptied our packs of books, photos of our families and friends, our journals, which they left undisturbed, perhaps not being a literary culture.

They sensed hesitation the way a hungry person smells food, and any defensiveness caused them to linger. I had fun listening to the passengers *ooh* and *ahh*, until the police located our years' worth of feminine hygiene products. He held a cotton tampon high in the air and turned it over in his fingers.

I was so grateful the crowd blocked the Tuareg's view.

My face turned red, *"Ce sont pour les femmes."* These are for women.

When that only made his face twist in confusion, I looked for another way. *"La lune, les femmes,"* The moon, women…

*Oh!* The youngest one discreetly told his comrades. But the women heard and pushed closer to see, unfamiliar with tampons. They turned to one another in heightened chatter. After the police had turned the backpacks inside out they thanked us and left. We repacked, gathering the strewn-about items, some from the hands of passengers.

My Tuareg friend in blue seemed to absorb from the ethers only what was essential; the superfluous, like white girls' tampons, had no bearing on his survival and therefore no occupancy in his mind. I read in my *Nat Geo* that where the indigo-colored cloth bled its dye onto the skin, it provided a sunscreen stain. Black skin also burned. Their women must bleed. If I felt naked before, now I felt translucent.

I noticed that neither he nor the older man with whom he was traveling stood in line to verify their citizenry. Perhaps Mali did not consider them citizens, since they lived beyond the nation-state and arbitrary borders. Nomadic people must cross imaginary lines drawn in the Saharan sand every day, not adhering to the collective or individual ownership of land. A nomad might spend as many nights in one country as in another. How would a government assess taxes on them? They appeared to me too free, too proud, to belong to nations, incapable of being possessed. Citizens owned land, demarcated boundaries, kept the distinction between this country and that country, this citizen and that citizen. Chattel. The division was absurd when viewed from the black eyes of the desert nomad. Perhaps the formation of the nation-state contributed to our civilizational dysfunction, suppressing our inherent desire for freedom and movement—forcing us to assimilate as nations, and as nations control resources, create tension, even war.

Mental train wanderings ... apparently, I had this thing with freedom.

We slept until six a.m., when the train abruptly stopped. The glowing orange orb hung horizon-level. Outside nothing but red desert forever—not a single bush or tuft of life sprang up. So quiet. The early light hit the glassy surface of the sand. The Tuareg rose to his feet, adjusted his head covering, then pulled it over his nose and mouth—protection from the sun and wind. Even more mysterious, he strode smoothly toward the back of our car and with indigenous agility jumped out. I looked through the opening to see him and the older man walking into the distance, into desolate, wonderful noth-ingness. Beyond the indigo-robed men floating over the desert-scape, horses stirred the dust, muscles glistening in the morning light. The men mounted the horses and rode across the sun, robes streaming like ribbons.

The emptiness of his seat and withdrawal of his attention left me less interesting, alone, and far from home. The world expanded into universes of past and future, of strange peoples and their lives. Lives lived in deserts, mountains, cities, seashores, houses, huts, caravanning tents. It was all suddenly too much. An overwhelm of possibility exploded in my tight, small mind.

I felt lost in its vastness.

Yet somehow found.

# Four | Boys, Men, and the Feminine

*Nine a.m. Bamako, Mali. Final destination.*

WE HAD COME to Mali to visit the ancient libraries of Timbuktu, which housed some of the world's original literature and spiritual texts. Supported by the Trans-Saharan gold and salt trade, Timbuktu flourished in the fourteenth century as one of the most prominent cities of Islam. The Sahara Desert once enabled the city to experience profits, but its encroachment now threatened Timbuktu's survival. In 1990, UNESCO put Timbuktu on the World Heritage List as "in danger," to conserve and safeguard the ancient buildings. The Sahara, indifferent to the listing, kept spreading.

Trapped with everything we owned, people who were either indifferent to or fascinated by us, scenery that had no beginning or end, the train's forty lulling-rhythm hours had settled us into surrender—another layer of conditioned American skin shed.

We grabbed our packs and headed for a Catholic mission run by nuns. Backpackers favored the mission because of its location near both the station and town center, and because missions promised refuges of peace.

But outside the train station gates, six boys about our age closed in on us, their shirts torn, eyes burning red from sniffing glue or drinking.

They shouted in French that we needed to pay for guide services. Kas looked to me as the boys spoke over one another, delivering a confused tirade of demands and taunts. I showed them we had a map. No need for guides. It may have been smarter to use their unnecessary services, but we protected our budget and our independence.

*"Nous ne sommes pas loin de notre l'hotel."* I tried to reason that we were not far from our lodging. We pushed through the ring of intimidation, but they followed us, yelling, raising the panic in our hearts until we found the mission and its enforcing ten-foot-tall iron gate. We rang the buzzer twice, three times. A nun, wearing a heavy cross around her neck, hurried us inside. The boys retreated, walking slowly backward, squatting in the nearby shade of a building's eave.

I took my pack off and slid it down my arms to the floor. The nun seemed overly cautious, looking us over. I am normally annoyed by this type, but because of the harassing boys, I welcomed her diligence. The nunnery hadn't felt sunshine in decades, it seemed, all locked up and gray inside. The cool felt good.

"Those guys—" Kas said, a little out of breath. "I haven't seen that sort of desperation since we've been here. And it's so flipping hard with these heavy packs!" she whispered as the nun across the counter watched our mouths, trying to untangle our quick American English.

We sped it up.

"Yeah, sniffing glue really messes with the head. I read about that. It stinks that they waited for us at the train, and now we're trapped in here." I wrote my passport number and signed the half-page, then slid it across to the sister.

The stark brick mission exaggerated the soft curves of the surrounding adobe buildings. A refuge of order. Nuns scurried in their dark blue habits with folded towels and small bars of soap. No smiles. No greeting. Everything 90 degree angles. A small center courtyard remained empty, the chairs set awkwardly apart. A plant struggled, dry in a pot. The rooms bordered the yard on two levels. Kas and I were given a room on the second floor. Before picking up our packs, we glanced back beyond the entrance gate—the boys' silhouettes still there, unmoving.

What a stark contrast to our first night's lodgings. No mold, no dirt, no rats. The single beds were made up, tight, white sheets starched and pressed—not the sort of bed to bring a lover to but rather to convalesce from illness, or even die. We took the key and the rulebook for personal conduct, noted the ten p.m. curfew, napped like liberated pack animals, and went in search of food.

We crept from the mission gate into the evening, the stillness, murmured voices, and the ample hiding spots of nightfall. Where were they, I wondered. Where was everyone? This desert was not the sort that inspired you to twirl, open your arms and fly the breeze; it was concealing, struggling for a breath. A one-room restaurant a few doors down from the mission had customers. We ate anxiously, hurrying the peanut stew into our bellies as fast as possible, and returned to the mission.


In the morning, Kas seemed less concerned about the boys. She said playfully, "Well, let's get this Bamako show on the road, shall we? We need fuel for our stove. The nun said we could fire it up in the courtyard." Her joy reminded me that perspective is everything—and so we went. The dirt street meandered around simple mud houses. Five old men squatted under trees, playing this stringed, banjo-style instrument, singing. They smiled and waved as we passed by, genuinely happy to see us. I started to like Bamako.

We trudged across a huge dirt field, hot but happy, each with a finger looped around a fuel canister top. The sun beat down on our brows, so we watched the kicked-up dust mostly. I was telling Kas about a dream I'd had when we heard shuffling. And voices. There they were, walking fast, about thirty paces back. The taller boy from the day before made a beeline for us. As he neared, I could smell him—a mix of layered sweat and something acrid, poisonous as his intent. His glue-sniffing pals followed right behind him. I had a moment to consider how we found ourselves in such peril and it pissed me off. Kas and I were being hunted simply because we didn't opt to pay for unnecessary services? If fear hadn't hoisted my hackles, my indignation might have run headlong into a skirmish. Dirt-field wrestling.

Eight thugs formed a ragged ring, surrounding us. Kas snugged her shoulder right against mine.

*It smells like the zoo, I say quietly to Kas—the volume adjustment on my voice not conscious but instinctual. Evening, hues of light-gray and blue dim the savanna.*

*Yes, she whispers. Did you notice how the warriors stay closer now?*

*Maybe it's just a herd of goats? My mind and intellect try to stall, but my senses know.*

*The lions are waking, he says. They'll be hunting soon. You smell them. He widens his eyes until the whites shine brighter. A playful gesture, an attempt to reassure us. He knows we might be afraid.*

*Joking, not joking, I say to him, Maybe you should chew some of that leaf? It could keep you more alert—*

*He laughs. I know you are a little afraid, but this is my land; I know these lions. We walk everywhere with them, even when we don't chew Miraa. Okay? He smiles simply, zero fear in his face. He grabs my hand and forces me to walk at his pace for a while—to move nervous energy.*

*Ploote, always smiling, takes Kas' hand into his long lithe fingers.*

*I attend to his spear and* rungu—*they are more than interesting decor; they will save our lives. How exactly will he use them?*

*In full darkness, the warriors huddle around Kas and me.*

*We will see better by moonlight, my lover says. And the moon will be rising while we walk.*

*It calms me to know he has lived with lions his whole life, knows exactly what phase the moon is in and when she will rise.*

*Mama Jolie and Papa Duane will have their daughter back, he assures me as he scans the brush. Constant vigil. Animal scents fill every breath.*

*He draws a diamond in the sand with his spear. We will walk quickly, he says. It's safer that way, but not running. Kas and Micah, you walk one in front and one behind. There will be one warrior in front of you, same line, and one behind you. I will be on your left and Cousin on your right. Do you understand?*

*A trotting diamond. We understand.*

*I am ready. If we are meant to survive this moon's night, we will. But, cocooned in the middle, flanked on all sides, I suddenly start to feel how critical this all is.*

*What will we do if there is a lion? I rush the question before we start walking.*

*We protect you. You will not do anything different but stay with each other.*

*I trust and don't trust in one breath.*

*Do you need to hold a stone to throw? he asks, reaching down for several large stones, handing them to us. If a lion comes, throw this direct to his face. It can help you.*

*If I am close enough to aim for a lion's face, natural order has won out! I take two stones, one in each hand, as fear threatens to paralyze my legs. Imagine being so close to those eyes, that mane, the teeth. Oh God!*

*Ploote raises his spear.* Mapetin! *Let's go! We form our diamond and begin walking into the dark—into lion, leopard and hyena-hunting night.*

*The night splits open my awareness. As we fast-step into the unknown, both heart and mind demand my attention. Mind tugs me closer to panic, but heart opens. I stretch my senses desperately, as far as they will go, listening for every sound, the roaring and the barely audible. The savanna grows louder with the night. Every bush hides a threat. I hear movement, weight shifting, animals or night birds calling. Even the insects' clicking and scurrying grows louder. Everything so unfamiliar. What savage beauty in those calls.*

*The warriors keep us walking. They do not sing or speak. He does not look at me but stares ahead—pure instinct, honed awareness. He is more animal now. I am still pretending. I do not know how to hone my senses. My people lost their animals, abandoned them, self and other and all. I cannot even get real with the real. But before self-pity takes another left jab—*

*I hear something.*

The eight Bamako thugs wasted no time. I cursed our luck as they nudged us apart, five on me, and three on Kas. Their elbows and legs jutted out to keep us fenced in, like thorns on branches. Sneaky, patient fuckers. As they yelled, spit flung from their mouths.

"Micah, what are they saying? I don't understand."

I lunged toward Kas, stepping over a guy's leg.

"Pissed we didn't hire them yesterday. More of the same." I took her arm and feigned calm to diffuse the feverish energy; the boys would leap at the chance of any heat.

The leader towered above us, his shoulders cinched back. His bravado only made me puff up taller. I knew bullies. I'd fought with half a dozen in grade school. I fought until they were beaten or I was dragged into the office to explain myself. My fourth-grade school picture shows a compact Irish girl grinning for the camera with the purpling remains of a black eye. No shame in her smile.

When Boy Poison launched his fiery threats, and the others shoved me into him, I let my body bounce limply off him without reaction, but inside me, pressure mounted a defense. Someone shoved me again, hard from behind. I kept steady, my feet apart and heels light. I slid sidestepping between two of them, trying to reach Kas. The odds were against us, stuck in the center of this dirt lot far from view, far from those singing elders.

"Hold on," I said, keeping my eyes on them, "I'm coming." I skittered toward Kas like a passed soccer ball, weaving between bodies. I did not feel the rage till then. But once at Kas' side, I'd had enough. Kas could handle her own, but she didn't speak French.

I planted my finger in the tall boy's chest and began shouting. Shouting anything and everything that came to mind.

*Je te frappe!* he screamed back. More spit and vitriol.

"And if you do, I *will* hit you," I said in French, holding the fuel canister high to show I could reach his head with it. Metal meets skull—

He blinked. A moment of doubt, and the mob flexed in place.

Then I did the repugnant. I went for the lowest blow. I told them we were Americans—rich, powerful, protected Americans. I stressed every syllable. When he nudged closer, I held the canister higher. I pushed back with a torrent of words and tormented him with his impoverishment. It was the best French I had ever spoken; my brain flooded with forgotten words. I moved nearer and turned into them, a rabid, inconsolable girl who feared nothing and bullied the bullies with my stinging, acidic tongue. Kas moved when I did, turned and taunted them with her arms, her body poised for a fight. No cowering. We would be beaten—or worse, raped—or we would walk away. In those moments, it did not matter. We put everything in, and a strange sort of valor marked us in our commitment to the fight.

Five boys fell back, leaving the tall one and two others. I said that if one finger touched us, an American woman's rage would howl down on them. Not a muted rage but full-on maelstrom. As I bluffed, I began to believe myself, which made me more convincing. Then I hurled my last shot at him, landing it right in Poison's face—we would report them to the American Embassy.

Ridiculous, of course, but it worked.

Their exaggerated view of US dominion penetrated whatever they'd sniffed. It crushed the mob. They left, occasionally looking back, almost like they were making sure the whole thing just happened. The space between us grew like boats drifting apart in rough currents.

I looked at the maze of scuffle marks in the dirt. We had pushed back and forth for twenty feet. Only now the pounding in my chest broke free. I breathed from my mouth, the sweat on my belly streaking down my legs. My body shook. I looked at Kas but stayed silent a few moments longer, then said, "I've never been that afraid of men. Out here. No one to help."

"I hate it," she said. "I hate not being able to speak. I swear I would have punched them had they attacked us. God you were intense. I heard you repeat *American*."

"I know." I reached my arms up high to stretch out the tension of fear. I shook my head. "Gross. The lowest blow. I told them they were nothing. Insignificant in comparison. The sad thing is, they believed me."

"Oh well, fuck 'em," Kas said as she touched my shoulder, then added in all absurdity, "if they can't take a joke."

I shouted to the wind, "Ha! Yeah, guys, I was just kidding. You too, right? Nothing to see here, folks."

We laughed like hyenas, which felt kind of like a prayer, like gratefulness.

"*Je te frappe*, my ass," I said under my breath, and our laughter resumed. "*Frappe* may mean slushy drink in English, but it means *I'm hitting you* in French." I tapped the empty, lightweight canister on her head. "Apparently, a good phrase to know in Mali."

"I've never seen your ugly American side. Attractive. Especially in your flowery dress."

I giggled. Then I said in all seriousness, "Let's get out of here."

Our course took a quick reverse after that. Local news warned of desperate youth in Timbuktu, and that was all we needed to hear. We'd had enough of the local youth. Mali's historic libraries would have to be another trip. We repacked at the nunnery, received visas, and charted the path to Abidjan, Cote d'Ivoire. Our first mail from home waited there, and we kinda needed it.

Bamako did not welcome our departure. Or anyone's for that matter. We wandered through a wrecked bus yard at the edge of town, hoping to buy a ticket. The Ivory Coast border lay three hundred miles south. In the middle of the bus lot, a rusted, broken-down vehicle with its hood agape leaned unevenly on one flat and three bald tires. The place seemed more like a motor coach graveyard than a viable station.

Mali was poorer than Senegal. The lack of infrastructure, the unpaved roads, small villages, few cities, and illiterate youth competed only with Niger in desperation. We could not find a departure schedule anywhere. Several cobweb-covered doorways and broken glass windows hinted at businesses that seemed to have closed a hundred years ago. A few people milled about. Others looked to have slept in the compound, clothing dusty and wrinkled, hair flattened down at the sides. I confused them with the depraved sort common at stations everywhere, but they were customers like us, waiting for a vehicle to be repaired, waiting for more passengers or a reliable driver. Whatever the circumstance, they were waiting and had been for days.

Despite our desire to be conscientious world citizens, we could not undo our Americanness in two –and –a -half months. We could not comprehend the brokenness of the bus or the system. Our land of customer service, technology, and machinery worked too well. We did not see the scattered people, idle and loitering, as we saw ourselves. No, we were different—there to purchase real tickets with real money for valid destinations that the station assumedly served.

Hours later, when we still could not find anyone to speak with or a vehicle worthy of a voyage, reality settled in. Mali was in a bad way. We put down our packs, found a spot on the shaded ground, and assumed the same deflated posture as everyone else, leaning against the building's splintery beams. We were just as hungry, dusty, and flat-haired as the next person. Entitlement be damned. Time passed as we had never allowed it to do.

A man who did not look like a member of the Malian Bambara tribe huffed around. His thick eyebrows arched under deep furrows, a permanent and embittered scowl on his face. Despite his temperament, whenever he walked in and out of the less-vacant buildings, he inspired an energy, a bustling; he was a provider of faint hope. I asked who he was.

"*C'est le conducteur pour notre voyage,*" a middle-aged man propped against the same building said. He was also trying to get to the Ivory Coast.

Our *conducteur* tinkered under the hood of the minibus sporting white paint and busted-out windows. Kas and I sat up from our afternoon slumber. He looked mean, but we needed to buy a ticket, and he was the only person with a semblance of authority.

"*Excusez-moi, puis-je acheter deux billets a Cote d'Ivoire?*"

He kept his head in the hood, then growled something inaudible over his shoulder. He walked toward one of the shops with grease-stained hands holding random auto parts. So much for customer service; if he were a dragon, I would have been singed.

As dusk loomed, more travelers arrived. Among them I found one who knew something and was inclined to share his information with the rest of us. Supposedly the bus had been broken down for days; an earlier attempt to depart had been thwarted. Several of the passengers, not wanting to lose their money, stayed at the station, waiting to see if the driver would be successful in fixing the bus. Others had abandoned the voyage and had chosen different means.

Then it was early nightfall.

We read, slept, and lagged about the station for eight hours—an unintentional submersion into Malian lifestyle. The mean driver approached. Without a word, he picked up our packs and carried them to the bus, then slid them up the side to the top, where a muscled boy hoisted them by the straps. The backpacks were the first to be bungeed to the luggage rack.

Grateful for any movement, we were disinclined to demand more information—such as when exactly we would be leaving, how long the journey would take, and how much the tickets would cost. I asked anyway.

A crowd gathered. I found myself in a mob of French-speaking people, eager audience for the bargaining game, money gawkers—as though I would pull a year's worth from my pocket. I had already learned not to expose the full amount, ever. My humor withered. People tugged on my sleeves, coaching me, telling me they could do the negotiations for me. Some made pacts with the driver to ensure their cut. Too much attention on money, too much desperation. My one option, the same as always: surrender. Bargaining had to be done. We needed out of Mali.

I amused them all with my hardheaded haggling. The driver and I finally agreed upon an amount still too high. On top of it the blood-thirsty, snaggle-toothed *conducteur* added one thousand CFA more per backpack, smirking as he did. He called it a luggage fee—more like extortion. Of course, we had luggage; we were traveling. Everyone in Africa had luggage. Even if it was a plastic bag with groundnuts, it was luggage. No one else paid a luggage fee, but we were white. Tourist inflation.

"Take the packs off the bus. We'll find another way," I said, tired of injustice.

The crowd laughed, whooped, and waited for his response.

I'd already sat idle eight hours, been harassed in Mali worse than this. I felt a pulse of feisty in my veins.

He shouted for the boy to unstrap our packs.

But then he waived the luggage fee, with arms pumping like Popeye's, only because we were not expecting to pay extra, he said.

The boy on top waited. I saw the faintest grin.

I had already pissed off our driver, so I defiantly asked if we would be leaving soon.

He pushed the crowd aside and huffed out of sight. With our money.

The bags sat upright like people atop the bus for two- and –a -half hours. The sky darkened without memory of sun. People quieted. Kas and I kept watch, our luggage appearing more like hostages with each passing minute.

*Bwwobb bwwwobbubwub!* The engine revved a couple of times before turning all the way over. Then it died. Still, good. The brief mechanized hum woke the whole compound into action. Men came from shadows, from between the rows of buildings, carrying small bags and rolled prayer mats. *Luggage.* Most of the men were smaller, of Arabic descent, not the larger bodies of the West African men we had seen. They rattled in Arabic but spoke French too. One spoke a little English. Kas learned they were from Mauritania. We'd recalled our African studies at CRMS—though the government denied it, Mauritania still supported slavery. After Gorée, my stomach knotted at anything slave related. The lot overflowed—all men. Not one other woman anywhere.

"I hope this isn't another perilous Micah and Kas adventure," I said, half joke, half serious. "What do you think?"

"Do we have a choice? We've got to get out of Mali." Then, her face lit up with fun. "I've got it, act gay."

I had to admire her spunk after eleven hours on the ground going nowhere slowly.

"Being lesbians could be the best, or the worst, idea you have ever had," I said.

We piled on the bus—Kas, me, and thirty-two men. On the side, red letters beamed in English: "21 Passengars Ful Capacity." We were just getting situated when the driver told everyone to get off. Once we were off, he barked for Kas and me to get back on, as though that should have been obvious. The man had no time for idiots.

We took our seats, confused. The men remained outside, waiting for the ringleader's direction. They anchored their bodies against the window frames, hands gripping so tightly their nail beds whitened from pressure. We watched them below our window. Then, with a forward and backward rocking motion and a few grunts and groans, the bus began to roll. The driver yelled from his seat, *"Poussez! Poussez!"*

I laughed out loud. *"Push,"* I whispered to Kas, "though it surely sounds like the derogatory term for a woman's vagina." Which put the cherry, pun intended, on top of this ridiculous cake.

The driver yelled again, *"Poussez! Poussez!"* Kas stuffed her mouth with her scarf and tears rolled down her cheeks. I said dryly, "The *poussez* is sitting on the bus. No need to yell."

Kas fell into me, dizzy with laughter.

The bus gathered momentum, the engine popped, and the unknown road showed itself a few feet at a time. Men clambered in through the windows, snickering at the need to push and at the startled American girls.

I eavesdropped on conversations.

The bus traveled at night because this whole trip was illegal: the bus, the lack of a commercial license for the driver, the lack of appropriate documentation for the Mauritanians. Not only did we travel at night but we took back roads pitted with huge potholes and tree trunks that had fallen across. I felt calm. I can't tell you why. Maybe I'd always wanted to flaunt the law—here it was easier, not my laws. Small fires in villages twinkled in the distance. The smell of burning trash, which I'd begun to like, filled the air—sweet, like banana skins and apple wood. Kas settled into my shoulder to sleep like a good lesbian. We inched closer to the Ivory Coast.

Now, there are *Poussez,* and there are pussies. And we are neither of those. Kas and I had to slap away male hands like swatting mosquitoes within minutes of our departure from the graveyard station. One man reached down the front of my shirt. I turned to confront him, but bodies huddled together and I lost the perpetrator. Power in numbers.

All through the night, their hands flew in the dark, groping body parts, getting swatted, and after each attempt they chittered in Arabic.

On an incline, in the wee hours, the driver stalled the bus. Everyone except Kas and me unloaded to pray. The men rolled out their carpet mats; faced Mecca; cleaned their hands, nose, ears, and head; and performed the recitations. Post-prayers, the men shouted, *"Allez Poussez!"* and braced their bodies against the bus.

Mercifully, we all stopped for the night at a roadside camping site with open-ceilinged tents. Kas and I lay on cots, drank black tea, and stared into the sky. I imagined separating stars before sleeping on an empty stomach. Heart sated. Filled with stars.

Day two of the slow-going crawl, with the Ivory Coast somewhere before us, the driver stopped near a large shade tree and field. The two prior stops had been for prayer, which came five times a day—an amount true to the precepts of Islam. We remained on the bus, as prayers went by fast. But this time the *conducteur* exited the bus alone.

Five hours later, now under the tree, I asked the men, "What are we waiting for?"

The youngest responded, "The driver has gone into the field to look for his friend, who has something for him." As he spoke, I couldn't help but wonder if this guy had had his hand down my shirt. Kas was asleep. I had finished the books I brought, so I lay on my back, one leg crossed over the other, and watched orange and yellow birds flit from tree to tree. Twenty years later I still remember them. Some grand stillness pressed deeply.

Acceptance helped us with the men's wandering hands—not that we stopped batting them or even twisting a finger if we caught hold, but we no longer reacted. They noted our indifference and followed, bored. Sunset became our favorite prayer time, because for a few minutes, though it was dark, the men stopped harassing. Once daylight struck, they recoiled like boys, afraid of their mother's reproach. Had either of us had a history of sexual assault, we might have been traumatized by those long grope-filled nights, but oddly, we felt in control.

While the men prayed one night Kas asked, "What do you think your dad would say about this?"

"Oh, he'd kill them. Even my mom. It'll be a hard one to explain, that's for sure. They're just boys," I added smugly. "Old skinny ones."

We scooted across the Cote d'Ivoire border around midnight on the third day. The bus stopped outside a restaurant with a small hotel next to it. Kas and I thanked our driver, who grimaced like an axe. We waved with flitting wrists at the teenaged men who actually seemed sad to see us go. In total, we had ridden the bus seventy-nine hours for a meager three hundred miles. Four miles per hour. Well, actually, three-and-three-quarters. God speed the *conducteur.*

At last—beds, bucket showers, and privacy. No nocturnal hands reached over seats or down our tops. There was no strange language to decipher. We had space to stretch, to elevate our puffy ankles to let the swelling ease, but we were not yet in Abidjan—our first poste restante address.

Month three, and these long, arduous journeys helped us adapt to life in Africa and to relinquish our own. The change happened without our awareness: one day we were disgruntled and paranoid; the next we enjoyed whatever transpired.

# FIVE | SKIN

It was in Abidjan, the capital of the Ivory Coast, where I first felt ill. Though the city catered to an educated, cosmopolitan, falafel-eating population—in high contrast to Mali—it still had nasty water. We took all the necessary precautions, treating and filtering, pouring a little of the treated water back into the cap to coat the bottle threads. To no avail. I arranged my day between diarrhea and vomiting in our hotel room, and I admit I enjoyed the anonymity of Abidjan. The more educated and affluent the population, the less they seemed to care about Kas and me—about white people—merely for being white. For now, that worked.

When I kicked my parasitic flu, we flew outside. The dank, noxious room had lost all appeal. Rain drenched already drab Abidjan, the sky cold and as unfriendly as the harbor, the buildings the dingy cream of industry. Farther away than ever from our African village, Kas and I walked straight to the bus station, read the departure schedule, admired the brightly painted homogenous vehicles, and purchased two tickets to Accra, Ghana. Because I was well enough, we left the next day, on what Americans might call a whim. Whim is a relative of freedom. A distant freckled cousin. We courted our whims to move beyond them. We headed east—deeper into Africa and away from the peripheral security of coasts. Senegal's airport, our point of entry, disintegrated into memory. The trail back burned behind us.

We traveled for months, slept in cheap hotels, explored local ·fare and historical sites. In the evenings, we gathered with tourists at resorts for tribal dancing and drumming. We knew this was some kind of dues paying. We weren't yet primed for immersion. We only skirted the outside of the dream. When the buses lumbered through villages, we leaned out at the idyllic scenes from the eclipsed view of our window. But we seemed not to meet anyone from a village, hadn't been invited in.

From Accra we skimmed east again, saved a little time and skipped Nigeria. We'd heard it was politically unstable, so we took a plane to Cameroon. And here, even whim stalled out.

In Cameroon, we rested in a quaint turquoise-painted beachside hostel, owned by a retired Catholic priest. Calm and sweet, it sat entirely empty. If we were not to make friends in Africa, if we weren't going to stay in villages, we settled for relaxing by the seaside and enjoying the continent's exquisite natural diversity. We wrote in our journals as if it were a job, and the lull in constant travel gave way to deeper reflection. Three months in Africa had not extinguished the rigor of our cultural conditioning or our studies, which included a limited but staggeringly persistent second-hand view of Africans. I probed deeper, and the question of race, of skin color, of disadvantages due to both, kept pushing me to define my values. My favorite author at the time: William Faulkner, for his perspicacious (his word) portrayal of the American South, black and white. My degree from university: political science and French with an emphasis on West Africa, where a predominant number of American slaves originated. This journey: a need to be around black people and to *feel* being a minority.

All well-intended, but I was still a snob. A pedantic snob.

My mind overworked while my heart atrophied. My culture set it up that way. As much as I considered myself non-racist and liberal, I filtered Africans through my first-world bias, which was:

Educated.
Impersonal.
Elitist.

Ethnocentric.

Envied.

The Africans we saw through windows and from passing trains, even those living in cities, played and danced, they seemed silly, naïve, and full of joy. My judgment reflected my unease with play and childlike nature. My judgment ran against my heart. And as much as I hoped to have real experiences with African people, I felt I would first need a profound understanding of myself. Of that I was sure. I wanted so much to show I cared, but how do you care for cultures you still do not know how to respect? *Be still, my heart.* You wait until something pulls you to your knees with reverence.

*The village, the first time I see it—soft with early sleep, flickering light from hut fires tossing distorted shapes about. But the quiet warmth welcomes us in. His pace quickens. He heads toward the hut he calls home. He leads and we follow. He and his cousin stake their spears into the reed- and twine-woven stick hut. They wait. When no one stirs, he leans into the quiet dark and calls to his mother and sister in a hushed tone. A reverent tone. He steps back and waits. A girl's body fills the domed entrance. She falls to her knees, clinging to his legs with both arms, burying her tearful face in him. He keeps still and lets her do her crying. A series of aggrieved, exultant screams come from her. Not words. Uninhibited emotion, wailing. My body grows anxious, responding to another's sadness, tears start from my eyes, and I want to hold her. He looks at me as though he hears my thoughts. One day it will be me crying for him. And one day we will have our reunion.*

*She is my only sister, he says. I haven't been home for some years.*

*Lintan is exquisite. Petite, with a perfectly-formed shaven head, high cheek bones and a small nose. Strands of red beads around her slender neck, still brightly new, suggest she is nine or ten years old. Her beauty is both angelic and raw. In an oddly raspy voice she begins to find her way to words. I understand only,* brother, thank you, *and* God. *He reaches to hold her wet face in his hands and lifts her so he may enter the hut. Lintan stands, brushes off her leather skirt and follows him. He beckons with his hand for Kas and me to come. Ploote takes his spear from the side of the hut and walks away, into the night.*

*Micar… Miicah… Micah… Lintan practices my name and pats the calfskin between her and her mother, Natiyon. I take my seat, and Kas sits next to me. We fall silent in the dark while the family remembers itself with greeting, Lintan holding my hand. Hers is sticky with chai sugar, but chafed and dry, despite its smallness, despite her youth.*

*Natiyon's voice is feeble with long pauses. She sits, legs extended, crossed ankles, adorned with aluminum bands, soles black with fire's soot. The weak firelight reveals her a flicker at a time. She wraps a blanket around her shoulders not for modesty but for warmth. A saggy and withered breast is still partly exposed.*

*He talks to her. She hums and coos, encouraging him to keep talking. A kind listening. Gutok, a language of spirit and image, is not mine yet. I ache to understand anything said in his words. How to disentangle Gutok? Its breaks are unfamiliar, a rhythm like fire eating wood, no cadence or consistency that my ear can detect. Hearing satiates, and my need for understanding dissolves. As they exchange images, Lintan watches me and Kas, and looks with adoration at her brother. She grows tired, her dark eyes watery. I motion for her to lie down. She curls up near me and within moments is asleep, a faint whisper-like breath escapes her small body. Small but full of life, of muscle and will. Kas finds a dark corner and is asleep soon, too.*

*Natiyon makes us chai. The black tea aroma fills the space. The shock of the lion encounter and our three days' walk here finally settle into stillness and fatigue. My body grows heavy and leans closer to prone. I sip the chai as they speak for what feels like hours. I am almost sleeping upright when Natiyon breaks my delirium, motioning for me to come closer, cupping her right hand and scooping the air.*

*Wou ene, Micah, she says, her eyes tilted a little lower than mine. She is blind, tuned to a subtlety that speaks only to her. I slide nearer until our legs touch, our upper bodies facing one another. Her face is awkwardly close to mine now. I stare at the fire and avoid her blind eyes but feel her breath on my cheek. Maybe she wants to smell me? She clears her throat and begins touching my face with both hands, running her splintered fingers along the contours. I close my eyes. She is not gentle, not rough, but confident. Her hands read me. Beneath her calloused hands, I feel naked. She runs one hand down the length of my hair and says something. I open my eyes and smile.*

*She rushes her hands back to my face to feel the smile. I close my eyes again. Her fingers pull at the corners of my lips, brush past my exposed teeth. I close my mouth and swallow but she does not mind my spit on her hand. She traces the outline of my neck, lightly running her hands down my breasts. She says something to him again. I do not dare smile this time.*

*He laughs gently. She says you look like a Lokop girl except for your hair. Even your heart is like a Lokop. But your hair is more like a lion's.*

*I laugh too—even here the hair gets awkward praise!*

*He continues, I told her you have a beautiful face like us but not black skin like hers.*

*I wait. A splinter in my heart. Black and white. Still the distance—even in belonging.*

*She said that is because you don't sit and cook by fire.*

*Thank you, I say with my eyes. I would sit and cook by her fire to feel this found.*

Why had I come to Africa? I knew the kernel, the seed. My maternal grandmother adopted one girl from the many children she had fostered. Tammy was closer to me in age than my other aunts and uncles. Cool and pretty, Tammy took me along to hang out with her friends whenever my family visited Denver. I smelled marijuana for the first time and felt the thrill of the inner city. My grandma said Tammy could come visit us for a long weekend, in the mountain town where we lived. I wanted to show her off, introduce her to the boys I had crushes on. I was ten. We gathered at an arcade on Friday and Saturday evenings to ward off summer boredom. The boys played video games; the girls feigned interest. I told everyone at school, "My cool aunt is coming from Denver. I'm going to bring her to the arcade." I couldn't wait until she blew open their mountain minds with her city savvy.

I took extra time applying lip gloss and feathering my hair, not wanting her fourteen-year-old beauty to outshine mine. When we walked into the noisy hall, it turned quiet, as though someone had shorted the power. People looked at us and turned away. One boy I was sweet on left out the back door.

I approached one group, then another. "This is my Aunt Tammy. The one I told you about from Denver."

"Your *aunt?*" They interlaced arms and laughed as they walked away. Mean laughter.

Tammy and I froze. Eternity in a moment. Being snubbed in that rundown arcade with my so-called friends.

She gathered the courage first and said, "Let's go home, Micah. It's okay. Come on."

My mom found us in bed, that night, and asked how it went.

"It hurt," I said. Tears soaked my pillow. Tammy lay quietly next to me.

On Monday, my school friends asked, "Did that black girl finally go home?"

"Yes," I said, with an ache in my chest and a tightening everywhere.

My silence that night and the next day, and the lingering shame of it, gave me courage in my adulthood, drove my studies. Led me to bounce around Africa on a shoestring budget.

I never again stayed silent, but it did not mean I was whole. And I didn't yet have a plan for how to get there.


We met Guy. Guy drove the taxi from the priest's hostel into the nearest town, Kribi. We could have walked, but we wanted to buy vegetables for the week of relaxation we'd planned. The sun beamed hot, and the air filled with mineral mists of sea salt. Guy played funky South African music in his rattletrap car. The locals chose a particular commute vehicle not because of the car itself or the driver but based on which type of music played.

*"Aimez-vous la musique?"* he asked hopefully.

This was one handsome cabbie—broad shoulders, square jaw, high cheeks that made his face seem kind. His dark-brown eyes soft behind curled lashes.

I swayed to the rhythm, flirting with him as he watched in his rearview mirror.

When he opened the door for us, at the market, his muscles caught on his loose-fitting clothes. Guy asked, not in a pushy way, if he could wait while we did our shopping.

Lush hillside market. Strapping taxi driver. Plenty of time to explore. Jackpot.

Cameroon's climate grows nightshades, as well as tropical fruits like pineapple and coconut. We wandered the rows of hand-picked produce stacked in pyramids and woven baskets. A stubby-fingered, busty woman knew we wanted a pineapple long before our eyes betrayed us. Pineapple was expensive. We paid four dollars—more than our hostel cost per night. A river flowed through the market, and the stands lined the banks, offering meat and fish for sale, which was considered halal as long as the fish had scales and fins. Guy was Muslim, as were all the locals, but here, far from its Arabic origins, Islam was less severe, more tolerant—the women more expressed. Their gravelly laughter speckled the air.

As Kas shopped, I kept an eye on Guy. He stood by his car, twirling keys, speaking to someone, gesturing in wild blithesome sweeps.

We loaded our vegetables and the prized pineapple into his backseat, a luxury after carrying everything on our bodies, and relished the freedom of having a car.

"*Voluez-vous visitez les chutes?*" He wasted no time booking our next outing, though he played it cool—at least he thought so. A good salesman.

I asked Kas if she wanted to see the local waterfalls. I knew her answer. Kas possessed an internal compass whose true north was anything that supported adventure, enjoyed life.

"*Oui, d'accord. Dans deux jours. Pas demain.*" We agreed he would pick us up in two days' time, not tomorrow. We needed one day of doing nothing again.

Kas and I set our chipped, blue wooden lawn chairs to face the ocean. Day folded into dusk by the sound of green waves washing up, licking the gold beach. Streamers of pink and fiery orange saluted us. We planned for a full week in this haven of heaven, which was the longest we had stayed anywhere. A break from constant travel won out over exploration, at last.

Our beach cottage had two cots with mosquito netting and an oil lantern. A wooden desk tucked in the corner held dented impressions of so many travelers' letters home. I opened my journal. The security light above the door provided my first inspiration. A chartreuse gecko waited. A handsome, wily lad. He caught a flying insect on the stickum of his tongue. Then another. And another. One was an unusually large, colorful moth.

I scrunched into the desk and wrote: "Why do I always have to be aware of who is eating whom, no matter where I am?" Being vegetarian, I took offense to anything taking another's life, and I always saw it. I could be persuaded to pray for carrots. I rescued bugs from all sorts of endings: spiders from bathtubs, flies from windows, moths from flames. I often asked Kas to relocate insects. She was better at it and scooped them up without wincing. The world of the small broke my heart. How many ants did we kill, stepping on them unawares? Fellow workers grieved, gathered, and took the tiny snapped bodies back to the nest for an ant funeral. I have always seen it. I could exist in a perpetual state of grief, thanks to my senses. So far, Africa seemed unkind to animals: goats were slaughtered *en masse*; dogs and cats fended for themselves, living off scraps, tails tucked between their legs; momma's bellies hung heavy with milked teats—hungry babies somewhere. My sensitivity did not facilitate a carefree existence. But it was how I was wired.

The gecko turned his graceful neck to look at me. Big sigh.

Eventually I drifted to sleep.


We woke with the first light, the sun tracking through the mesh windows and across the sea. Kas bounded out of bed.

"Let's go for a run," she said, pulling on shorts, which I had not seen for a while.

We'd been running partners for years. I threw on shorts and sashayed out into a perfect African day—a little humid, not too hot. Sometimes our respect for different cultures gave way to the sheer exhilaration of freedom. Leg freedom. We felt unstoppable in sneakers and shorts. Grounded and sweaty and free. Few cars passed us as we ran, and the road contoured gently toward the sea.

The largest, most elaborate spider-web stopped us. Morning dew glinted there with tiny crystalline lights. Spanning three feet, it bridged the gap between two large bushes in a lush section of road shoulder. Marvel gave way to concern. Something moved in the diamond.

The spider? No. We walked carefully near. It was a bird—a red and orange finch with fear in its eyes.

"Kas, we have to try to save it."

This meant *she* would have to try to save it because I did not really like wrapping my fingers around anything pulsing. I might electrocute the poor thing.

As a kid, I found wounded animals, birds with broken wings, a fawn who was caught in barbed wire, a great horned owl that came to our property and stayed for a week, then died. I was always heartbroken, like most sensitive children. But I couldn't stop finding them. Everyone told me dying was part of nature. I still grieved. I am certain I inherited this trait. My paternal grandfather, Quentin, built homes for city squirrels. My father, Duane, was moved to tears by few human things, but an animal suffering caused torrents.

Kas and I neared the suspended, disoriented bird. In the corner of the web, camouflaged by the shade, cleaning her teeth-like pincers, sat the queen of spiders, as big in her majestic black body as my palm! Her sheer size paralyzed me. I stayed Kas' hand. I worried the spider might jump if we interfered with her potential meal.

We wanted to preserve the web and loose the bird, but nothing straightens out so easily. We threw stones.

I had shit for aim, but I threw one that knocked the bird's right side free, only to have the bird swing to the left, where the web ensnared it further. God, the strength of the spider's threads! Even as my heart sank in fear, I had to marvel.

That fast, the spider was on the move, heading to secure her prey.

Kas' hurried throw had the same effect as mine—swaddling the bird deeper into the glistening silk. "Shit!" she yelled. "This isn't going to work."

"Not unless you grab it." I believed in Kas, in her powers to save. I hadn't yet given up.

"But it will still be covered in the web and probably have a heart attack in my hands if I try to clean it off—"

The finch struggled, each inhibited extension of its wing a sign of defeat.

The spider stitched and wove her web where we'd broken the geometry.

*Her meal,* I thought heavily.

"Micah, I think we lose this one either way."

I said a prayer for a swift, painless death, though I knew it was unlikely. One fierce arachnid would avenge trillions of spiders everywhere, eaten by birds.

Why did this particular memory stay with me? As we walked away, a fleck, a memory, a strange awareness revealed some seasoning of my heart. *Accepting death was accepting life.* Africa forced me to consider my relationship with death, whether or not I wanted to.

Kas and I ran, fast and furious, so alive—the sea at our shoulders, legs strong, hearts at full tempo.

To cool our skin and ease our minds, we jumped into the chilly Atlantic. The water was dark from an overcast sky, the salt cleansing.

*Life is raw and wild, in Lokop land, every moment. I have never lived so close to death. Everything eats something or searches relentlessly for something to eat. Mother camels wear the skins of their dead babies on their backs so they won't cry all night and wake the village, mourning their lost infants. Death is simply natural law here. It is not tragic. Until I grow used to it, my emotions bounce hard, celebrating birth one moment, grieving death the next. No one here cleans it all up—makes it tidy. There is no shiny bow. There are no satin-lined coffins.*

*Where does the extreme belong, I begin to see, if not in the present moment? And why are we always running from it?*

*One morning, I stand grieving over a mother camel who has lost her baby to a lion. I see Natiyon appear at the camel pen. She speaks quietly to my lover and points to a baby, the color of mocha. The camel's awkward, ambling gait and large brown eyes with long lashes are so beautiful. I adore its coconut mousse swirls of wiry hair. Because camels are the Lokop's source of milk, the rugged pack animals are sometimes their transport but rarely their meat. For me they are safer to love.*

*Uh, Micah, he says, my mom is giving this camel to you to bring home to America. She doesn't understand that it is by plane and far. He laughs at his mother's innocence.*

*Really? Really, this one? It's now mine? Tell her that I will keep this camel with her and come to visit it often. And tell her to always milk it and think of me.*

*I now have something to belong to which belongs to me. I have my very own baby camel. A camel to prevent death by heartache. Who doesn't want that?*

*I ask him, How do you say* forever *in your language?*

*We say,* ntarasi. *Why? Is that the name of your new baby?*

*Yes.* Ntarasi. *Forever. Is it a good name? I ask.*

*No better name, he says and strokes the baby's soft head.*

Guy arrived to escort us to the waterfalls wearing a Michael Jackson T-shirt, the album cover art for *Thriller* on the front, and a pair of black baggy jeans. I chose to wear my finer dress, one of two, both threadbare now. We'd had new outfits tailored in Ghana, but I'd chosen poorly: satiny purple with black horizontal stripes and elaborate gold-embroidered roosters. I really liked gold. I asked the tailor for a pant and tunic combo because it was easier for travel than a dress. In it, I resembled a garish fat prison escapee, the stripes running the wrong way, the pants wide at the hips with elastic ankle gatherings. Kas actually liked her earth-toned ensemble. Embarrassed or not, I wore my horizontal jail jumpsuit—just not to the waterfalls that day.

I am at heart utilitarian—a conservationist. I had an obligation even to bad clothing. I could not waste the fabric, the person's time who tailored it, the money, etc. I knew early on in Africa that my self-esteem had to be more enduring than aesthetics; plus I liked the challenge of making the distasteful attractive. This dolling up for Guy allowed me to see myself a bit more truly. I might be slow to merge culturally. I might mix African textiles in with my blue jeans and wrap my heavy hair in colored scarves. But it was a start. And maybe that was how assimilation happened—first the outside, then the inside. My heart said, *Who really cares anyway? Do what brings freshness.*

So, I donned a threadbare dress, kicked my striped pantsuit in the groin and winked at Guy when he lifted my daypack into the taxi.

There was time to find African fabrics that welcomed my skin, flattered my body, and did not show my underwear like this poor old Laura Ashley sack. The fabric barely held. I knew that Guy, if he was anything like many of the Africans we had met, would be tolerant culturally and personally. Especially personally.

Was I nervous? Just a little.

*Thriller.*

# Six | MODERN LOVE

I CLIMBED INTO the backseat of Guy's taxi with Kas, a faint awareness alerting me to his attraction. And mine? I loved this part, the ambivalence, the teasing out of pheromones. You can't smell anything, but the cells open wide, awake to the hint. I'd tempted myself to sit in front but a slender boy named Joseph took up the passenger's seat tapping his fingers against his knee. He looked too young to be Guy's friend but feigned cool with the best of them.

Guy cranked up the music and talked in his slangy percussive French as we headed into the forest surrounding Kribi. Tropical monkeys howled and parrots fled from the grinding engine. I had to remind our intrepid driver to speak slowly. Africans were so gifted at understanding different dialects—an effect of various tribes converging. We had another reason to talk slowly and loudly; the paved roads were badly gashed by rains, the shoulders eroded and no signs of maintenance anywhere. Driving required his full attention, but Guy still sent up lilting words, hitting syllables like cymbals.

I sat back, smiled at Kas and remembered how it felt to be relaxed.

Random police checkpoints delayed all journeys. Their sole purpose was to harass the taxi driver and ask for a legitimate fee plus a bribe. Eying Kas and me, the officer asked for more—assuming the taxi had raised its fare. Guy paid it. I started to offer to pay but something in the set of his shoulders told me to stay still.

The *chutes*, as they are called in French, trickled over three-foot-high boulders—not exactly photo-worthy, but Kas got out her camera. Guy seemed proud of them and Kas obliged. Once her high-powered Nikon was out in the open, we attracted a thief. Joseph—still the tag along—kept looking over his shoulder. Kas and I might never have noticed the glue-sniffer behind us but Joseph kept close watch. There was this fascinating custom in Africa. You could spend all day with someone and never ask or be asked a question, not about their life, age, what they did and didn't enjoy, as if the friendship occurred in between anything spoken, simply, while passing time together. Joseph was no older than sixteen, baby-faced, completely unimposing. He served as a kind of support for Guy on the open road with all the police. And that day, he alerted Guy to the Malian-esque behind us. Guy swelled a little fuller, put a light hand on my waist and hurried us to the taxi. All kinds of shoots at the *chutes*!

Yet again, the sentry police in green fatigues and red berets hailed us. Guns draped like cages across their bodies. This time they asked Guy to get out of the car.

"Do you think they do this every day, or is it because we're here?" Kas asked. "I wonder how much they want."

I watched Guy pull his wallet from his back pocket, give them bills, and come back to the car. I hated to crash our daily budget again but I figured Guy had one, too.

"How much did they charge you?" I asked. "We can pay it … as long as it's not too high."

"It's no big deal," he said, smiling. Then he added, "It's life in Cameroon."

Joseph turned and cocked his voice low. "If we refuse to pay, we can't live. Life in Cameroon is money, clean and dirty." He told us Guy worked hard, leaving his house at dawn, sometimes driving as far as Douala, 200 km north, worn out by dusk, not home until nine or ten at night. Guy shifted in his seat and drove with focus.

"Guy is saving his money to finish his house so he can ask his father for a wife," Joseph tattled.

Guy's hand shot out and clubbed him on the shoulder. "It's no big deal," he said.

Marriages in Cameroon were arranged. Every bribe prolonged his dream.

We asked Guy and Joseph to come for dinner at Pere Gespar's and fired up the camp stove. I set a picnic table lit with lanterns near the sea while Kas made pasta, tomatoes and basil, and for dessert, a cinnamon, creamy rice we named "*riz doux.*"

"Hey, expert, can you pick the stones out of rice?" Kas tossed me the bag and a woven plate. She tittered, downright tipsy with joy to host our only guests since arriving in Africa—reciprocating some of the generosity that had seen us this far.

They arrived freshly showered. Guy smelled like powdery soap, his skin so clean it shone. He tried to involve Kas in the conversation, but her French failed her. So he repeated her name as a form of inclusion. She volleyed his name back and they played a sort of tennis. I watched him, so easy and kind. We impressed them with our portable kitchen and *rix doux*, especially Joseph who had a sweet tooth. Easy amusement led to friendship, and we began spending more time together.

When Guy discovered our budget had run out at Pere Gespar's, he said, "Come stay in my house. You can see how Africans live in Cameroon." We accepted—simultaneously a cultural study and a tribute to our burgeoning friendship. This time we would try not to mess it up. This time, the invitation was real.

Like many Cameroonians, Guy had built his home himself, a white, stuccoed square with two modest rooms: a dining/living room and a bedroom. Most homes did not contain kitchens or bathrooms because they lacked indoor plumbing. We set our backpacks near the door. His combined possessions, minus the bigger furniture, did not amount to what we carried in our packs, and we didn't want to draw attention to them.

"I've been saving to finish it and make another room, but it will take time," he explained and pointed at a plastic-covered opening in the far wall. Guy had a small table for dining, a wooden bench, wicker chairs missing the cushions, and a bed. On the wall, last year's calendar hung, framed with colorful Mardi Gras beads and two strands of Christmas tree tinsel—similar to the decorations we saw at the Sinyanis'. I thought, *One man's trash* … and caught myself. I did a quick mental flip and appreciated the few decorations he had lovingly gathered.

His family, who lived in the adjacent home, shared the outside bathroom, kitchen, and well. Guy asked us to meet them.

"Kas, there's only one bed," I whispered as we followed behind.

Kas raised her brow and laughed at our predicament. We had imagined at least two bedrooms with two beds. Silly Americans!

We met Guy's sisters a short walk outside, in the kitchen, Onerine and Eveline. Onerine, older and less friendly, cast an indifferent glance. Eveline was thinner and grieving, having lost her husband to malaria six months prior. She managed a shy smile. Neither one stood to greet us, but the space only accommodated stooping. They worked at food prep for an early dinner, huddled over the soot-covered pot on the fire. The one small window would have let out more smoke and in more light but an adjacent two-story building occluded it. The sisters, barely fitting, squatted on wooden stools in the dirt.

"Let's walk to the market to meet my mother and father," he said. We cleared the doorway and set off.

"Maman," as she was called, had a vegetable stand and sold Eveline's prepared food as well. Onerine was the seamstress. Their father had a butcher shop open seven days a week. Everyone worked hard.

Our walk to the opposite end of town took us past sandy stretches where sea fishermen brought in the day's catch. Blue and green pirogues wobbled ashore in the slow waters. We watched men unload nose-curling sardines into large aluminum bowls that women then placed on their heads. Once loaded, the women ran to the market, where they laid out the fish to dry. Kribi did well despite the corruption, Guy said. The economy was stable enough to warrant the large market and his taxi business.

Maman was a big woman. She rested her broad hips and buxom body against the counter, a dishtowel hung on her forearm. Guy had apparently never hosted women before, especially white. She listened to him as she packed up the day's unsold vegetables.

"Can we buy some of your produce?" I asked. Kas too saw this as our opportunity to please and filled a large plastic bag with tomatoes, squash, and eggplant.

Maman's voice remained low, her expression steady, as she looked Kas and me over. I saw business savvy in her clever eyes. His father gave a jovial shout and called us over the wooden bridge, to his stand across the river. He wore the Islamic cap called a kufi. Curiosity turned his body and then his voice to us. "Son, bring your friends to be introduced." He entertained a whole group of kufi-wearing men. The experience with Pa had seasoned us—Kas and I tried harder to show respect. We tempered our confidence as they asked us the usual questions—where are you from? how long will you stay? who did you vote for? We said, "Clington," because to Cameroonians that was the newly-elected president's name. They grinned. We spoke only when spoken to, answering with basic responses. I felt sure they were onto us, and they liked that too, American girls softening to African ways.

"Guy, do your parents approve of us staying with you?" I asked as we walked back.

"I am a grown man. I pay for myself. I didn't ask them; I told them. But I do like to treat them with respect." Saying it aloud, the self-possession caused him to buoy up his saunter.

He really could. Saunter.


I grew up with wells even though we didn't use them. Living in rural Colorado, a well was often a valuable part of any property. The trouble, it seemed to me, was that taps provided instant gratification. The tilt of a wrist or twist of a knob and *voila!* Water.

I spotted the family's well from the window. "Kas, I'll be right back. I have to check out the well." She looked up from her book, *The Temple of My Familiar,* and nodded.

The well dropped into shadow with the waning light. Cement blocks had been stacked and mortared into a circle with an iron bar across the top, the bucket suspended on a braided palm rope. I glanced around to see if anyone was watching, then stepped up onto the rock. With a tap, nothing beckons you to the water's source, no hoisting buckets, no time for daydreaming. But a well? None other than the abyss.

I peered into the black shimmering and caught glimpses of myself—strands of flying hair, lightened now, round gleaming eyes, a nose that looked—well, African, slightly wider nostrils and pudgy. In this watery crystal ball, I sensed the subconscious, some energy beyond my reflection. I waved my hand, pretending it was a dowsing rod. Well water burrowed down, deeper down and carried part of me to it, channeling all life, seeping from the ground, filtered by roots, purified by the Earth—a cycle complete. Evaporation. Transpiration. Condensation. Precipitation. To feel this complete, this layered interdependence—

I felt truly peaceful, maybe for the first time since arriving in Africa, swirling my hand around.

No one should ever build a square well.

I walked back to the house to tell Kas about it.


That evening, Eveline knocked on the door, pushed it open before we could stand up, and set a plate of steaming somethings wrapped in banana leaves on the table. I hoped it wasn't fish.

"*Merci beaucoup, Eveline. Qu est-ce que c'est?*" I asked, saliva slicking with the aroma.

"*Le coquilles*—" she said, shyly. Ground quinoa mixed with dura palm oil, spices and salt, steamed in banana leaves. Beauty incarnate, beside a heap of sautéed vegetables—the very ones we'd bought for the family.

I *tss*ked. "Eveline, these were for you. A gift." Still I couldn't help myself from digging in, which pleased her.

Guy came home and sat to eat with us. We played African house.

"Will Eveline eat with us?" Kas asked me to translate her question.

"No," Guy said, "she eats in the kitchen with Onerine."

The image formed: a widow alone with her unfriendly sister, cooking in the dark for Americans. I did not like it. *Okay then, give Eveline extra kindness*, my heart said.

I cleaned my *coquille* plate. Once I'd tasted it, it was all I ever wanted. I honored Eveline's efforts by devouring her food and carried our dishes outside to ask if I could help. She laughed, covering her mouth like a school girl, and shook her head no. Impossible. White girls with soapy hands! Never.

I said, in broken French, "Thank you. So delicious. Best meal yet." Broken because for once I was thankful past words.

When I returned, Kas and Guy sat across the table from each other in high spirits.

Guy tried English on for size. "Kas what you want to chomp, Kas?" She giggled at his pronunciation. The house sweltered. Our bodies were used to the cool beach breezes. The bed thing was on my mind. Every time Guy said *chomp*, I thought, *I like to chomp AND sleep, you know.*

Kas looked calm and breezy as the sea. I could not begin to approximate it. How was this all going to go down? They played like school-kids while I stewed over the lack of bedding at hand.

Moonrise toyed with the window, and I blurted out, "Guy, is there another bed, and where would you like us to sleep?"

They both shot me a glance—his eyes amused and astonished at my bluntness. He said, "There's only the one, but I planned to sleep here," and pointed to the cushionless wicker, which by morning would leave reedy indentations all over his smooth skin.

He was the only one working. We were luxuriously free.

I glanced again at the single, sloping bed. Three might be fine in it.

What an awkward deal, God help us. We should have known—we were staying in an African family's compound. How much first-world pampering did we think we deserved?

It was Kas' compassion that determined we three share the bed. When I translated and told her Guy's plans to sleep on the wicker, she said, "There's no way we are making him sleep on that hard thing." She smiled like an African Cheshire cat. "You're sleeping next to him, though."

I already knew that.

We hadn't considered mosquitoes when we agreed to stay with Guy. We were used to hotels with netting or fans. Guy slapped at his face or leg without thought and kept conversing, though the bugs buzzed our ears with abusive whining and their high-pitched battle cries. This was one insect I delighted in destroying. What creatures eat mosquitoes? In my opinion, not enough.

We brushed our teeth, preparing for bed. Truth be told, I love sleep. Without it nothing works. And the thought of sleeping three abreast under a swarm of *moustiques* bummed me out. I wanted the beach and breeze so badly, but this was what we came all the way from the States to experience. I had to make the most of it—Guy's life.

He did have a fan in the corner. Guy turned off the lights and turned on the fan. Evidently we did not have electricity for both. I grabbed our flashlights from the packs and shuffled my way to bed. The fan rotated limply—not enough to move the thick air.

We lay there, stiff as poles, trying to avoid one another in the tiny bed. The minutes dragged by. Just when I felt the faintest hope of sleep, Joseph appeared and upset the order. He had a habit of doing that. We greeted him in the dark, the three of us in our plank-like proneness, still fully clothed. He asked about the day and heard we enjoyed *coquille*. Then he sat on the edge of the bed and pushed down next to Kas, squeezing us tighter. I suffocated my laughter. It was so absurd! My body shook Kas, causing her to laugh. Guy said good night. I turned toward Kas, my back to Guy, and stifled all laughter and judgment.

Joseph secured the edge—a body bookend.

I started to sweat. The screaming mosquitoes mocked the fan with their agile flight. Smearing either blood or sweat across my brow, I closed my eyes, conjured a prayer, beseeching whatever power existed to help. I could not bear the thought of hurting Guy's feelings by leaving, but I could not abide mosquitoes or my sudden malaria obsession. I sank into thought, weighing my options, when an unexpected generator whirred in the distance and powered up the fan—blew the mosquitoes back to whatever stagnant pool bred them, triumphant!

How many people slept without generators, fans, or netting that night? How many without beds or friends? Circumstance brought me to where I could not endure another moment, but in the next, salvation came. I had never prayed before—I'd never had to.

We slept well, imitating packed fish until around four in the morning, when the generator powered down and weakened the fan. The hungry mosquitoes found us. Kas and I woke with the first sting. Neither Guy nor Joseph moved. Laughter snorted out our noses while we pretended to sleep, feeling almost lucky. We weren't yet sure how to be around one another on this new morning, a little awkward with expectation, and I really didn't want to face Guy, in case he heard me giggling during the night. Four to a single bed.

"Guy left a note. He and Joseph are off to taxi," I said and showed Kas the paper as she straightened the bottom sheet.

"Joseph tried to put his hand up my shirt," Kas said with a smirk.

"Oh, brother. Really?"

"Yeah, but he's harmless—like the men on the bus. I pushed his hand once, and he went to sleep. Mosquitoes were worse."

"Not Guy," I said, surprised and a little miffed. "He didn't move—sleeps like a mummy." I wasn't sure how to feel, squished in, fully clothed, pressed against his virgin body all night long.

In Cameroon, life expanded. The well seemed always full. Fecund soil grew nourishing and bountiful food. Roadside police bribed in daylight—conspicuous in their corruption—and Kas and I allowed ourselves to be more playful. *Les Camerounaises* seemed to suffer less, so we could laugh and feel light. Our conscientiousness, the heaviness of first-world shame still lurked, but levity and friendship took precedence.

That morning, we cleaned Guy's house. Two rooms with nothing to dust was a cinch. We washed the painted walls and cleaned the concrete floors. I asked Eveline to help me clean the sheets, my ploy to access the well, to submerge my hands in that Earth water. She grinned at the request as though she knew its power, and my manipulative cunning. How could she deny me her assistance?

Eveline led me. I hoisted the bucket up. The water sparkled cold. I poured it into a blue basin at my feet and added powdered soap. She bent over, leaning elbow on knee, and folded the sheet into the sudsy water. With a series of swift wring-outs she squeezed the dirtied water from the sheet into the basin and handed me the folded heaviness. I practiced wringing and slinging and splashed us both. She hid her disappointment. I practiced it over and over until I got it, but not before sloshing most of the water out of the basin and sweeping the sheet corners through the dirt once or twice. I could tell when I found the rhythm. Tiny bounces of Eveline's body. The sound the sheets made moving through the soapy wetness. A *swish, swish* that was strangely calming.

I scrubbed, using my knuckles as a washboard, my body bent forward at the waist. She added water. Eveline danced in little steps to the pattern. She rinsed with a fresh basin and hung the sheets to dry, starched stiff by the open air. When I took them in, I was aware of the friendship they carried, a well-water bond. So pure.

The next day it rained from morning until night.

*The brown water boils. I don't care; I want to hydrate. As fast as it cools he hands me my bottle full. I drink hastily, water spilling over my lips onto my chin. Instantly, it evaporates.*

*My lover looks up and down the dry riverbed.*

*Micah, let's find a bath. I'll show you a bath for Lokop womens. Bring your little soap, he reminds me, and takes my hand to lead the way. I think he is looking for running water. We walk down the riverbed.*

*When we are out of sight of the others, he says, You will wash in this place, and I will go further, but don't worry. I will be where I can see you.*

*He is serious about bathing apart—any judgment by me that finds the notion ridiculous, genuflects. His reverence is so new to me, and compelling. But my heart does snag on his occasional disinterest.*

*Can I show you how to make your hole?*

*He takes off his red cloth and beads, laying them on a nearby boulder. The wavy mirage air bends space back and forth. He finds a place in the dry bed and gets on his hands and knees, pushing and pulling the sand back and forth. He mounds the heavy dirt away, his naked hips lifted, his chest brushing the ground. Moisture glistens on his back. A trough opens under his belly.*

*Satisfied with his efforts, he stands and says, Wait until it fills, and then you splash the water to your back and head and whole body. You know how now?*

*I nod, smiling shyly. Who knew water would emerge from sand? My lover. Who slings his red* shuka *over his shoulder, with beads in hand, and saunters downriver naked. I could cry, he is so beautiful! But instead of crying or running after him, I vow to bathe well, like a Lokop woman, not together with her man but alone in sacredness. I want to make him proud.*

*We are like desert sun and river water. One devastates the other in the end.*

*I follow his instructions. I do not glance at him, giving him privacy and taking my own. I undress. The water rises slowly into my sandy basin. I squat, cup my palms, splash this cool, urine-scented water onto my shoulders and face. Water used by everyone. Goats, camels, hyenas, lions. I don't care, smelling like a candy cane at the stock show. The breeze invigorates the cooling soap, and I shiver. Shivering chill in the desert. I think of the camels and goats that might taste the remains of the mint in the water. I sit on the rocks with my eyes closed. The sun dries my eyebrows and lashes. I dress. I replay the image of his body pushing through the sand in preparation to bathe.*

*He is here without warning.*

*Do you feel fresh,* Nanyorai? *He comes near and looks at my cleaned face and kisses me with intensity and heat. My body flushes with desire. The way he builds a fire, creates a bath, the way he watches over me—this passion a courtship that I have never known before.*

Three weeks brought us all closer. I suppose three, sometimes four to a bed will do that. Guy and I still had not even kissed, but he slept most nights with his arm draping my waist, spooning. His pace, right out of a Jane Austen novel. One evening Kas and I worked outside, helping Eveline peel manioc. Manioc is a tasteless, dry root grown throughout Africa, a drought-resistant non-yummy starch.

Guy came home early, mouth tight with irritation, his forearms particularly pumped after wrestling the car on those swervy-curvy roads. He seemed grave, as he often did, with fatigue. I had spent the day with Guy's sisters preparing the *coquille* and another dish with even more ingredients. They sang songs and giggled as we cooked, no trace of our somber first meeting. I wanted him to absorb some of the taste of our afternoon, so sweet and simple.

But instead he sighed and asked us to come inside. Kas looked worried.

We sat on the wicker chairs without cushions.

"Micah, an African man with two white guests—especially American women—raises suspicions. These people have small minds. I understand we are only friends, not lovers, and that your intention was always to continue your travels and fly away. No one knows what we do in this house, and it is none of their business. But they do believe certain things—" He paused, then added, "You have to forgive them or they will frustrate you. I don't want you not to like it here."

I asked him for a minute and translated for Kas. He had never been this direct. He looked like Muhammad Ali after a long round. Kas handed him some water.

Then Guy offset the mood by laughing—but not with his usual heartiness.

"I know you are innocent." Here he looked pained. Did he wish I wasn't so innocent? "Most of the time we are speaking Bamileke and you do not understand, but the dish you learned to prepare with my sisters this afternoon is what a traditional woman learns to prepare for her husband. She practices preparation for the wedding night. My parents want me to marry you."

I stood, turned away, and hid my face in my hands. "Oh, God, Guy! I mean, *mon Dieu!*" Shock coursed through my body. Shock and sheer frustration at the stupid way I'd responded. It was not easy to react in a foreign language. The timing was off. Time was altogether off in a land of its own making.

He stood, too, and put a hand on my shoulder.

"Guy, I'm so sorry. What a mess!" I looked in his eyes, grabbed his hand and silently hoped the world would be gentle with him, with us.

"Our intentions have been innocent—all of them. I'm not concerned with how the community thinks of me, but I need to find a way for my family to understand."

Pa and Maman. His generous sisters.

"What can I do to make this right? I am not familiar with your culture. I don't know how to make this right." I sat down to settle my nerves and think, but the reedy wicker poked my ass. I stood. It all seemed so absurd. *Me? Being groomed for betrothal?* Mothers of sons at home never wanted someone like me. I was a handful—too spirited, way too obstinate. I longed to step outside to walk and think. But Guy looked so lost, and I could not stomach the attention outside the compound just then.

Kas said, "Uh-oh, something big is happening," and asked me for the details. I was too concerned just then to play translator.

"Should Kas and I leave immediately? Would that help?" I didn't want this, but I would do anything to restore the peace. Of course, his family did not understand two rambling girls with nary a plan! They must have thought we were husband-hunting.

Guy massaged his temples, looked up, and asked, "Do you trust me?"

I translated to Kas, and we both nodded ardently.

Then he spun out the path of our escape—involving an aunt, a very long drive to Bafoussam in two days' time, a red dirt village, and a flight to Kenya.

I felt suddenly loved by him, his deep concern for our happiness. Despite all the difficulty and adventure we'd brought to his doorstep, Guy set us free.

The next evening, Guy came home vibrant with happiness. He was smacking his gum with a wide-open mouth. I asked him where mine was and he touched his shirt pocket—the place my grandpa made me search for gum as a child. To my delight there were two pieces, one for me and one for Kas.

Guy said in English, "Kas, what you chomp, Kas?" and extended the gum to her. She laughed and said, "I chomp gum, Guy. Give it to me."

It was then that I thought of kissing him.

Guy's father insisted that we dress in our African finest for the last evening we shared—not the jailbreak cock outfit but a new one that a Cameroonian tailor had made. This time I had followed Kas' advice on material and pattern. The fabric made my body proud. The entire family wore traditional clothing—the waxy colorful sheen of fabrics rich with palm trees, forests, and hard-angle geometric designs reserved for special occasions. We took photos in front of their glassless window, Kas and I featured in the center.

Guy's father put a cassette in the tape player and taught us to dance—Bamileke style. It's a scooting, line-dancing sort of shuffle, arms at your sides without any saunter and even less sex appeal. His parents thanked us for accompanying Guy to visit his Aunt Rose, the next day. Maman's sister was very dear to them. Ever the manager,

Maman asked me when we would return from Bafoussam. Guy told them we were flying to America first. He had agreed to do all of the lying, for which I felt deep thanks. I just kept smiling innocently, pretending my French was worse than before. This satisfied everyone and helped those around us make sense of our unconventional friendship. And so, I danced.

Kas did too, taking the hands of Guy's sisters, singing songs she did not know. His usually conniving mother jiggled with joy around the open room. Cultural celebration! Deep deception! The stuff of life? Who was I to pitch a fit about integrity? I would soon be on a plane to the other side of Africa.

I watched Guy dance, close enough to see there was something alluring in the clear control of his hips.

Bafoussam lies 600 km northwest of Kribi. We started out early, beating the police to their corruption. No one manned the first station just outside Kribi—a favorable omen for our journey. Kas and I flew the finger at the years of harassment Guy and Joseph endured—our American salutation to autocracies—as we drove by.

Guy laughed and shook his head. We knew we were being cute. We all felt the slash of freedom as wind whipped in the windows. We moved deeper into the green forests that fell in hills toward the turquoise sea. Men carried dirt-covered tools from fields. Women towed babies on their backs, balancing large bundles of banana or pineapple atop their heads. Older children skipped behind them. Contentment sprang lightly in their steps.

I remembered something I had once read in my religious studies course: "*Ora et Labora*." "Pray and toil." *Thus God finds you* was the inferred part. This prescription summed up wisdom seekers and spiritual aspirants worldwide, physical labor deemed an essential part of their spiritual equation. I had not done anything physical in too long. We played soccer in the dusty compound with kids from Guy's neighborhood, but I was pretty sure the authors of this philosophy were not speaking about sports or workouts. It had to be in service. Use the body to serve something grander. Make beauty in your world. As far as prayer, well, I never really knew how.

Everything outside the car moved like ritual, an effortless undulation, like breath. People walking, animals in fields, trees swaying. Guy's music played as much for the scene, the living rhythm outside the car window, as for us. I was thinking about God more. I knew that.

A six-hour drive through dense forests brought us and our provisions to Guy's aunt's house in Bafoussam. Guy and his family said provisions were the gifts we bore while traveling—gifts as modest as tea or coffee, a chicken or a sack of sugar. Even a journey as near as the neighboring village, fifty minutes' drive, say, demanded gifts upon arrival and return. An invisible web of products and commerce exchanged across a large landscape despite the lack of infrastructure. Think desert, think Sahara hundreds of years ago, and you find the origin.

Africans served one another, served anyone arriving. Travel caused discomfort even in the youngest bodies. Too many bumps on the road, and too many vehicles without shocks. It followed that guests arrived in need and were given something to drink. If extended family arrived with an agenda, which it often did, needing money or whatever, only after drinking, honoring our humanity, did they discuss the reason for the visit. This simple practice is power-packed with intelligence and grace.

Bafoussam is a dirt village—red soil dotted by dark-green trees. Argent sky. The rainy season ushered deep purple clouds flashing with lightning. The people seemed wholesome "salt of the earth" types. They gathered about in circles near the few buildings. Easy conversation dropped from their mouths. Their dwellings were made from the same red dirt that spread itself amid the anchoring roots of ancient trees. I relaxed just watching them from the car.

I smoothed my dress and felt good. The Earth, celebrated from top to bottom and back up, seemed to lift the people into celebration, too.

Guy got out, stood next to his door, and waited for us to realize we had arrived. Village. A field with rectangular red dwellings not in any recognizable formation. Jungle greenery embracing the huts. We inched the car into an opening, which was hard to find, as lush as this place was. I loved the quiet, quaint feel of Bafoussam already.

"Well, Kas. What you chomp here, Kas?" I said, grinning as I got out. We stretched our backs and legs, dusted ourselves off, and felt hungry.

Rose was younger than I had expected, prettier than Guy's mother, with slender, toned arms that eased out of a short-sleeved tunic. Her bright mid-calf skirt looked like an upside-down hibiscus blossom. In the eyes of many African men, slender women were less desirable than fat women. A man in Ghana told us thin women worked too hard, worried too much, were too wiry to be wives and mothers. He told us, with glowering eyes, "Eat more meat."

Rose welcomed us with an unexpected hug. No standoffish respect from her! She called to a young man to help with our backpacks. The house appeared humble, but inside rare textiles and angular furnishings mixed with ebony masks. Guy's aunt must have traveled to acquire such art. The masks hung like personalities on the walls. Rose showed Kas and me to our very own room. I fancied stretching out, the bed so big. It bordered a sunken, tiled-floor family room with plush pillows for sitting. Tile was one of the region's industries, along with soap and cacao. Propped on pillows, we ate chocolate squares and sipped our tea, arriving and settling.

Rose lived in exquisite, modest beauty.

I smiled at her. She returned the grin. *Men and their opinions be damned,* I thought.

Guy excused himself to work on the car.

Kas took a bath. I read about East Africa and waited for dinner. The room had no netting or fan, but the elevation was too high for mosquitoes—the temperature and lighting perfect for naps. I showered with a metal bucket, changed into my jeans and T-shirt, and peeked outside at Guy, who was leaning over the engine with a puzzled look on his face. He had taken off his shirt.

Shaved head, broad shoulders, thin waist. What is it about a man leaning over a car?

"Why don't you sleep with him? He's handsome, he's generous, you can speak with him, and he likes you," Kas said as she plucked her eyebrows. I kept looking out the window.

"What then? Learn to make the *coquille* and get married?" I said with bite. "How are we possible? We don't have the same life experiences, reaction to things, filters. I think about it, I think about it plenty, and do nothing." Guy shifted to wipe the grease from his hands, folded the cloth over and wiped his head. His very smooth scalp. I'd slept next to Guy for weeks, and still my mind wasn't open enough. I would imagine touching his face, holding his shoulders, and freeze. African man, no, make that Islamic African man. This mind-ceiling, though vaulted, weighed heavy.

"Or you could see it as *just* sex. It's been a while for both of us. You can tell me all about it—" She lifted her eyebrows mischievously.

I closed my eyes. I let her words reverberate in my head. If making a vegetable dish connoted marriage, what would sex imply?

That evening we had rice and vegetables in coconut milk sauce and relaxed on the oversized pillows. Guy ate meat with his hands—a little barbaric, certainly not daintily, the grease from the car faintly visible on his black skin. His aunt inquired after her sister.

On our way to bed, before we parted ways in the hall, Guy said, "I'll miss our family that sleeps together. Sleep with good dreams, Micah and Kas."

I fell asleep reading Chinua Achebe's *Things Fall Apart*.

I wear no shirt, crawling through cool grass in gray lightweight shorts that I sleep in. I am so turned around. My feet and knees covered in red mud, cool wetness. I know my eyes are open because I touch them to make sure. Darkness. The tall grass lies trampled where I have crawled. My palms sting and bleed from parting rough grass blades. I have to pee urgently. Squinting in the darkness, I am looking for a building, a toilet. Why am I outside? All this mud. Where's my shirt? Where is Kas? I need to get something on these cuts, or they will become infected. Don't risk open wounds in Africa! I look behind and see the outline of the roof against the now lightening sky. Fear and nerves and cold propel me toward Rose's home. People wake early. I have to get back before someone sees me. I race the sun. I squat low in the grass, splattering the edges of my muddy feet. Relief. I can think now. I make my way back to the house, covering my breasts with my hands, find the bucket used for showering and fill it with the tap outside to wash. My heartbeat slows. I know where I am. My hand stops bleeding with the soap and water. I tiptoe back to our room to find my shirt bunched up on the floor near the door and Kas deep in sleep. I lie down and try to untangle my confusion.

Distant sounds and low voices in other parts of Rose's house woke me. The sun had fully risen. Kas had risen. I said, "Kas, come with me. I have to show you something." We walked to the outdoor shower. I pointed to where I had crouched on all fours. My disoriented prints marked the red mud, mud which still edged my toes. Bloody lines streaked my palms.

"I can't believe you walked that far before you woke up. That's scary," she said, looking at the flattened grass in the distance.

I started sleepwalking when I was young—when my parents were divorcing. I did it again after having sex for the first time. Whenever the edges frayed in my fastidious psyche, I sleepwalked. I had not sleepwalked in years. It's more surreal than the strangest of dreams, a stumble around the mysterious subconscious, this world and that world.

What had frayed this time?

*"Avez-vous faim?"* Guy asked if we wanted breakfast. He wore a plain, dark gray shirt. He looked sexy.

"Oui. Chomp," Kas said, and wiped her bare feet on the woven entry rug.

French baguettes, jam, tea with fresh milk, and the pineapple we brought. I had asked where Rose's family was, but the effort to understand Guy's slapdash French was greater than my desire to know; I let go. I often let go. I translated things for Kas all through our trip, but I missed important nuances. Sometimes when I felt lazy and Kas wanted to know something specific, I would make stuff up. A more efficient story. Kas no doubt came home with a slightly skewed version of Africa—or at least French-speaking Africa. There is always something lost in translation.

We went to the market later that morning. Beauty everywhere. The fertile Earth knitted in the sheen of the green pepper and tomato skins. Guy disappeared into the crowd. Kas and I hardly noticed, lost in the glistening veggies. The latticed roofs, the bold clothing, jovial chatting, the ground packed smooth by generations of festive market.

I held eggplants, papayas, cucumbers, and lastly the rough, hand-made soap Guy brought me, waxy and uneven as our plans. He surely had taken his time choosing it. I had begun to think he might let me leave without so much as a kiss.

The following morning, a weak sun edged into the gray sky. We said goodbye to Rose, a most gracious host, and drove to Yaounde, Cameroon, to catch an international flight to Nairobi, Kenya. Guy asked us, while driving, to stay one more night—all together in one bed, and something about the forlorn way he asked let me see into him, finally. I understood this language, his will beaten down by police stops and injustices. Guy was resigned to letting me go, like he paid the bribes and toted Joseph around. And when I saw it, I knew I couldn't change his life in Cameroon, but I had the strangest urge to blow him up from the inside so it all wouldn't hurt so badly, so I wouldn't be just another unreachable dream.

The nourishing land of Bafoussam sloped to a drier, lower land of industry and factory. Yaounde was the capital and business center of Cameroon—not an ideal setting for a last evening, but our friendship beautified the hazy, smoke-filled air and drab buildings.

Guy asked the nerdy hotel clerk for a large bed for three. Staring at the clerk's light blue polyester shirt, I swallowed hard and interrupted Guy. I asked for one double bed and one single. Guy did not argue but I could see his mind doing circus math, feeling disappointed. We hauled our things past the tangerine walls that brightened the hotel like a Florida beach resort. We'd chosen this lodging because it looked happy—a good place for an indefinite parting.

We left the luggage in one room and went for dinner. Kas and I hoped for the *coquille*. Guy said we would not find it in Yaounde; the dish was regional. Kenya would not serve it either. We ate sautéed vegetables with our hands. I still had trouble keeping mine clean, though we'd relinquished utensils months ago. The porridge dried in a starchy grit under my nails. Guy's hands stayed clean, so firm and muscled. He caught me looking at them and held my gaze longer than he'd ever done.

He reached into his back pocket and gave us a cassette of Bamileke music—the traditional music from his village. My throat tightened at the thoughtfulness, but I couldn't grab it because of the manioc cement on my fingers. He laughed out loud. Kas smeared a globby mess of manioc onto the back of my hand, and I got her back. We decorated each other, all the while sopping up his generous affection.

We three walked back to our tangerine hotel. Storm clouds pushed into one another, pressing a blue-gray darkness to the ground. Rain came like tears.

Kas asked me to translate. "Guy, you are our first and only real friend in Africa. We will never forget you. Wait for our letters. Please tell your family we appreciate their hospitality."

I then bid Kas good night and walked with Guy to our room.

"Can you find a candle and a condom in this city?" I asked.

"I will come back with one or die!" He ran down the hall like a world-class athlete and made me happy.

I loved him that night; we loved each other. Our black and white bodies merged, drawing the wonderful unfamiliar further in. I smoothed the disappointment and defeat from his skin, caressing his muscled thighs and strong hips. I would not look away, nodding gently, begging him without words to believe in me, believe deeper, to let me love him with the tenderness he'd taught me. He pushed so intensely his male heart blazed. His saunter, bold and unyielding. We thrust injustice far away from us and the whole room caught fire with our gratefulness.

I belonged to him for that night and realized that some kinds of belonging, the pure kind, felt exactly like freedom.

In the morning, he said with clear eyes and big lungs, "Thank you. That was the best sleep—no stress, no tension, enough space."

I hit him with the pillow. "Guy! You should have said something. I never knew you were kept awake. I didn't even know if you liked me!"

"*Je t'aime*, Micah. *Vraiment*." He shrugged and reached to twirl a strand of my hair between his fingers. My ringlet curls held on.

The plane taxied. I watched him, this beautiful black man I now knew in scent and sound. The engine's wind whipped the trees. Guy stood by a fence outside the tarmac, waving with sadness in his body. Sadness, but not defeat. This time we won, and the fulfillment would really carry us, I felt.

The plane lifted off.

Guy would return to his family's expectations, the corrupt Cameroon police, and his unfinished home, which would one day be ready for a wife.

# SEVEN | KENYA

*HE AND I lie under our favorite baobab tree on the beach—an entire village could live in its expanded branches, the base so mighty in circumference that ten adults can encircle it. We lie again, today, talking. I want to pull this tree's branches into forever.*

*When Nilotic people, people of the Nile, cross paths, they ask a series of questions. This ritualistic greeting honors the greater community and serves as news delivery. First they seek the family name, which will sometimes denote the specific clan. Then they ask about the region of origin and details about the family, livestock, raiding tribes, and water source. Now they are known to one another and might share a meal or a song.*

*He says, You live in Boulder, Colorado, now, but your mother and your sister, Desiree, live in Carbondale, which is in the mountains. Your father, Duane, lives in Denver not far from Boulder. The mountains and the cities get snow and also much sun. There are wild animals in the mountains but not many in the cities. You have four climates and summer can get almost as hot as here. We see the same moon. Most days you go to university and become a waitress in the evening, getting tips. He recites while I rest my head on his stomach, taut with the fluctuations of speech and breath.*

*Mmhmm. That's it, I say encouraging him.*

*How often do you see the whole of your family? Are they staying with you sometimes? Do you get lonely because you live alone? He asks this question more than others. Lonely.*

*I have answered him several times, but he never tires of the images forming and keeps asking. He gleans something from the telling and retelling; nuances arise from the recitation. The first time the story is told for the mind, the second for the body, and then spirit infuses the words. He needs the people and places of my life to know me. They are my ancestors. This never occurred to me before now. With a hint of shame, I say, I don't see them enough, but we speak on the phone at least once a week. Usually on Sundays.*

*We will travel to Mombasa to call them on Sunday. We can find a phone where you can call international. Then I will greet Duane, Mama, and Desi, he says. He takes the stick from behind his ear and begins brushing his teeth.*

*Desi is in Argentina now—another country, not America. But we will call my mama, and she will tell Desi. Duane we will have to call at a different house, I say, imagining my family hearing his voice, his accent that mixes British English and wild.*

*Then, we will talk to Desi and Duane another day, he says with satisfaction.*

*He spits the toothbrush splinters out and continues, Cousin and I will escort you and Kas to the airport in Nairobi,* Nanyorai.

*So little time, I think. The waters of the bay shush my thought, take it out to sea.*

*We must see you all the way, to keep you safe, so that you can return to your lovely family and tell them about you and me.*

Kas and I had both imagined we would skip Kenya altogether on our trip. The country, on the east coast of Africa, nestled under Ethiopia and Somalia, above Tanzania, was already famous for Westerners, which translated to: not as much to discover. Or so we thought. Nairobi, the country's capital, boasts game meat restaurants and Karen Blixen historic sites. Mombasa and Lamu rely on exotic Indian Ocean coastlines to draw tourists. We had no interest in either. But Guy knew the cheapest tickets out of Cameroon, going east, were to Kenya.

On the plane to Nairobi, a British expat concerned with our safety adopted us. Nigel was one of the many wealthy outsiders who crowded Kenya. The Brits, it seemed, took their snobbery everywhere they went. Nigel, in his mid-forties, was a place snob. He casually dropped the names of places, not people. The wildlife safaris awed tourists, he said, and lavish hotels there doted on them. The Jomo Kenyatta International Airport, he confided with some pride, bordered a wild animal safaripark. Planes landed as giraffes with gangly legs ambled beside the runways. The tourists loved it.

I looked out the smudged window and felt rattled, though I couldn't say why. I didn't yet have a reason. The cheery expat invited us to stay one night with him and his wife to orient ourselves before we launched into the diesel-dirtied city of Nairobi. I suddenly became self-aware—sat with better posture, dusted my lap for imagined dirt, peanut bits, stray hairs. I rummaged around my memory for proper behavior. With Guy and his family, the proper had withered into irrelevance. I liked it there.

We drove to the expat's home in a shiny leather-seated Mercedes. I thought of my sandy feet on Guy's dash, arms out the window, surfing the wind through my hands. I could even have spit, though I never did. He would have laughed! These liberties fell hard in the confines of a swanky German vehicle. Nigel was "civilized," like our parents, and his presence evoked a manner of being, evoked manners *period*.

His home was like his car, an architectural tribute to elegance. Flat-roofed and angular, the one-story house zigzagged around a bougainvillea courtyard that separated wings on either side. Glass windows partitioned the rooms. An open kitchen joined the two wings near the center of the courtyard, the floors slick with slate tile under soft Persian rugs.

We left our backpacks outside. I brushed the bottom of my shoes more than once upon entering, asked if I should remove them. He gave a dismissive wave. His wife was not yet home. Nigel showed us to our room in the right wing. The queen-sized bed looked enormous. A glass-block shower stall lit by a small window opened to fragrant wisteria vine.

"Let's have dinner together. Maybe in a few hours?" he said. I was distracted by his shiny wrist watch. It kept casting rainbow prisms around the walls.

"That would be lovely," Kas said with a particularly British phrase. Kas never used *lovely*.

I protested mentally. Sleeping in this opulence even one night might negate all of my hard-earned tolerance for squalor. Kas flung herself into an oversized chair to read while I took a hot shower, letting the water cascade down the back of my head, luxurious after cold bucket showers. The shampoo smelled like aseptic cleaner with fruit on top. The Earth hid itself in my pores and hair, protesting. We, the Earth and I, had been reacquainted. I did not want to wash the acquaintance out.

But, my how the puffy bed fluffed itself with down comforters. Egyptian cotton sheets pulled tight over a dreamy mattress. What if the dirt in my hair, on my being, seeped out in sweat and stained everything? Oh God, I missed Guy's family's toughness. And his realness.

Our host's pretty wife, in her early forties, arrived home at dinnertime, carrying Indian food takeout, her brown saucer eyes and dark hair pulled cleanly into a barrette, her business suit still pressed despite the travel.

She slipped off her pumps. Admiring the garden view from the terrace, she said, "You both appear so young to be traveling alone in Kenya."

Too young? In an attempt to see myself, I looked at Kas. Her skin showed no wrinkles, and her eyes still held innocence. We differed there. I did not look innocent though I chose to behave innocently sometimes. My eyes could see through people even when I was young. The couple believed they were doing us a favor—and they were—but we were trying to break free.

We ate fatty Indian curries. Our hosts offered beer, which we declined.

"Oh, right, you aren't yet old enough to drink, but you can vote," he said. "You Americans!" And the night proceeded in the strangest parry, jab for jab, as any Western cocktail party would.

"I've never acquired a taste for beer. I liked drugs—which I gave up when I was fourteen. In fact, I gave up anything that altered me except for sugar—" I winked. The sponge cake Nigel was slicing into slim wedges said that they liked sugar. "It's the most addictive drug yet, behind love." I'd thrown in the drug bit for shock value, which worked. Our hosts looked at us anew and sharpened their tongues.

When at last I flattened my body on the pressed linens, that night, I felt no comfort. The tête-à-tête had been harmless enough. It was the speed at which I destroyed all softness I had learned, all surrender, that troubled me. Our conversation jabbed and outsmarted. They led. I followed. No heart in it, no true humanity. But my arrogant snob rose to their cordial challenge.

Cameroon's green, fertile heart lay so far from Nairobi, and so far from me.


With coffee and a wave from the driveway, the couple left for work. Grateful for their hospitality and the contrast it provided, we thanked them and resumed our adventure by walking into downtown Nairobi, with youthful spunk and the freedom to spit.

Not so easy to maneuver our heavy backpacks in the fury of city life. Kas took stunning photos of the chaotic streets. She had to be sneaky. Photos had value. Plus, our perpetual state of awe prevented us from being more respectful, though we sensed the immorality. How would my parents feel if backpackers stopped outside their home and took a few snapshots of Mom hanging laundry or gardening?

Among the African locals, magazines did not hold sway. Instead, people gathered photographs. Kas and I had watched an old man on the train from Dakar to Bamako sell his photos of strangers to strangers. Passengers scrambled to flip though his album of three-by-fives. The photos exhibited every variety of human on the planet: all races, ages, males and females, together and separate. For a few CFA, a photo was yours to keep and allowed you to fabricate a story about your connection—an African version of the Western world's celebrity magazine. Did they see in that stilled moment something that reminded them of themselves or a way they wished to be? Without magazines, television, even sometimes mirrors, people used photos to link the continent. Kas and I played our part.

People wanted our address as often as we wanted their photograph. They needed a US address to apply for sponsorship, and we needed theirs to send a copy of the photo. Kas tucked a manila envelope with addresses into her pack. It contained hundreds of folded and dirtied papers scribbled mainly with post office box numbers—men who worked construction, people we'd met on trains and buses, a man who helped us locate a post office in Ghana, a mother who wanted us to sponsor her children through school. On the back of each crumpled address we made notes so we would remember to match the photograph once home and send them a copy of themselves.

This proved to be an adventure. People who did not have an address—never having the need—began a desperate search for a PO box they might borrow. The search for a box to receive one uneventful photo could take hours. It was their hopefulness that kept us sitting on a bench, watching them run to and fro. The need for that frozen image, somehow dire.

Nairobi was cold in October. Stained gray with the exhaust of diesel fuel, most of the buildings needed washing. A few tribes in Kenya were Nilotic. Their features were finer, their bone structure thinner, and their skin lighter shades of brown with red undertones as opposed to the people of West Africa. Other people were of Bantu origin, agriculturalists from the central continent. Nilotic tribes moved nimbly, at home in their long limbs. Their watery namesake flowed in their nomadism too. Bantu people were sturdier, with wide noses and full lips, muscled and compact. Bantus stayed put, given any say in the matter.

Diversity equaled beauty in this far-from-beautiful city. Forests need all types of trees. Mono-crops were unsustainable. Surely humans were also examples of the need for variety. Body and facial structures captivated me. Living photographs. I started seeing vivid shades of dark and light. Physically, Kas and I looked sturdy, like the Bantu peoples, but we were without solid roots like the Nilotics. We flowed here and there, as they did.

In Nairobi, we caught colds, consulted a map of Kenya, and discovered just how far north—how close to the Saharan heat—public transportation could take us. We hopped aboard a minibus (*matatu* in Kiswahili) and rode it roughly ten hours north of Nairobi, to what felt like the last frontier.

We wound up in a strange, Western-feeling town—John Wayne's horses swapped for Lawrence of Arabia's camels. Lamaresh, at our first viewing, was held hostage in midday languor. Everyone halted to cower from the passing of the sun overhead. It gave us time to gawk. The town encircled a roundabout of discarded lorry tires. Old men gathered there, wrapped in nothing but blankets. One man had earlobes hanging down to the bottom of his jaw, large holes hollowed by plugs from many years ago. Another man anchored his earlobe loop up around the top of his ear so it did not dangle, and a thin strand of cracked, dirtied beads hung to his breastbone.

Kas and I had never seen anything like them. The roundabout tires doubled in utility as benches where they held court, chewed tobacco, and watched the constant tide of *matatus* as they U-turned at the end of the road. Where were the women? The children? We kept to the shadows and kept our questions to ourselves.

We'd traveled as far north as the Kenyan government and the US embassy in Nairobi advised. No further public transport was provided. They cautioned against the Somali bandits at the border who, for the last few decades, since the Shifta War in 1963, had been responsible for kidnappings.

Kas and I felt a curious need to travel as far north as Yangaloi—a city we chose arbitrarily due to its amusing name, and the fact that it bordered the eastern shore of Lake Outran, Kenya's largest body of salt water. Finding transportation could have proven difficult except for the impressive amount of relief food the US trucked to the lake weekly. We found a truck, full to the brim of American-flagged sacks of wheat. A local boy tipped us off—the driver was lazing by the discarded tires.

A bulky Indian man with vacant eyes and an apparent disinterest in us, if not life itself, talked with the old men. We knew we had no business traveling to Yangaloi—this land of no tourists—which is why we had to go. We loitered, not wanting to interrupt his conversation. Then I tried, politely, to get his attention.

"*Tafadhali*," *please*—Kas and I were picking up a few Kiswahili words—"can we pay to ride in the back of your lorry to Yangaloi?" I whispered it, knowing that travel north of Lamaresh was ill-advised. He did not speak but his raised eyebrows, showed he considered the proposal, and the eye arch made space for a devious twinkle.

The big man walked away and gestured for us to follow. He demanded privacy in order to inflate his price—no one liked conducting shady business in broad daylight. We paid one thousand Kenyan shilling, which was the equivalent of twelve dollars—a good price, considering everything but our budget.

The large tarp-covered truck would certainly launch us out of John Wayne territory. As sturdy as a superhero, with tractor-like tires that could stand up to the uninhabitable country, the truck gave us pause about the type of terrain we were entering. I thought of Mexican immigrants who risked their lives for opportunity—many died in trucks such as this. We waited until no one was looking and climbed up the attached ladder and slipped under the tarp. The sacks of wheat made hard seats but felt cool to our legs. We hid and avoided a section of pulled-back plastic, the air thick with hot stagnation.

"Friend, why are we going to Yangaloi?" Kas asked from the dark corner where she sat. She knew we had no reason, which caused her doubt to swell.

The guidebook relegated four whole sentences to Yangaloi. It listed one three-room hotel run by a Somali family. It did not say if they were kidnappers. We'd have a place to sleep and could eat the relief wheat if we met dire conditions. Sitting on the sacks, we waited for our driver to hit the road. Sweat ran from our chests, gathered at our bellies, and seeped out from behind our knees. Forty-five minutes passed. Panic nudged me close to the edge. I kept eyeing the opening. When suffocation threatened, we poked our heads out to breathe and saw the driver playing a wooden board game in the shade. Late afternoon. A few men slept against trees.

"How long do you think we should wait?" I asked, looking at our water bottle reserves.

Kas wiped her dewy face and shook her head.

As if psychic, the driver broke tempo and hopped into the cab of the truck. The diesel engine only increased the heat and trapped fumes under the tarp. Kas looked at me wide-eyed: *Time to abandon this stifling diesel-filled mission?* Gasping, I grabbed my pack to jump out, but the way was suddenly blocked—by women, men, children, boys our age piling in and scrambling over us to find a grain-sack seat.

The boys tightened down on their laughter, seeing us covered in sweat and angst. I was too proud to quit now; if they could do this journey, Kas and I could as well. We hunkered down.

Most Africans are hardwired for hardship; Kas and I—it remained to be seen.

The engine roared, and the passengers stayed quiet to conserve energy. My ass hurt. My lower back jammed toward my upper on the bumps. The hollows on the rock-littered road could swallow tires whole. Even superhero tires. I braced against each jounce with fatigued arms. Sometimes the truck drove down a dry riverbed and screamed up the other side, the sacks shifting crazily underneath us. We tumbled into one another, and after the third or fourth time, I stopped apologizing. Resilient children slept, clinging to their mothers' cradling arms. Everyone looked at Kas and me, curious about us, curious if we would make it, yet no one spoke. We smiled through the slimy grime coating our teeth.

At one difficult pass in the road, the truck stopped, stirring up dust, and the driver got out to assess. Kas and I peeked out from under the tarp. In the distance three bare-chested young men walked with determined strides, gripping spears, mirage-like. Ornate beadwork covered their toned bodies. Bodies that glinted in the sun as they moved. The bright red cloths wrapping their waists snapped sharply as they crossed the barren land, pace unhindered by heat, unhindered period. They turned and looked directly at us with fearsome indifference before disappearing behind a hill.

"Kas, what was that?" I said quietly, mesmerized and confused by the vision.

"That was crazy. I feel like we're suddenly on a movie set. They had spears!"

Anthropologists say the American Indians did not see the three ships sailed by Columbus until the ships were at shore, as consciousness could not assimilate so quickly something it had never known.

I assimilated as quickly as I could. "I bet they know where we can find a village."

We ducked under the tarp. The truck roared.

When the truck stopped in Lowaa, a half hour later, everyone unloaded into the night. The driver was hungry. While he ate, two girls our age boarded. We stayed to keep our good seats on the grain sacks—now just the four of us. A street lamp shined into the uncovered lorry.

"Kas, are you hungry?"

"Yeah, but beyond. You know when you should have eaten hours ago and now you just wanna sleep?" she said, reaching to rub her eyes but remembering her hands and face were filthy.

We didn't eat in front of people on these long journeys unless we had enough for everyone. I unloaded the top part of my pack and offered peanuts to Kas and the two girls. They shook their heads, declining but smiling.

They were tall and slender, waif-like willows—Islamic girls of Somali origin. Nilotic. They laughed with that easy quality familiar to vacation. We could relate.

"What are those you are eating?" one asked in perfect English as she pointed to the unshelled peanuts, her voice smooth and low.

"I think you call them groundnuts. We call them peanuts." I extended the few in my hand to her.

Her face was full, soft like the moon. She was submissive when men were present, the opposite expression of feminine than me. Where I was flirtatious and bold, she was demure and taciturn. *Fire and water,* I thought. I didn't believe men superior, and although she may not have either, her culture demanded she behave like she did.

When the truck loaded, silence descended again. The two girls stared at their feet unless someone spoke to them. I caught them looking at us several times. We were safe to peek at because we were foreign.

Under the tarp, in the pitch black, one moved toward us.

"I am Hawo," she said. "Mary and I are traveling to Yangaloi to stay with our cousins while we have a holiday from school." She introduced two boys about our age, Hussein and Ambrose. I had noticed them earlier, lighter skinned young men, likely Somali. Hussein had a male model's build, Ambrose was as thin and asymmetrical as a newly planted tree.

"I am Kas, and this is Micah. We are also on holiday from school and visiting Yangaloi for the first time."

Hussein said, "Where will you stay? We have a large house, and my mother will let you stay for less than the hotel. There are bandits who rob tourists. Sometimes they take them and their money. Yangaloi is safe because everyone gathers relief portions at the mission, but you can't go outside."

I hoped he meant outside of Yangaloi, not out of doors. Too late now. Africans often took pleasure in alerting tourists to the danger of travel. Not because they enjoyed scaring us but because by their assistance they were becoming trustworthy, differentiating themselves from the bad guys.

Kas gave the okay with a glance, and our night's lodging was settled.

*We sip our Cokes from straws, easy lulling waves, but there is nothing easy in my heart as I listen. He says, I was forced to go to school. One child from each and every home in this country, even if the family did not want it. I hid in the bushes from my father for days, refusing, trying to survive like a wild boy with wild animals. Elephants chased me and I became tired. I could not speak my mother tongue or be called by my real name. They called me Stephen and made me wear your clothes. I thought it was only British who dressed this way until I came to Mombasa and saw Germans and Italians. Now Americans.*

*I feel three inches tall. Kas and I know where he is going with this sad tale. Africa fosters our truer selves. Where had I sacrificed this part of me, a wisdom, something so natural to all humans? School.*

*He says with a sternness, a disregard not for our feelings but for placation in general, This type of education I don't think it is working for people. He looks directly at me, winks and asks, Do you?*

*He continues and I thank God his question is rhetorical. And he does mean* people, *Kas and me included.*

*But this language allows me to ask you if you are understanding me. That has to mean something, but to take a child's only name, to force him to put on clothes and make him feel ashamed to speak his language, to know his own songs, his own God—to me it is not a balance. He sweeps his hand through the air and says, But we are here now, speaking together and enjoying this tourist beach. He begins chanting a sad song and the other warriors swan their necks back and forth to the memory, to the time before school, a time totally unknown to me.*

*Something about the way he bridges worlds, sipping a carbonated Coke that causes air to push out of his nose, this tourist beach and the timelessness he carries in his eyes, make me want him terribly. I have to have his wisdom on my body.*

We tried engaging Hawo and Mary in conversation, but they would not talk until the boys fell asleep. As soon as we were free of the men, our conversation flowed like water downhill. I gauged their zeal for Islam. In subtle ways. But I learned only this: Hawo's sister Habiba was staying in Yangaloi, and they were going to collect her for their parents. Hawo dusted the relief sack she was sitting on. "They want her to come home, but she doesn't want."

"But she doesn't want" accompanied me on that hard sack over the last miles into Yangaloi. I hoped that Hawo and Mary could provide a gateway into their language, into foreign feminine thinking, believing and being—the inherent value in being female, which every woman knows even when generations of oppression and abuse have denied it.

I already liked Hawo and Mary. But Habiba's rebellion, her big risk, stoked my feisty curiosity.

When the engine shuddered to a stall, the tarp flew off the truck and a warm wind swept in. We climbed out with our packs and helped others unload. Wind rattled tin roofs and tossed pebbles as though it were juggling, spinning rocks from ground to sky to ground. Voices strained, lost in the howl, everyone shielding their eyes with scarves and hands.

Yangaloi was a dry, nomadic-people's trading post dependent on relief-food distribution—not exactly a mecca for tourism. The landscape had sand, wind, three wind-whipped trees, and boulders from nowhere. One talkative boy, when I mentioned the big rocks scattered in the powdery dirt, said, "God became angry and threw boulders and stones down to Earth, and they're still here on the way to Yangaloi. Everywhere else got trees—green things."

My eyes grew wider absorbing this surreal landscape, an immense flat sea of whitewashed boulders, sandblasted smooth. The lake glimmered, a near full moon provided the light, reflecting her beauty off the backs of salt water, land-locked crocodiles. Fine as talcum powder, the dirt varied in shades of white. Because the wind blew fierce, Yangaloi had no mosquitoes and no malaria. To the east, the shadow of a densely foliaged mountain expanded out of flat ground like a Hershey's Kiss.

Hussein and Ambrose carried large sacks of grain, sugar, and tea into Hussein's mother's store, which was also her home. They said to follow. We ducked under stiff laundry, still hanging from the day. They led us through the storefront to our room, one in a row of others. The wind had blown the windows closed. Even the normally cool concrete floor felt warm from trapped heat as though in a Ziploc. Everything echoed. Airborne sand sprinkled over the tin roof like spill from an hourglass. It was eerie and fantastic.

We thanked Hussein and Ambrose and said we'd pay their mother in the morning. Before he left, Hussein squared his strong shoulders and asked, "Micah, what will Kas take for breakfast?" I could see he had a crush. Men tended to measure the bond between us and present their requests to the one they were less interested in, subliminally asking for permission to court. Kas and I granted them our respective blessings unless that certain *nope* look stopped us—then we would give the suitor "the slip." Back home it worked like this, too. We were guardians of each other's solitude, sentries of chastity, unless we had no interest in being chaste.

I said Kas and I liked anything vegetarian, keeping the permission general.

With the howling, rabble-rousing Yangaloi wind, we disintegrated into sleep.


Morning. No wind. Nothing stirred in the glaring sun. Flies took advantage of the stillness. Kas still lay in bed, her head ducked under the lightweight blanket, thirty or more flies resting on her body like deer poop in a field. I had to giggle.

Tapping on our door, Ambrose greeted us, carrying two buckets of well water for our showers. He bounced effeminately, light on the balls of his feet. He laughed but sounded like a muted horn honking. His cheer felt distasteful and forced, to me. He wore the same pink shirt he had worn on the truck, a little grayer now. I did not trust him but hid this even from Kas. I had learned that cultural differences could often lead to hasty first impressions.

Dried palm reeds served as outdoor shower walls, the gaps wide enough to expose our white butts. A concrete slab sloped away, discouraging the water from pooling. Even without the wind the air was cool in the morning, and with water on our skin, cold. The water changed color as it ran off my head—rusty. My hair captured dust like a butterfly net.

Kas' hair, jet black and shiny, hid its filth no matter what. Once, in Abidjan, a throng of children followed Kas, shouting, "*Chinoise! Chinoise!*" The children were Muslim and totally innocent of Kas' Jewish heritage. Initially, we went to great lengths to conceal it. But most of our fears proved paranoid; there were other pressing threats to our health and happiness that we never considered.

The newest threat appeared to be wind. Hussein said many tourists left because of the wind. Unique to the area, it blew from ten in the morning through the evening, coming to an abrupt halt in the early morning around three or four. Everyone slept and dreamed best then. The constant wind stirred anxieties, as if our inner selves were also subject to the ferocity. The ceaseless gale made you seek shelter. Question your safety. Long for quiet. How the guys with spears we had seen dealt with this wind lured my imagination. Maybe walking against it so often informed their stride. I'd never seen such syncopated determination; a lee of its own design.

Before breakfast, we hid large bills in the bottom of our packs and left a few on the steel support stays, secure in the internal frame. The bedroom door had no lock. A thief would have to pass through the store entrance, manned by day, enter the courtyard and search rows of rooms to get to ours. But Ambrose watched more than he spoke and had slinky timing. He lurked when we discussed money. Kas and I decided to trust. In what, I was not certain.

We met, Hussein, smiling in the yard, his clothes clean, scalp-short hair still wet from his shower. He said, "Good morning, Kas. We have chapati and chai for breakfast." Then he taught her the word for *wind* in Kiswahili—another sure sign of attraction. "*Upepo,*" I said under my breath and wondered if there was enough breakfast for me.

It had always been this way. Men either found her attractive or me, never both.

Hussein set a full pot of milky ginger chai on the coffee table with a lace doily under it. Ambrose carried the plate of steaming buttery-smelling chapati. Maybe he wasn't so bad after all.

"This is good," I said in French, stuffing chapati into my mouth, referring to the whole situation. "Make sure not to disappoint him too quickly," I added in English, winking at Kas as I sipped my chai. "But don't learn how to make any betrothal meals."

Kas thumbed through the guidebook as we ate.

"That mountain we saw when we arrived is called Mt. Laku. That's where the men in red cloths and spears live. They're nomadic shepherds called Lokop."

More than anything, I wanted to go see the Hershey's Kiss mountain and her warriors. "Why don't you ask your new boyfriend how to get up there?" I asked.

Kas dismissed Hussein's flirtations, though she might string him along for a little ginger chai and chapati. She mastered this sort of romancing, and I had known many men who never received a kiss before their hearts shattered at her youthful, reckless feet. Kas was not cruel, however—just beautiful and noncommittal—a fatal combination for those who loved her.

I was more serious about love. I never indulged a well-intentioned man even for a moment, if I was not interested. Too much mess. After a year or longer of being in a committed relationship, I might break a heart, but I was black or white when it came to love—no frivolity, few flings. To date, only circumstance had broken my heart. True heartbreak had yet to come for me.

# EIGHT | PRIMAL LOVE

AMBROSE ARRIVED AGAIN with his strange timing.

"Well, hello, Ambrose," Kas said, laughing. The guy was random as rain. Only later would I appreciate his catalytic talent. Buck teeth, shrunken shoulders and all.

"Yeah, my family lives in a field not far, and I thought you would meet them and see how traditional people live. We call it *manyatta*. The warriors are at home," he said, casually. "Do you want to see them?"

*Red-clothed, spear-carrying nomadic warriors?* I shot Kas a look of disbelief at our luck.

"Thank you. We would love to," Kas said, giddy as a kid.

Ambrose sucked his teeth and waited. Apparently, he meant right then, not someday in the near and uncertain future, so we got ready.

The few tourists who did venture to Yangaloi came to view the traditional pastoral people of the region; they hoped to gain a portal back in time to our common beginnings. Ejocho, Lokop, Samburu, Pokot, and Rendille made Yangaloi a stop on their way to their various lands. Each tribe proudly boasted their differences. The Ejocho wore ostrich feathers for headdresses, the Pokot capped their spears with giraffe tails, many chose red as their preferred color, but some favored blue. They all gathered, peaceful while they collected their wheat ration, then all bets were off and raiding one another's livestock ensued.

"Shall we go, then?" Ambrose led the way through the courtyard, clothes still blowing on the lines.

Hussein waited outside. We walked into the drying sun away from the salty lake and its white shores. They set the pace, strolling, showing off the two young American girls to the town. No one seemed interested.

"Those are Ejocho mens," Hussein said, pointing at a row of idle elders. Sleep and night clung to these elders. Strange sticks poked out from their mess of brittle, matted curls. A bluish mud covered the back of their heads like thick pomade to tame the unruly hair. Most lay in the wheat-colored dirt, sleeping, blankets strewn across their naked bodies, their heads cradled on a homemade prop.

Hussein explained that nomadic people used a wooden stand with a downward bowing top as a pillow. The contoured curve cradled the base of the skull. Supportive? Yes. Comfortable? Impossible! When they were not sleeping on their *pillows*, they squatted on them as seats. Their pillows hung by a leather strap from their fingers, ready for board games and spontaneous naps.

Other than the distant hills sloping up to Mt. Laku, we saw nothing green—no bushes, no foliage. Yet I wouldn't call it vacant. I still remember feeling something inviolable lurked beneath the land's apparent barrenness. Yangaloi felt rich beyond resource. We walked away from the town toward the alluring mountain, which captured all the rain on its sides, leaving little for wind-beaten Yangaloi. We passed a dirt soccer field and turned into an open area. Between the town and the mountain we saw our first *manyatta*, the Lokop word for village—a *traditional* village! A misshapen circle of domed, arched-entrance homes made from palm reeds, cow dung, leather skins, and mud, sturdy enough to withstand the wind.

We wove among them, entranced.

"It's here. This one," Ambrose said as he neared one of the huts.

He called us closer, said to duck our heads inside. We smelled earthy, bodily, animal scents, scents that in the United States we always cover over.

Kas shot me a wide-eyed glance and a pleased drop of her jaw.

Nothing would be as it was before.

A warning came, a timidity in my chest that caused me to pause before entering the hut. A brief caution but nothing more. Nothing declared, *Careful. You will be awed and altered, broken and humbled. Now is the initiation, a genesis. Heartbreak is the passageway.*

If a cat has nine lives, innocence has one.

I ducked into the hut.

It was dark. Deep darkness after the blinding sun. Kas and I hovered in the doorway arch, unable to see. Ambrose spoke to a woman in quiet, kind tones.

I imagined what he might be saying.

"Hi, Auntie, I've brought two white girls to see how you live because they come from a different part of the world, and they are visiting here for the first time." Or maybe he was more cunning. "Hi, Auntie, these girls have a lot of money and come from a country where the homes are sturdy and clean and expensive. Maybe if they see how we live, they will choose to help us and give us some money or create a charity, or make something useful of themselves later, when they are no longer students traveling for sheer pleasure and adventure."

We never knew the nuances that trimmed these conversations. Their language was beyond foreign, not only in lexicon but in rhythm, texture, and history. I had never heard this language before, but I loved it at first word. It bewildered and relaxed me—the gentle cooing and coaxing and the way it floated back and forth, no hard landings. Hussein, being Ejocho, didn't understand it either, save for a few words the Lokop and Ejocho people shared.

Mama did not speak Kiswahili. So it was up to Ambrose, who coached us proudly. "Say, '*Supa*, Mama.'"

Kas and I responded. We needed that greeting to proceed and enter her home. "*Supa*, Mama," we said from within the doorway, still not able to see.

Like a vision she appeared, sitting with her legs extended and crossed at the ankles, threading red and white glass beads onto a nylon string. She was older, about fifty or sixty, or perhaps younger but with withered skin that had seen a lot of sun. She tucked her legs behind her to the side and made room for us to join her around the fire pit, the fire reduced to burning coals. We sat on hard cow skins—Kas and

Hussein and I—spotted brown-and-black hide hair. The leather must have been new, not yet softened with use. Soot blackened everything.

Kas and I fell silent, trying to be respectful. We had no idea how to be. I petted the leather, running my hands with the hair, smooth, and then against it, causing it to bristle under my palm.

Mama poured water from a calabash—a leather-covered gourd—into a large pot and boiled it on the fire. Her chest was bare except for the layers of multicolored necklaces that hung heavily on slim shoulders. Her skin, hard and scratched in places, showed age but her hands were steady and her eyes still sharp. She fingered the necklaces and asked Ambrose questions in an understanding tone. He answered her quickly. She absorbed us, through some sense beyond her eyes, not looking up from her beads. I could feel her taking us in. Her breasts were withered and well suckled—she'd probably nursed many babies. Mama set the necklaces aside, wiping her hands on her dark leather skirt. She asked Ambrose to open a metal trunk in the corner. He pulled from it black tea leaves. Chai. We had not been asked. And yet we were invited.

Kas smiled. I smiled. Finally, the village of all villages! Fearing this might be my only time in a Lokop home, I absorbed it with full presence—the smells, the odd containers I could not identify, the colors, the steam from the tea—all of it. The extreme strangeness. Strange in land, in culture, in custom, in language, in dress, and even God.

How had the same God created us all?

I felt like a chicken in the presence of peacocks.

Did they believe in God? What was their God like? How could this planet be large enough for us and for them? This hut was a home so unfamiliar, I thought at times it was all grand theater, a performance. But, no. Mama beaded, tended a fire, wore animal skins with exposed breasts whether or not Kas and I were here as audience. What a miraculous thing!

I felt like a prop in the exhibit at a Natural History Museum, only this scene lived and breathed. *Incroyable!* Mitochondrial Eve and me.

We did not want Ambrose to represent us, but we had no choice. In Kenya, those chosen to be students learned English and Kiswahili in school. Otherwise, only vernacular languages were spoken.

"Hussein, what are Mama and Ambrose speaking? What do they call their language?" I asked.

"They call it Gutok. It is a difficult language for tourists to learn because it is not written."

Not written. Spoken only. Stories. Thousands of years of stories. *Les Raconteurs*. Dream weavers.

I wanted it.

When I was two, my family was stationed at Sullivan Barracks, Mannheim, Germany. One day my father, the handsome, cigarette-smoking, uniformed man who normally paid me little mind, asked my mom why I had reverted to gibberish baby talk. The German landlady stopped him. She saved my intelligence from further insult. She explained that I was not speaking gibberish; I was speaking Deutsch. It turned out learning language was one of my talents.

Kiswahili seemed familiar now, my intonation and structure strong. Kas and I acquired more vocabulary like language thieves. But Hussein was right—one Gutok word began and blended into another, without edges. They tended to run together like a pack of dogs. This didn't deter me. All of my anxiousness quickly surrendered to the sound. The sway of words, the soft, subtle words, lulled me. I listened and rested as easily as grass lies down in a field.

My eyes flew open from half-mast when a warrior stuck his head inside the archway and looked at me with piercing precision. His eyes had needed no time to adjust to the dark.

"*Supa oleng!*" he said in a deep voice, a raspy voice that broke one spell and began another. He asked Ambrose our names, then personalized the greeting. "*Supa, Micah, Supa, Kas. Karibu sana.*"

I said, "*Supa . . .*" and looked to Ambrose to fill in his name. Ambrose stalled. He was not happy about it. Had he felt the immediate zapping between me and the warrior? *Oh no*, my heart protested, *Ambrose has his grimy sights on me?*

Ambrose spit out a tea leaf and took his time. "Well, I'm not supposed to call his name but because I have been to school it is forgiven. Lochili. My cousin's name is Lochili."

"*Supa, Lochili. Supa oleng!*" I sang out. To the warrior. In the doorway.

In a village in Kenya. I was flirting—in his own language—with one of the red-clad warriors we had seen from the truck! Flirting for all my life. Flirting like an expert, calling in all charm.

Lochili's fulgurant smile brightened any sadness, excited all boredom. His confidence attracted me like a bee to borage, the gleam of his milky teeth. Tall, broad across his shoulders, a sculpted waist, a red sheet covering his chest, his muscles flexing with grace and sensitivity. Pure impulse. He squatted where he entered as though he might leave just as easily, another sheet tucked between his long, toned legs. Crude sandals made of used car tires looked as durable as his feet—both made for this inclement land of boulders and spiky acacia needles.

*Please, Lochili, stay. I have never seen anyone like you.*

The almond ovals of his eyes caught light, declared his intelligence, and beamed full-hearted wisdom. He dominated the conversation, eager to devour, not patient as his mother was—he did not move his eyes from me.

I flushed. His intensity forced me to look away, reminding me of the Tuareg. I felt tenderized, melting like a piece of chocolate in his mouth. His maleness softened something unfamiliar in me. Demureness, not typically a quality of mine, ventured out. In contrast to Lochili's power, Ambrose grew more effeminate, slighter, retreating into passivity. The warrior's way affected us all. What was this invisible balancing, causing even me to curtsy?

*So this was male?*

I felt wildly female. Be-*wild*-ered.

Mama removed the boiling chai from the fire, then mixed in milk and sugar from the trunk. She poured it back and forth between calabashes, to cool it, then handed me mine in a metal mug.

Lochili said, *"Karibu chai, Micah America."*

Everyone's laughter rang out when he rhymed my name with country while inviting us to have tea. Clever Lochili. He awed us with his raw wit—the type of man that turns the room. The type girls love. Light-brown skin and a nose more Roman than African. I saw it. *Nilotic.* All eyes were on him now, and they were laughing eyes. I wanted to understand his every word, for him to break me open with his humor. He would not let Ambrose alone, cornering him and demanding answers about who we were, and what were we doing here. Ambrose responded respectfully, as Lochili's wild confidence chased him into submission, no matter how reluctant he felt.

When I dared to look at Lochili, his eyes locked mine without fear or intimidation.

Then, a wounded Ambrose turned to me. "Lochili wants you to come again this time tomorrow, and we'll put Lokop clothing and beads on you, and some paint on your faces. Do you agree?"

This was one huge step beyond Hussein's advances, teaching Kas a word or two of his language. But Kas had forgotten all concerns about that, about my courtship cooking and marriage muddle with Guy's family in long-distant Cameroon. She was in cultural anthropology heaven, a shine in her eyes of pure wonder. "Yes, we'll come tomorrow," she said.

"You'll escort us here, please, Ambrose," she added, needing him for translation although Ambrose was, at best, sparing with words and, at worst, we feared, dishonest.

Hussein had watched the entire scene utterly silent. He left then, hunch-shouldered, without acknowledgement, a tamed boy amongst a warrior, who felt his displacement sorely.

His exit made room for Lochili's brother, Loiboku, who must have been waiting outside. He greeted us with reserved certainty, unlike the luster Lochili generated. He watched Kas from the periphery, his skin dark black with black eyes that resembled Kas'. Loiboku wore white, which lifted the black of his skin, made it shine. His long hair, braided down his back, was bound in the front with a beaded plastic visor, which he adjusted, making sure it was in place but without vanity—more astutely. Loiboku dressed for God's eyes—the rest of us were fortunate to see him. Whereas Lochili was boisterous, Loiboku was deep, quiet. Intense as his brother but the intensity buried inside.

Full of chai and beautiful novelties, we rose. Like a gentleman, Lochili rose as well. He taught us *goodbye* and *thank you*, and we practiced our pronunciation on Mama. Tomorrow afternoon felt like an eternity from now.

If there was an edge to the universe, I felt I had just reached out and tapped it. So very different. Everything. I swear I saw that desert with different eyes.

Kas and I walked with Ambrose, saying nothing. When he strolled ahead a few paces, I chanced being ridiculous.

"What happened in there? I feel drunk. Who are these guys? Did you see the way Loiboku looked at you, visor and all?" I hoped she felt the same. This instant, rampaging attraction felt too far-fetched to go it alone.

"Looking at me?" She laughed. "Lochili was fucking you with his eyes. He wouldn't stop staring at you. He's intense. But I liked his brother. I like Loiboku." She said his name, savoring it like a dessert. And then she spun around, eyes to the sky. "How could I resist a man who wears plastic on his forehead and dresses in a white sheet?"

We cracked up. Ambrose turned to see us holding onto each other to avoid falling over.

Now we only had two problems—Hussein and Ambrose. How would we visit the Lokop and still be welcomed at Hussein's home? There was one other small problem. Language. Our Kiswahili vocabulary consisted of common phrases but only six singular words, one of which was *mamba*, which translated into crocodile—not especially necessary in matters of love, one hoped.

Kas and I connived to remedy these challenges when we arrived at the compound, where we found Hussein engaged in work at the shop—a little colder in his temperament than when we last saw him.

"Wow, that was interesting. You and Ambrose did a really nice thing introducing us to people who live so differently. This is what Kas studies in school—people from other cultures. It's also why we decided to travel to Africa." I cloaked our tangible attraction in scholastic curiosity, nothing more, and praised Hussein and Ambrose.

"Let's have chai, and you can tell us about your culture, Hussein. Ambrose can tell us about Lokop culture," Kas added. We were a dangerous combination.

The four of us sat on a shaded concrete patio next to the shop—a sort of cafe and another of Hussein's family's businesses. We talked about everything except our girlish desires for warriors. We learned that warriors were part of the age set, a generational grouping which the Lokop used rather than acknowledging individual ages. Ambrose was also of this same set and technically a warrior but chose education over shepherding. *Lmurran*, or warriors, were responsible for the safety of the livestock and the villages. Lokop men were circumcised when they were older, between age fifteen and seventeen, and that ceremony marked the beginning of their warriorhood. They watched over the cows—protected them from wild animals and brought them to water and to distant places for grazing. The men spent most of their time away from home, sleeping in the bush, risking wild animals and neighboring tribes. And because of polygamy, Lochili and Loiboku had different mothers but the same father.

"Cowboys," I said to Kas.

"At home on the range," she replied.

"They are only here to visit their mom that we took chai with, and then they return to Mt. Laku again. Lochili has a girlfriend there—" Ambrose watched my face as he divulged Lochili's secret. I remained one step in front and managed to hide the intensity of my disappointment. "And maybe Loiboku has a girlfriend, too. But I don't know."

We persuaded Hussein and Ambrose to give us lessons in Kiswahili, starting with the word for water and, much later, sneaking in the word for love. We needed every possible assistance. Hussein's mood picked up; he was pleased Kas showed such an interest in his language. She memorized some words, and I, others, feasting on dinner and chapati, and sweet chai for dessert.

Then we feigned fatigue and said goodnight.

Kas flopped onto her bed scribbling the words we'd learned, while I searched the back of the guidebook for translations. We still lacked the glue, the words that linked the story, but what we lacked in words became an adventure in creativity.

"I can't stop thinking about his face and hearing his raspy voice," I said.

"At least you know what his voice sounds like. I'm in love with a mute. Ohhh, I love his silence and those big black eyes. How do you say *eyes*?" Kas was keeping me busy hunting new words.

"*Macho*," I said.

She shot me a puzzled look. "You think? No! They weren't macho—they're the real deal. *Eyes*, Micah. The Swahili word for eyes."

"*Macho*," I said again, with a raised look, waiting for her to catch on.

She laughed. "Oh. *Macho*? Yeah, definitely their footwear. Where the rubber meets the road!"

Those tire shoes sent my mind to my wardrobe.

I frowned. "What are you wearing tomorrow?" My choices were dreadful and few. "Well, I am wearing impractical, hot-as-hell jeans. My butt looks good in them." If Lochili's traditional clothing was the red sheet, jeans were mine. I wondered if the Lokop warriors were like American men. Did they even like butts? "Lochili might have a girlfriend on that mountain, but I'm guessing she does not wear jeans." His girlfriend had no threat in me. It was an innocent flirtation. I had not considered sleeping with Lochili. He was untouchable, an *objet d'art*. How would I move around his war paint and beads, hold him, let alone kiss him?

I tossed the book to Kas. "Kas, look up how to say, 'Take off your jeans.'"

"You're hysterical. We're both nuts!"

That long night, short on sleep, we exchanged wonders.

"I wonder what their lives are like on the mountain. Do they spend most days near the village or away? It's good they can have girlfriends." Kas sounded dubious and generous at the same time.

"I wonder if they're allowed to have sex."

"Well, it's cool they want to dress us up like Lokop girls. That's a good sign."

Long silence. The winds had died down by then.

"Kas, what has happened to us?"

"Maybe they put something in our chai—"

"I am not kidding. These guys are lithe, black, muscled, and beautiful. They've known us all of half an hour. They carry spears and wear beads and decorated, makeshift tennis visors."

"They are wild," she said.

"And I can't wait to see him again! Lochili Lesepere, what will I say to you, and more importantly, what will you understand?"

"I wonder how old they are. Same age as us?"

Before drifting to sleep, I asked Kas one last question. "Can you imagine telling our fathers about our new boyfriends?"

"Dad, he carries a spear, doesn't bathe really, and is more decorated than a male peacock. He doesn't have a home, job, or any money. He can't read or write. I love him, Dad. Oh yeah, I forgot, he was circumcised without sedation when he was fifteen."

We giggled and drifted off, intoxicated.

In the morning, we headed down toward the lake and out of town for a run, winding on footpaths barely distinguished from the white, powdery earth surrounding them. We neared the lake and saw Hawo and Mary and others, wading out and bathing.

"We hoped you were still here," I said, hands on my hips, a little out of breath. They stood at attention wondering why we were running, then realized it was for enjoyment and not to alert them to some danger.

"Can we run with you someday?" Hawo asked, timid but determined. I tried to imagine how that would be with her hijab, the Islamic head covering that both she and Mary wore, trailing behind her like the tail of a kite. "Why not?" I said. But Mary never showed any interest in running, her frame frail, her spirit subdued. Mary seemed an extension of Hawo, and content with that.

"This is my sister, Habiba—the one we have come to collect for my parents," Hawo said. Young Habiba was not as pretty as either Hawo or Mary. She was shorter and fatter, with mischief's glitter shining in her eyes. She didn't wear the hijab—her hair and face were free. I could never be sure, but Habiba seemed to know things, her innocence manhandled. Perhaps she had had sex—it was that kind of knowing. She possessed forbidden knowledge, one apple after another.

Habiba certainly lacked the deference her sisters carried. She spoke right to us. "Maybe we can travel together to Lowaa when you leave Yangaloi."

I sidestepped her demand and pried into her life instead. "Why do you want to stay here, Habiba? Lowaa is nice too, and not as windy as this place."

She grinned with excitement. "I have a man here. He's older and married, but he loves me."

Once you've tasted the crispness, you have a sixth sense of other apple eaters.

"And your parents know and have sent for you?" I asked.

She shook the middle and ring fingers of her hand to make a snapping sound, the sign for "beating." Many Africans did this same gesture, allowing their hand to fall limp at the wrist, the two fingers hitting against each other in rapid succession—Snap! Snap! Snap!

"Yes, I will be beaten badly when I go home. I must go home. They know already."

She asked to travel with us because if she arrived chaperoned by two American girls, the punishment might be less. Clever. I sighed. She had spirit. Its wild expression neared an end; she would be beaten into assured submission.

"Hawo, maybe you can help your sister not be beaten," I said, feeling some kindred need to meddle.

They laughed, including Habiba. My ignorance was funny to them. Their shoulders shook with delight. Why not laugh at two white girls romanticizing their culture and then trying to intervene to change it? They could huddle up and howl. But when it came to being a woman, being born an American woman was the very definition of fortunate. Period. Kas and I knew it. Not to have known it would have been a much grander insult than trying to intervene where we sniffed injustice.

"We will pass through Lowaa eventually, and we'll look for you there. Tell your family we are coming, and maybe they will punish Habiba less," Kas said, offering what we could.

A Jewish princess protecting a hedonistic Muslim. Lovely world.

Americanness, of whatever ancestry, carried clout. No one ever cared whether Kas was Jewish. They seemed unconcerned about our ethnicity, this deep in the interior of the continent, far from the Saudi kingdom, Jerusalem, and Palestine. The truer conflict here was tribal—disputes over control of resources rather than grievances with where, how, or to whom one prayed. Amid the daily suffering, God the concept held less significance; to be devoutly religious was a luxury for people with time—not for those struggling to survive.

Kas winked and sat the sisters down on a large piece of driftwood. They leaned in when she said, "We have some unfinished business here in Yangaloi." We retold the feverish events of yesterday. Hawo cautioned us not to tell Hussein or Ambrose; they would try to sabotage.

The sisters all agreed Lokop warriors were proud and attractive.

Kas directed a question to Habiba. "Do you think they have had sex already? Or is it forbidden to warriors?"

"They all have girlfriends that they sex, but they cannot get her pregnant. Also, she cannot be married," Habiba said, matter-of-factly. Her sisters blushed with each English word.

"Are they good to their girlfriends?" I asked.

"Yes, of course," Habiba said, but I sensed our respective notions of "good" were different—maybe even unbridgeable. But Kas and I took their word for it. We traveled in their land, immersed in their culture, and we wanted to believe the brothers would cherish us.

We all looked up at once. A large ostrich ran toward us, her massive brown wings flapping chaotically, her feet flinging outward from large bony knees. Boys ran behind her, not in torment but play. Her long, muscled legs brought her closer. Ostriches peck the top of a person's head to kill them, I recalled, as the distance between her and us whittled away.

"Run! Run!" Hawo jumped up from the log she was seated on. She must have heard the same thing.

We all ran toward the lake. *Ostriches fear water?* Hawo plunged in from fear. We looked back to see if the feathery mass was still coming. The ostrich turned and headed off to hunt the younger boys, then passed them, never even slowing her speed, not chasing anyone, simply exercising her legs.

Habiba laughed. "Town ostrich!" she said. "Crazy one. The people let her run to and fro." Yangaloi's benevolence had in fact preserved her life. Ejocho ate that meat. Perhaps it was the wind that drove her mad?

"Crazy ostrich!" Hawo giggled, wringing out the bottom of her dress.

"Bye, *kwaheri*," we said to them. "See you later." We ran back toward a shower, chai, and our new warrior friends.


I washed my jeans when we got back. Everything dried, even the heavy denim, in less than ten minutes. The wind picked up, howling her way across the lake, blasting everything airborne.

We walked with Ambrose into the *manyatta* with anxious hearts. Hussein joined us only in order to spend time with Kas. We found

Mama's hut and entered with ease, knowing the layout and expecting the dark. She sat there in the same place and greeted us with mugs of chai. Within moments, Lochili ducked his head inside and unnerved me.

"*Supa, Micah. Supa, Kas. Serian ake? Teperie N'kai?*" he asked without hurrying, teaching us. Hearing his voice, my belly rose to my throat.

Loiboku came in.

Ambrose translated with a hint of bitterness that was not lost on Lochili. "He's greeting you and asking if you slept with God, or did you sleep well, I think. It's difficult to translate our language because it uses pictures. It is more for the eyes than the thinking."

"How do we say 'yes'?" I asked and learned *yes* was a simple *ehhh*, drawn out a little at the end. This was why the language sounded like a song, the cooing and humming. All the harmony of agreement.

Lochili's eyes smiled. I lowered mine. I tried to channel Hawo, but I cannot assume it suited me. He came to sit by me, and as the space between us closed for the first time, I smelled him. Fire and Earth.

Loiboku followed Lochili's lead and moved closer to Kas, scooting Hussein aside. Lochili told Ambrose to translate. He said they would apply face paint, and we could borrow the necklaces worn by the young girls. He then asked if we'd brought our camera.

Kas said, "*Ehhh.*"

Beads of sweaty dew gathered on my nose. It was hotter in the hut, due to the fire, the chai, and my damn jeans. Lochili wiped them with his thumb and said my name in a whisper as if we were alone. I followed his hand with my own trying to clear away any ugliness. He chatted, entertaining the others, except for Hussein who sulked at Loiboku's side.

Then Lochili unwrapped a packet of colored clay from his red *shuka*. He spit on the powder and, using the soft end of a whittled branch, applied the red clay to my cheeks in various patterns. He laughed when I winced as he smeared spit on my face. I was as still as a statue otherwise. A fly landed near my lip, and he brushed it off with the pad of his thumb. My breath caught in spasm, trying to hide my arousal. Too late. He felt it, then persuaded it. His skin was hot, fingers long and deft, painting the designs with ease while he told stories in a language I longed to understand. I wished my face were larger. Everyone broke into laughter at something Lochili muttered.

"Lochili said you will make a beautiful Lokop wife," Ambrose said, resistant and terse.

I shook my head *no* and made Lochili smile, interrupting his painting. *Here we go again with the wife thing*, I thought.

"*Mi-mi* American, no wife," I asserted, still shaking my head, letting the hut know that being an American woman eclipsed their cultural expectations that I should be married. Everyone laughed at me, including the painter. Kas and I intimidated men with our confidence, and most African men did not know what to do with us. Lochili seemed to tease the intrepidity out as a matador taunted a bull. Fearless.

Loiboku painted Kas' face. Her dark eyes glowed in the hut. His precision contrasted Lochili's coarseness. When they were satisfied, and our faces looked like Navajo rugs, Kas and I were given red sheets to wrap around our shoulders and strands of bright red beads, concealing our T-shirts underneath.

"I feel ridiculous in this. Very pale," I said to Kas playfully. "These definitely are not your colors."

"It's a toss-up between this and your prison deal." Those fat purple stripes.

Kas handed her beloved camera to Hussein. We stood against the straw house backdrop with the warriors, while the sun scorched. Then we switched partners and stood next to Hussein and Ambrose. Lochili learned quickly and snapped the shot. I saw it in the photos later. Our bodies leaned away from our two hosts and into the spear-toting Adonises.

We all went inside away from the sun. Lochili grew bolder, touched my knee, which poked out from the red sheet I still wore, and put Ambrose to work as translator.

"What do your fathers do for work?" he asked. I wondered which father I should describe—the one I lived with or my dad? Should I talk about divorce and having two fathers? I decided to tell all, bare my soul. Why not? In order for the cultural exchange to be real, we had to be honest and reveal ourselves to them, warts and all.

He nodded without judgment, eager for knowledge, an unrealized world explorer. We listened between the words for pictures to arise. It amazes me still how complete expression mingled in the silence with so few words. Lochili's being hummed with newness, understanding the complexity of Western lives, needing Ambrose less and less. Neglected, Ambrose sat off to the side, pouting. In smatterings of Kiswahili, English and Gutok, we talked for hours, evading the heat outside, trading it for the fire between us. Lochili consumed our stories as though he had been starving. He anchored his new knowledge by translating to Loiboku, who nodded.

Kas and me traveling alone, so far from our families, impressed them most, I think.

"You are like Lokop with planes," Lochili said, linking the travel—they by foot and us by all other means.

Hussein, who had not said a word since the photographs, fidgeted. We had been there all afternoon. "I'm getting hungry. Let's go." He interrupted the deepening connection that abruptly.

Kas and I said reluctant goodbyes and removed our Lokop clothes, not knowing how or if we would see the warriors again.

The sun suspended near the lake's edge, waiting to go down. We returned to Hussein's and ate an early dinner in our room.


"His hands were chapped but warm, and he kept finding ways to touch my lips. And when he looked at me it was powerful, electric," I said as I rolled a chapati and dipped an end in the broth. Electricity required no words. Lochili made me yearn to wander a labyrinth of unfamiliar. It did not matter that we were from opposite ends of the Earth. Hearts, primordial desires, subtle body and nerve impulses, the rise and fall of the belly's emotional elevator, the hunt and the capture. Was love anything other?

Hussein joined us for chai. We were all three talking about travel, when someone knocked at the door.

"*Nani?*" Hussein said.

I heard his voice from behind it and felt a body flush of heat. Lochili opened the door and greeted us. He wore an extra blanket over his shoulders for the wind. The tone of his skin was flatter, softer in this light.

"Karibu, Lochili," I said, taking control. Hussein looked as surprised as we were by Lochili's visit. Lochili had no fear, even though, tribally, Hussein was his enemy—the Lokop and Ejocho had forayed for each other's livestock for decades. Either he was brave or as desperate to see me as I was to see him. Or both.

I moved closer to Kas so there was room for him on the couch. He quickly scanned the room and sat down where I intended. Kas moved across to Hussein's bench, facing us. I poured chai for Lochili from the thermos. He said he had already eaten.

Our Michelin map lay open on the coffee table between us. Lochili's eyes widened. He pressed his finger over the borders, and I called out the names of the countries. Some names he repeated without effort, having heard them before, while others were brand-new: Gambia, Togo, Benin. We struggled a little, so Hussein translated in Kiswahili, which Lochili had learned by ear, never having been to school. When Hussein interrupted, which he did frequently, I vied for Lochili's attention using my hands, my face, my few words, and the pulse of hormones.

Kas wanted to know about Loiboku. I could see the question forming in her cherrywood-colored eyes. Why had he not come? After Hussein explained our ambulant travels, interrupting me again, Lochili asked him to tell us that he and Loiboku would leave tomorrow to return to the mountain. After they grazed their cows—a day, a week?—they would return and find us.

Kas tightened her mouth in frustration. I caught her drift. We couldn't be left behind. We both wanted to go with them. Herding, in all its traditional hot dusty glory! With our Kenyan cowboys? We could climb the mountain. In the hut, I had told him we were from Colorado—the Rocky Mountains. We loved to walk, to climb.

Lochili did not take the bait.

"It must have to do with girlfriends,—" I whispered to Kas, "—the reason he did not invite us."

Kas leapt into the fray. Hussein, tell Lochili we'll walk him back to the *manyatta* tonight. We need a good walk after dinner. Micah and I know the way."

Lochili rose as though he understood. He adjusted his sheet and prepared to go.

I wanted to hug Kas, my patient pal, so willing to go with the flow—until she wanted something—then beware. Hussein translated, forgetting chemistry, which had a language all its own.

Kas and I followed Lochili's lead into the dusky night. Once we cleared Hussein's sight and the town, we tried to speak, the sentences and sentiment staccato in their simplicity—see Dick run. As our confidence grew, we tried to offer more complex ideas like why Hussein was so protective of us, his interest in Kas and her interest in Loiboku. I understood that Lochili had never been invited to Hussein's home. "*Mi-mi looking we-we,*" he said as straight as an arrow. I came to Hussein's looking for you.

His courting tastes, like everything about him, were clearly direct. Lochili seemed taller to me tonight, walking upright and proud. Grabbing my hand in his, he directed us toward the hut. I liked the feel of his rough fingers, slightly dirty. The grip was strong, his pace fast.

"*Micah, nataka we-we,*" he said.

It took me a minute to translate. Shocked by his boldness, I looked back at Kas, who had allowed a gap between us for intimacy.

"Kas, Lochili just said he wants me. What do you think that means? Does it mean he likes me, or is he asking me to have sex?!" I still held his hand, slowing him down when I turned toward her.

He sensed my confusion and made himself clear. "Micah, *nataka we-we* okay? Kas, okay?"

I learned later, he asked Kas for her permission as a show of respect—we three were walking together. It was completely plausible to him that we stop for sex right there.

"I think he means now, friend," Kas said to me. "Okay with me, Lochili." Playing with my trepidation, she gave him full permission. I laughed at her audacity and felt a thread of excitement. He was moving full speed ahead.

For years, since AIDS had reached the US from Africa, I had walked diligently twice a year to the Boulder clinic. On one occasion, the volunteer nurse asked in a deadpan manner, "Have you had unprotected sex with multiple partners?"

"No, I've been with the same man for two years," I said.

"Have you had rough oral or anal sex with other partners?"

"No."

"Have you shared an intravenous needle?" she asked, without looking up from the clipboard; if she had she would have seen I didn't look like a heroin addict.

"No."

"Do you have *any* cause for concern?" she asked with a little frustration.

"No, I just like to know."

They drew blood and informed me it would take two weeks for the results, and I should come back for those in person.

I prayed for the strangers in that waiting room, two weeks later. I watched slumped backs follow the young nurse's lively ponytail into the small confessional, guilty and frightened, sexually tabooed, shamed potently. It was all so wrong.

When they came out, I did not look at them. I was too good a detective, and this was one caper I didn't wish to solve—knowing the outcome of the results.

Years later I discovered that, while I had been loyal to the same partner, he had been unfaithful to many. Maybe I was not as good a detective as I believed, or maybe his infidelity was exactly the reason I compulsively tested for AIDS the way people with Obsessive-Compulsive Disorder wash their hands. Just in case.

Lochili's grip tightened, and he turned me off the wider path onto a smaller one, motioning for Kas to wait. My desire for adventure, my nerve-spasm attraction, jarred against my reasonable Boulder-clinic-obsessed conscientiousness. The internal decibels rose. *Does he mean here, in the bush? Does he have a condom? How long are you going to leave your friend standing in the dark alone? You can't even speak to the man. Micah, what are you thinking?*

Something louder surprised me. *You crave everything. Why not this?*

We were out of sight when he took the blanket from around his chest and set it on the ground, then led me by the hand to it. The Earth was cool, the few shrubs surrounding us, about waist high. I kneeled, then lay down on the hard ground when he repeated a word I had not learned. *"Toa, toa."* He pulled at my jeans. I took them off. *Oh! That's how they say it!* He lay down on top without a kiss or a caress and tried to penetrate me. He did not look at my body, to protect a modesty I did not possess—which was why he was shocked when his penis jammed against my blockading underwear.

He said *toa* again, tugging at my underwear, when someone passed nearby. He covered us with the sheet from around his waist and lay over me, holding my face, pushing it to his chest while his other hand pulled my underwear to the side.

I gasped. Desire compressed, heart confused. Voices mumbled in the distance. He rammed himself again and again in rapid succession. After six thrusts, he came! The passerby must have seen us—if not my face, our two bodies fumbling in the sparse bushes.

We listened to footsteps moving toward the village.

Then he helped me to my feet. I put on my pants, numb with overwhelm.

He said, *"Pole sana, Micah, pole sana."* I was not sure why he was apologizing—for the lack of foreplay, his determination to have sex when a stranger was near? Or was he apologizing because I did not even think the word *orgasm* let alone have one, or the fact that he had ejaculated inside of me—a hasty decision that could impact the future of our respective lives should I become pregnant!

"Me, too, Lochili. I am sorry too," I said in English, as though speaking my own language would help make sense of it all.

We walked to Kas, who was standing like a windsock where the path split.

She whispered with eagerness, "Did you see that man pass by? Were you having sex? What happened?"

"I'll tell you in a second. The whole thing was too strange."

Lochili felt my unease and asked gently if there was a problem. *"Iko matata, Micah?"*

I said, "No. No. You?"

*"Hakuna! Hakuna!"* He chuckled, saying my name as he did. Satisfied.

He held my hand and led us faster toward the village. We found the hut and greeted Mama, who was nearing sleep. Loiboku sat ready, as though he'd been expecting us. Fire provided enough light to see silhouettes but obscure the details. Kas snuggled in next to Loiboku. He pulled her down and covered them both with his sheet. All pretense between us had been dissolved by my bush romp.

I sat next to her and whispered, "So, is this where we're sleeping?"

"I guess so. He covered me up. Sleep well." She tittered like a naughty kid.

I still hadn't had the chance to tell her about Lochili—more like warn her. I remained sitting up, waiting for Lochili's direction, when Loiboku rose, pulled Kas by the hand, and led her out of the hut.

"See you in the morning, I hope," she said in a low tone. The cultural anthropologist was headed out for "fieldwork."

Lochili motioned for me to lie down next to him. He situated me on my side facing him and wrapped his legs and arms in a tangled twist through mine. He pulled me closer in each time I felt a little stifled. Normally I could never be held this tightly, in a deadlock spoon. Mama was asleep, I hoped. I didn't hear her at all. My eyes dried from being open too long, my mind sifted the parts, wondering about Kas and replaying what just happened. I clung to this warrior who in one reckless moment had stripped me of my clothing, my reason, and my need to control.

Rather than feeling violated, I felt new. I liked him. More.

He did not make another attempt at sex, though he held me through the night and asked several times, *"Micah, sawa? Iko matata?"*

I would always respond, *"Hakuna.* I'm okay. Kas? Loiboku?"

He reassured me they were also *"sawa."*

He slept when he was not reassuring me. I grappled with reality, with the fact that I had fallen for a man I could not speak to, the worst lover I had ever experienced. My best friend had been whisked into the night by a stranger who spoke less than his brother. I don't know that I slept at all, but if I had, it would have been with awestruck wonderment in my heart and a smile. This life song, grand, full-voiced, and sweet. Mine, now ravaged by the intoxicating power of primal.

I had just been fucked by a lion.

# NINE | SCATTERING MOLECULES

I MUST HAVE fallen asleep because I woke to find everyone together, including Mama. The wind whistled, tossing the fine dirt through the hut slats. When it finally settled, Loiboku brushed the dirt from Kas' body with tender diligence and lay down again. He loved her in such an uncomplicated way, simple, attentive.

Gray light broke. Lochili woke me, helped me to my feet, handed me my hair tie, and hurried us out of the hut while Loiboku and Kas said a cryptic goodbye, the sort that leaves you lonelier than before you met. We walked with messy hair and sleepy eyes back to Hussein's, looking like released hostages. So much for chaperones. The warriors were hiding us. We didn't need language to know this, but the effect was evident in our slinking bodies.

On the walk, we stayed silent so as not to stir the town. We hoped to avoid all witnesses to our early flight from the *manyatta*. We would still be seen and talked about. It was inevitable. The town was too small, and we were too white.

Because Kas and I spent every moment together, we both savored this prolonged silence.

At Hussein's, everyone was as we had hoped—still sleeping and unalarmed. We snuck to our room and got into our beds, turned toward each other, and began the delicious recounting.

"You first," I said.

"No. You tell me what happened in the bushes with Lochili. You were first to do something, so you should be the first to tell. I'm all ears."

"Okay, the bushes. Well, *Toa* means 'take off,' and he kept saying it. I wrestled off my jeans and then without anything, even a kiss, he climbed on top of me and ran into my underwear!"

Kas laughed, her eyes watery with astonishment.

"Then a guy ran by! Lochili threw himself over to cover me, pulled my underwear to the side and came! Inside me! I swear. Six thrusts, no sound, no grand finale. It was like having sex with a wild animal—" I doubted this would shock her, so I went on. "Not like anything I've ever felt, Kas. And the strange thing is I like him … more. How does that happen?" I snuggled deeper into my bed, full of joy and disbelief. Kas laughed and I said, "Your turn."

In the low light, her face glowed as mysterious as a genie lantern. "Loiboku took my hand and led me up a path into the woods. There was a pool of water and it was warm, like a natural spring. I couldn't really see. I was excited to get in, but when I jumped in after him, naked, he ushered me out like an unwelcome guest, shooing me until I understood that I shouldn't be in there."

It was my turn to laugh. "What? Why?"

Kas shrugged and leaned in. "I figured out that he wanted me to sit and watch him from the side, like he was involved in a cleaning ritual or something. Thank God it's so hot here, or I would have been freezing. He took his time in the warm bath. After he was done, he put his sheet on the ground. I lay down, and it was over. I think, maybe, four," Kas said, twisting her mouth. "At least you got six! I know what you mean by no caressing, no noise, no tremble. His penis was long but not much thicker than a fat finger!"

"Did he keep his visor on? You're in love, too, aren't you?" I said, hopeful, not wanting to be alone there.

"Terribly," she said as she bit her bottom lip.

"Kas, this is crazy. These guys would be shunned at home for their poor sense of foreplay. One kiss would have been nice, anywhere."

"Oh, I tried. Kissing is out of the question, and don't touch them on the small of the back or the back of the neck. It made Loiboku break out into convulsions. He had to stop me a few times from touching him. I didn't know what to do with my hands, so I put them out to the side like a limp snow angel. He smells sooo good. I'm crazy about him, and we can't even speak to each other."

I asked, knowing the answer, "So, no condom? Crazy girl. I think we're safe though. Our cycles only ended yesterday or the day before, right?"

"Yeah. We're safe. This time." Yangaloi's distance from the world we knew made it seem too far for AIDS as well. AIDS was a city disease. We never considered it.

"Lochili held me all night. He also did this really sexy thing and buried my head in the front of his throat so that all I could breathe was him. Their smell! It's earthy and smoky, but somehow clean too. He kept asking if everything was okay. I know I should have been worried, but I wasn't. I lay awake smiling at the absurdity and the aliveness!" We heard someone walking to the toilet outside the room.

"What do you think Hussein'll do when we see him?" I asked.

"I'll win Hussein over. We'll just tell him we got tired and fell asleep and woke early to come home. Shouldn't be a problem. We'll make time for him now that the warriors are going back to Mt. Laku." Kas knew how to play this game.

That afternoon Kas and I went into town. Old mamas sat in a row, beading necklaces. Kas said, "*Supa*, Mama," and they responded in unison. After reviewing their wares, we shopped with our hearts, settled on a price and left satisfied. Overlooking the lake, we perched atop boulders and strung midnight blue beads onto remnant nylon strands from corn and wheat relief-food bags. I remember missing Lochili more than I had missed any man. We daydreamed about their lives, creating possibilities from our few observances, piecing the puzzle together.

"I'll bet they're tired climbing up that mountain," Kas said.

"What do you think?" I held up the strand of beads. "It's long enough for him to wear diagonally across his chest." I imagined again and again giving it to him, the way a hungry person eats, until I was sated by the vision.

"It's nice. I hope they'll wear them. With our luck, blue is probably the color for girls," she said.

Her necklace hung better than mine. Though Kas and I were of equal creative caliber, neither of us rated very high. The sun crept around the corner of that Hershey's Kiss mountain and would blind us soon.

I admired my handiwork. I would never be able to share subtleties with Lochili, to explore the nuances. I believed that he knew me anyway, saw my heart; I pretended he saw parts of me, the romantic in me cooking up fantasies. To be seen, to be known. But for me, Lochili inhabited the enigmatic from beginning to end, inside and out, and no matter what infatuation I suffered, I knew his mind worked differently.

Days dragged like years in Yangaloi's hot wind as we waited for the warriors to return. Hussein warmed to us, and we practiced our Kiswahili. One evening he told us a movie was showing outside the mission—a Bruce Lee film with dramatic martial arts, no storyline or advanced character development, and therefore perfect for a non-English-speaking warrior audience. The moment Hussein suggested the film, I knew Lochili would be there.

Night fell. We walked to the mission, a one-room cinder-block building rising from the barren clearing, trodden flat by relief-food distribution and movie audiences. Weird. A Yangaloi drive-in with no cars. Kas and I left Hussein and hid in the middle of the squatting people. Chinese actors kicked ass, throat-chopped villains, and cried out victoriously, badly dubbed. Why was the mission showing such violent trash? Maybe they told their parish this was how you behaved if you had not found God?

I hadn't yet seen Lochili, but I felt him, energy entangling long before eyes. Bruce Lee and his block-breaking courage actually spoke to my situation, me and my doubt. Did Lochili like me, or was I about to get the karate chop?

People laughed, oohing and ahhing, eyes shifting between the film and Kas and me. What did we think? We laughed just to belong.

When it ended, as credits flashed erratically on the screen, shooting bright sparks into the dark desert night, I saw him from my periphery, his silhouette. I already knew this outline but as to the outcome? *Crap!* I could only wish for his affection.

Instead of turning to him, I turned away, heart jumping, waiting to be discovered. I heard his voice even at that distance—masculine grit that scattered my molecules. He spoke louder than he needed to. He laughed, and it became too much. My head spun against my will. What did my warrior look like when he laughed? Forget hard-to-get, I had to know.

Mischief sparkled in his face.

I smiled.

He disengaged from the conversation—all mine now—his desire shimmering brighter than the screen. Oh, such relief!

Kas and I walked away from the light and the crowd toward the *manyatta*, one slow step and another. I heard his quick footsteps behind us. My back arced with anticipation.

*"Kas, Micah, tunaenda wapi?"* Lochili asked where we were headed in his raspy playful way.

My smile spun around, then my body. *"Lochili, Supa. Supa oleng! Ni na kutafuta."* I told him I had been looking for him.

"Mi-mi looking cows mountain," he said in the most English I had heard him speak—probably he had also been studying.

Kas asked after Loiboku, who was still on the mountain.

Lochili grabbed my shoulders affectionately and straightened the edges of my long hair while repeating my name. I extended my hand and slowly opened my fingers, exposing his blue-beaded gift.

*"Zawadi kwa we-we. Unapenda?"* I asked timidly if he liked my gift to him.

He grabbed it, held it up as though to catch remnants of the moon's light, then handed me the blanket draped over his shoulders. It was full of his smell and warmth. He wore the beads exactly as I'd intended, against the others—new and polished on his muscled black chest.

*"Asante sana sana, Micah. Napenda mingi,"* he thanked me, glowing, smiling, assuring me he liked the necklace.

I got stupid then, gesturing to myself, saying *mi-mi* and stringing the beads for him on the sky canvas. I wanted my creative endeavor notched somewhere. *I made this!* Lochili laughed at my emphasis.

Then he gave us a gift. An invitation.

I pieced together half of his words. Something was happening in Moloi—a village on the shores of Outran. Kas and I had seen the name on a map. We would walk there tomorrow, accompanied by Hussein, our translator. Lochili would sing once we got there—some sort of celebration, many warriors and their girlfriends. Loiboku would come. We would stay together—sleep there. Fun!

We learned the phrase for "don't tell the secret" that night: *Usesimi siri.* Lochili said it as he pressed his index finger to his lips and made the universal shushing sound. We mimicked him in complicity, not exactly certain what we were protecting.

He touched his finger to my lips, which caused them to part slightly, and he repeated, "*Usesimi siri*, Micah."

My molecules scattered again.

# TEN | DANCE WHEN YOU'RE BROKEN OPEN

HUSSEIN SAW OUR light. "Did you enjoy the movie?" he asked, poking his head inside the doorway.

"Yes, thanks. We decided to leave you to visit with your friends. It's hard having to translate for us all the time," Kas said sympathetically.

"Yes, but people want also to meet you. They ask about the American girls that have now really stayed at Yangaloi. Ha-ha. Residents—" he said, and he really did look handsome in his green polo shirt. Just not our kind of handsome. "Tourists don't stay. The wind chases them." He laughed and continued. "You are becoming like us."

I shuffled items in my backpack, thinking, *We are trying like hell.*

Hussein excused himself so we could head to bed, but before leaving he added, "Hawo and Mary took Habiba to Lowaa today. They came to say goodbye but you weren't here. I told them you would see them in Lowaa later."

*Good luck, Habiba,* I thought. *I hope the sweetness of love served you well.*

Hussein leaned against the door with something else on his mind. "And I saw your warrior friend, Lochili. He asked me to join them for a wedding and a dance at Moloi tomorrow. He said to bring you. Do you think you can come? We will do a walking safari."

"A wedding? Is it really okay for *us* to come?" Kas asked. "We would love to come." She fretted over the appropriateness of showing up uninvited. I fretted immediately over the right attire for a nomad's wedding, not dance—wedding! We had missed that word.

I had to know. "Hussein, how do you say *wedding* in Kiswahili?"

"*Arusi*. And yes, it's okay for you to come. They will be happy," he said as he left.

*Shukas*. We would wear our *shukas* like a skirt. Part American, part Lokop.

The Moloi were the smallest tribe in Kenya. Though they resembled the Lokop in dress, they subsisted on fish, which the Lokop detested. They suffered health problems and comported themselves less proudly. The Lokop name for the Moloi translated to "the people who exist by means other than cattle." A new tribe for us to meet. A walking safari. A wedding to attend.

Kas and I spoke in hushed tones—more like prayers—before sleeping. We hoped Habiba would not be beaten, that we would enjoy visiting Moloi with the warriors, and that Loiboku would meet us there. Hussein was welcome if he translated and … disappeared at night.

Lochili arrived while we were eating breakfast. He looked ready for safari—not because he carried anything, but his virility filled space. He told me to bring water so we would not have to drink from the lake. Usually independent and well prepared, I felt distracted that morning, unconcerned with pertinent details like water, which proved a crucial part of a wedding safari.

Hussein with his small pack and Lochili with his spear paced ahead. Our walk to Moloi was thirteen dirt-scorched kilometers. With full packs. Locals made the journey with heavy rations of relief-food during droughts, so we swallowed any complaints. Every so often Hussein turned back, asked us a question, and gave the translation to Lochili. They spoke the entire way.

Kas worried about seeing Loiboku and whether or not he would attend.

"Lochili is getting all kinds of info. He'll tell his brother, and that's best because you guys can't really talk about anything that deep," I said, trying to make her feel better.

Hussein asked, "Did you bring a tent to sleep in? Lochili wonders if you know how to camp."

Kas raised her voice, spanning the distance, and said, "Yes, we love camping."

"Wonder what Lochili's got in mind? I can just see our shiny, no-tear tent set up next to all the dung huts," I said.

The funny image worked to bring a little levity to Kas. We would get our own little home set up and get out from under Hussein.

Sweat left salty layers on our skin by the time we reached Moloi. The village appeared even smaller than I expected—with homes made from palm fronds and mud, not animal hides. The Moloi were not shepherds. Their statures were stunted from the minerals calcifying the lake's water. Fish dried atop the homes on small wooden racks.

Lochili reached back for my hand, then led us to one hut in particular. *"Micah, arusi hapa."*

"He wants to introduce you to the bride and groom," Hussein said, feeling useful.

Two very short people came out from inside the hut, alight with wedding joy. They wore sheepish grins, their bodies decorated evenly with beads, paint, youth, and anticipation, waiting to be introduced. Not knowing how to greet in Moloi, I said, *"Supa oleng!"* They laughed but appreciated my eagerness. Lochili told them the essentials of our story, encouraging our welcome at their celebration, which they sweetly offered.

He then disappeared to prepare for the dance. Hussein followed a few paces behind him like a cub after a lion.

Kas and I were alone. Since we had nothing in common with the nomadic, marrying youth, we strolled toward a rocky hill rising between the village and the lake. We rounded the bend and were soon out of sight. Time to check in, to return to center, regain equilibrium. There were days we meandered in a low-grade perpetual shock—an altered state, with nothing, absolutely nothing, familiar.

We dropped our packs. We wondered if we'd missed the ceremony. The couple were already hanging out together. Maybe visiting warriors danced at the reception?

The sun baked our brains and made the shining black water appear cool.

"Let's get in." Kas said, daring me.

We had grown up skinny-dipping in the lakes and rivers of Colorado. But here? The only white people for hundreds of miles, within a rock's throw of a wedding party?

The sun beat modesty into submission.

Our clothing in a pile, we waded out. Shadowed and murky with sediment, the salt water was safe from Bilharzia and other bacteria. The salt acted like a salve on our sunburned, tanned, re-sunburned skin—as cool as aloe vera. Time passed. We played, dunking our heads to stay cool, shading our faces from the sun's reflection.

We looked to shore and saw people coming, slowly waving us out.

Kas waved back. I laughed at her dismissive gesture.

When we stayed put, their pace and intensity increased. They shouted and moved their arms up and down. We waved again, wanting to reassure them we were fine. Up to our necks in salt water, we had no intention of exposing our nude bodies, wedding day and all.

I tried to make out words the closer they came, more from intellectual curiosity than concern. I heard "*mamba.*" The word seemed familiar but I could not place it. In a life-saving flash, I recalled seeing it on a beer in Nairobi. I had asked the waiter the meaning, and he pointed to the label: a wrapped crocodile, its verdant, scaly body squeezed the belly of the bottle of cold suds.

I screamed, "Kas, they're saying *crocodile*! There's a fucking crocodile somewhere!"

We spun to see not one but three pairs of stealthy, bulbous eyes resting on the glassy surface of the lake, about 25 feet from us. We flung ourselves at the shore's edge, violent thrashing fueled by those chomping jaws which might already have dived down to drown us, crocodile style.

We scrambled, clawing and kicking, and crawled onto the rocks, hearts pounding, breath short, naked but alive. Safe at shore, compelled to look, we shivered at the sight. The prehistoric reptiles sank insidiously into the dark water—their jagged teeth and man-eating bodies vanished.

*"Iko mamba tatu! Iko mamba tatu!"* My adrenaline-fed brain only now translated all three words. "There are *three* crocodiles!"

A young girl ran to wrap my *shuka* across my shoulders. Then she covered Kas. I steadied myself on the salt-capped boulder and picked up our remaining clothes.

All we could mutter was "Thank you, very much." *Asante sana. Asante sana.*

Language, even through great limitations, can save lives.

The group chaperoned us to the huts beyond the rocky hill and served us salty chai. The shady huts we'd judged as poor, felt utterly safe and womb-like. When the shock subsided, we laughed at the irony of being saved by a beer label—that and the locals' providential timing.

Note to self: Lake Outran is a body of salty, volcanic water, and monstrous, hungry crocodiles thrive there.


Nearing three, the sun was no longer kicking ass overhead. We amused ourselves by braiding my hair, taking photos of young Moloi girls near the lake (not in it), and awaited the wedding, which may or may not have already occurred.

Kas put coconut oil on my hair, a fashion mistake. My scalp burned, and all the friendly curls around my face flattened. With my hair pulled back, greasy and stark, my cheeks and nose beamed the same color as the heart necklace I wore. My mom had given it to me when I left Colorado. Kas teased me about taking blackmail photos. I said I'd slather her Ashkenazi eyebrows in coconut oil.

Hussein found us sitting in the scant shade of a boulder, picking at our toenails. He straightened his back, bearer of important news, and said, "Because there is a wedding today, the women also do a circumcision ceremony. They have told me to come bring you to the hut."

I looked at Kas wishing I were glued indefinitely to that cool boulder.

She exhaled heavily and asked, "Are they doing it now?"

"Yes, over there," Hussein pointed to a hut that looked just like all the others.

Before Kas and I left for Africa, I'd attended a rally at Colorado University to protest women's circumcision, or, as they called it, "female genital mutilation." I left that auditorium embittered, fist-waving, and ready to take a stand. It's rough being a pacifist do-gooder. You'll recall that I couldn't hurt a carrot, and I failed saving even a bird from a spider.

Kas stood up, anthropology on her mind?

Our steps had never been so careful as we inched toward the opening of that hut, women of all ages spilling out and filling the archway. The gathering heaved with the feminine—breasts and cheekbones, shoulders and buttocks, round and soft. Hussein left us and stopped in front of an invisible force field many feet away.

Kas whispered, "Jesus, Micah. What we've only heard about and been horrified by! And suddenly we're part of it. Right there. In that hut!"

A woman with honey eyes turned and saw us approaching. She hurried, fetching and pulling us in, proudly clearing the way for us to see. I know my breath tightened. I squeezed closer to Kas.

Inside the archway, framed by it, in fact, a young girl reclined in two older women's arms, legs bent and apart as though she had just given birth, blood-soaked cloth surrounding her. And women, so many women. I think I halfway expected this to be a ritual led by men. The girl looked limp, her smooth face and shaven head so quiet there, like a body free of nerve endings, the verve gone gray. But also strangely confident. Belonging.

I thought I might faint. They kept giving her something to drink.

A harsh voice and tight grip moved Kas closer inside the hut, or tried to. A joking mama. I grabbed Kas' arm reflexively as she dug in her heels, immovable. Everyone laughed at our resistance. We tried to join them. But the twist in that mama's grin—*Next one,* it said. Her eyes glinted, *You or you?*

We backed away from the gathering, the swallowing, bleeding womb. I smiled gently at the girl before turning away. She had had the knife, she didn't need to see my sharp dismay. But as I smiled, I wanted to pull all young girls like her, not yet married, from this ceremonial web. Forever.

"I nearly lost you to a throng of blade-wielding women," I said to Kas as we walked away.

"Thanks for the save. Micah, wait till my professors hear about this. Nothing like the stinking books," she said.

We high-tailed it past Hussein.

"You know who that was, right?" she asked, with a tremor in her voice.

"No, I didn't recognize her. Did you?"

"Yeah, it was the bride."

In our year of travel around that continent, we met men who wanted women to defy the circumcision tradition and women who fought to keep it. What became clear to me: the fight was never mine. And belief is a magical thing, belief lights the densest of practices. I had to loosen my tight-fitting self-righteousness, my manufactured disdain, and get real. Women create initiation rites which protect, nourish and sustain. Uphold the tribe. Unite and exalt women. I prayed that circumcision would one day fade from this tapestry of belonging.

For being American, I felt so very grateful, again. The entire world benefits from the exaltation of the feminine, men and women alike—who bring back the love of Earth and Moon. And women, including me, needed to lead the way.

The wedding party had gathered in a circle, and the center filled in with warriors. Lochili, head high, stood smack-dab in the middle. Blue and black strands of beads crossed from hip to shoulder, mine among them. Charcoal accented his black almond eyes, and orange paint streaked his cheeks. His sole voice rose out of the crowd, with his hand cupped at his mouth, he caused a tremulous bellow much like a blacksmith fans fire. Then the chorus rang out, stomping their feet, the drum of humans on Earth. A rhythmic chant. The entire circle pulsed, trembling. I had never heard anything so ancient, rooted in infinity, so raw.

Locals gravitated to the dance. We followed them. I watched Lochili, but he seemed focused only on singing. His booming voice filled the space, echoing off the rocks. I strained to understand something, anything. Despite my desire, I remained outside the secret. Outside the circle. The words of his songs opened him, keys to hidden locks. The landscape was suddenly very old, the boulders so still, holding thousands of years of song in their volcanic texture. Porous. The red dirt, black water, smiling sky and people who fashioned themselves from it all—and Lochili, sonorous soloist. He sang out, stretching his neck back and forth. Warriors stomped percussive feet. One split from the group, convulsing, and collapsed into women's arms. Then another warrior. An outer circle watched for these ecstatic warriors and braced their fall to the ground. The seizures seemed to relieve some emotional pressure—it was evident in the calm that overcame their bodies afterward.

Warriors bounded from the circle, jumping straight up, feet dangling for a flashing moment at eye level, whooping exultation, Lochili breaking out of the chorus leading everyone into another layer of belonging. Girls danced all together, shifting in a gentle, cascading crescent moon. Their soprano voices rang, chins jutting forward and back against the multiple strands of necklaced beads, shaking. It would be them in that hut one day, being held and holding.

*Shushing, Shushing, Shushing.*

Kas and I never looked at each other. I was fearful one self-conscious glance could interrupt the mystery. Mesmerized, I followed, swallowed by rhythm. I was dying, dying by layers to Lochili's summoning.

Delirious—from lack of food, crocodile fear, the haunting chant, and unavoidable sway of my body—I lost hours. Everyone did. The sense of *I* vanished for whole moments, and time delved beyond that suffocating awareness, so free. Then logic entered, penetrating and derisive: *Are they watching me dance? Do I look stupid, dancing and singing with tribal people? Is it okay to go this far?* I closed my eyes and rocked. Lochili's call touched deeper than doubt, and my body lost its skin, its segregating edges, and I swung into that wide-open ancient field with them.

*Shushing, Shushing, Shushing.*

Loiboku came. Kas took his hand. They climbed the hill together. I closed my eyes engulfed in Lochili's melodic voice and me. Everything disappeared, dissolved into a chorus of aloneness. This chorus everything, primordial circle and song. I saw complete surrender—all essence—and did not marry it. Not yet. Lest I be the first white woman to crumble into ecstatic fit on the margins of a tribal dance.

Doubt circled in the dirt with us. Deep down, I feared no one would be there to catch my shaking, sweating body. *One day, all the chains will fall at your feet.*

I left the circle, when dusk descended, in love—the raw wild in everything intoxicated me. Kas returned and we scrambled up an outcropping of boulders. We sat without words, bathing in starlight. Oh, these marvelous stars beaming across the night sky without competition. In one day, we had almost lost our lives and discovered a sharp, rampant, desire for living.

By evening, the warriors disappeared. No glossy tent for us that night. We slept on cow skins in a hut with Hussein, who was a gentleman despite his wishes.

"Do you think they left to be with their girlfriends or their cows?" I asked Kas over chai the next morning. The warriors hadn't returned. We asked, all through the morning, and heard, "They are coming." They didn't come. So we watched Moloi children outside, giggling without care, and prayed that they never tasted sweet water. Ours had run out. The lake water curdled our veins.

"Kas, do you think Lokop wives are jealous? Or does everyone get along?" The Lokop were polygamists. "I would be a possessive Lokop wife, well, if I were marrying for love, and it hadn't been arranged. If I were Lochili's wife, I can't imagine sharing him. I know it's probably the higher path, the more admirable but not for me."

"No way!" Kas spat in the dirt. "That would be awful. And think of when you grow old and he moves a pretty virgin into your home. You would never see him. He would always be with her. Maybe sex is not as good without part of the clitoris. Maybe that curbs jealousy?"

We had read that both Lokop and Moloi girls were circumcised.

"Well, even with a clitoris, if sex is as bad as we've just had, who needs it?" I laughed, but the truth was that I wanted to make it better— if he could sing to my soul, he could love my body.

Long past noon, people moved to the flattening of Earth where we had danced. The sun quieted. I had not seen Lochili.

"Let's stay here until the ceremony really takes off," I said. "I want to wait to hear him."

From our perch outside the circle, there it was—that distinct voice, singing and projecting his sound past my mind right to my open body. We turned from our view of the lake. He faced toward us, the crowd around him, his eyes fixed on the horizon as though he found his inspiration there. I grinned and accepted his affection in this sort of impersonal, personal serenade.

The villagers welcomed us in. We stood as before on the margins. The Lokop warriors used the dance to seduce girls. Between songs, when he looked to me, Lochili seemed to be searching for something. He held his head higher than the other warriors, who tightened the space around him. I closed my eyes and heard the grainy, almost dry sound and pretended the raw courtship songs were for just me.

As Lochili sang the last, young couples wandered into the bush for rapturous lovemaking. We'd danced until our bodies were wet with sweat and supple from the vibration.

He stopped singing, spoke with a few people, then made his way over.

*"Micah, Supa. Unapenda kuimba? Kas wewe?"* He asked if we liked the dance, his voice hoarser than usual. I did not have words. His exhaustion softened him, infatuation softened me. I allowed him to lead me by the hand to a nearby hut. *"Mabe ... Twende,"* he said in Gutok and then corrected himself in Kiswahili. Either way, Kas and I knew *Let's go.* I reached back for her hand as the sun dropped behind the lake's edge. We crouched down to enter and took seats on the cow skins.

A fire glowed with resistant cedar embers. Lochili tried to speak but I put my finger to his lips telling him to rest his tired voice. He ignored me and yelled through the hut walls. A young girl emerged and began to pour lake water into a pot and stoke the embers. Chai. Dinner. Kas asked about Loiboku. He gestured with his arm as though he were shooing something, then laughed at our pinched faces.

"Kas, sorry. You seem to have fallen for the only workaholic warrior. I think he's with animals somewhere." She told me the evening before, when they disappeared from the dance, they had sat overlooking it all. He kept his hand on her knee while they laughed and repeated each other's names like invocations, their own primal love song.

Lochili told us to sleep and then, before leaving, said, *"Kuimba kufanya kasi."* To dance is to work.

I woke in the night with someone next to me, feminine and slight. Other girls had joined us, all sleeping off the dance. Strangers spooning, unified in our common vulnerability, we shared two truths: we were all daughters to fathers, and we loved that dance.

*When I fall asleep, Lintan is resting next to Natiyon. Now she pokes her wild head into the hut and calls loudly to me in Gutok.*

*I sit up and whisper, I'm sleeping, Yeyo, Mama is sleeping, too.*

*He calls through the hut walls. I straighten my* shuka, *then duck my head out the opening into the starry sky. He glows, eyes fiery with spirit light, newly applied face paint and ochre-stained hair, recently in ceremony with the warriors. He takes my hand and leads me to the dirt clearing where warriors gather with their girlfriends. Lintan chats with girls her age. Ploote greets me and asks for Kas.*

*My lover sends Lintan to wake her and grabs my hand tighter. His energy is abrupt, all male tonight. The warriors begin singing. They jump up and down facing one another and synchronize their movement, breath and chant. Girls dance the outside, directly behind their warrior boyfriends, throwing heads forward, their layered necklaces clacking like maracas. I stand behind him, close. When Lintan returns with Kas, she stands between us, holds our hands and laughs with surprise to see we know the movement. The dance mesmerizes—coupling, culture, sexual tension and desire witnessed by the whole village. On the outskirts of the circle, the elders gather and move minimally, dance to an aged, frail beat, but still they dance.*

*The full moon casts drumming shadows on the Earth. I close my eyes, more confident than in Moloi. I know this rhythm now. We practiced it on the beach daily. Kas' neck muscles loosen, tribally, which causes poor Ploote to love more deeply if that is possible.*

*My lover cajoles me from my midnight timidity to mimic the girls. This village knows me, knows my name. I kick loose to his jumping, the Earth around me breaking time with his thudding feet. I kiss Lintan's head. She reaches up to where my lips had been and giggles with delight. Kas kisses her head. More giggles. The warriors form a long line, grab their girlfriends' hands and bellow like lions as their heads sway back and forth. We mimic their movements, make shushing, clicking sounds. No throat. We push sleep further away. I know some of the songs, some individual words. We dance for hours. We dance until we are wet with effort and pulse. When our energy fills the desert night, the dance ends. Couples fall away into the bush to make love. Kas retires just moments before Ploote becomes mad with desire. She is clever with timing this way.*

*He sulks off to sleep alone. Kas lies with her back to us when we duck into our hut.*

*My lover brings the dance to us. He fucks me more intensely than before—breathy, pushing gasps escape from him. I smell the hair at his neck, ochre, sweet and earthy. He kisses me on the mouth, neck and shoulders, Western kisses mingle with desert breeze, enough to cool our sweat. We come together over and over.*

*Our love is now as serious as our very lives.*

*I want to become the wife of this Lokop man. I see it all. I can carry water on my head, bead for him, strap firewood on my back. I can get used to dirty clothes, dirty water and goat meat. Nights like this, the way our bodies merge, obliterate everything and every way I have ever known myself. As he enters me again I imagine babies. Children, wild and free, playing, the kind of free I long to embody.*

*He covers my mouth with his and I come back to him. Just him, just me.*

*He reaches up overhead for his wooden pillow. I settle for my forearm and bunched up clothing. He becomes eerily quiet, his body wrapped tightly on mine like sinew on bone.*

*He falls asleep, a stone dropping into a lake—all the way in, deeply down. I am awake. His wild intoxicates me, true, but my favorite is when he looks at me with quiet possessiveness, like I am the only thing in the world he has to have, will have, and as he knows it, he knows it weakens him. A little chink in his warrior armor.*

In the morning Hussein announced himself through the reedy walls. The girls had all gone. "Kas. Are you ready to go home?" he asked, urging us to journey to Yangaloi before the heat rose.

He smiled when he saw us. In times of uncertainty, we welcomed Hussein. Today he traveled with a quiet, sweet-faced warrior named Lapalat.

"Lochili told me where he left you to sleep. He has returned to the mountain with his brother. They have many animals that need grazing. He walked last night."

*To dance is to work,* I thought. He must have been so tired after singing, and then he climbed that mountain afterward?

We left Moloi without a farewell, unsure whom to thank. Many had housed, comforted, and even saved us. It wasn't customary to say goodbye. Nomads simply left. Before leaving, we filled our water bottle once again with salty, lacustrine water. While walking, I considered the Moloi's choices. They lived within walking distance of sweet water in Yangaloi. They hunted Nile-originating crocodiles. One of their rituals involved a man killing a crocodile before he was worthy of marriage. Having now seen both a groom and a crocodile, up close, I knew where I would put my money. The Moloi's reason for staying at Lake Outran? I never knew. Today the tribe risks extinction.

We walked through the vastness of stone and powder; fine dust engulfed our feet and made the tiny hairs visible. If my vision fell too myopic, focusing on a single dead space, I missed the beauty. When I opened it, the scene expanded into shining blue sky, cotton clouds, and a cemetery sea of white boulders. Red shapes of warriors and their girls wavered in mirage. The rocky hills of Moloi dropped into the distance.

Hussein and Lapalat strutted ahead. Anton, another warrior we met along the trek back, walked behind. He strode like a Greek god, I thought, brazen, muscled, and ever ready for battle. He didn't speak English or Kiswahili but his silence and steady pace shepherded us home to Hussein's.

Yangaloi's simple structures indented the skyline. Once we reached the compound, Hussein arranged lunch. Famished, Kas and I devoured food the way vampires suck blood. A walking safari is no small undertaking.

They knew difficulty, the Lokop—went extended periods without food and water, walked impenetrable distances with their animals in the heat, endured painful initiation rites. Were we the same people, essentially? Or had our Western opulence changed all that, distinguishing those who lived with the Earth, within her resources, from those who lived on the Earth, perpetually taking? I did not live within the Earth's resources. From the skin to the spirit, the Lokop and I differed. But when we danced, when Lochili sang, we were one.

In our room Kas and I checked the pack stays for the taped larger bills. Everything was there. We thanked Saint Ambrose. And stuffed ourselves with chapati and fresh water.

# ELEVEN | ALCHEMY OF SILENCE

LOCHILI AND LOIBOKU had a sister named Everlyn—at least they called her their sister, but Africans' sense of family extended out like sun rays, and the terms were often tossed with more recklessness than veracity. She might have been a cousin. However, she was related, and she knew things.

"My father will not let my brothers to see you. They love you but they are forbidden. This is why they stay with the animals," she said, emotionless, casting a glance toward the mystifying Mt. Laku.

"Where is your father?" I asked, spinning in semicircle as though he were there now, the ever-watchful eye.

Everlyn shrugged her thin shoulders under the red T-shirt. She adjusted her *shuka*, straightening the knot with hands that looked to belong to someone much older. I had guessed her age was the same as ours. She did not know her father's whereabouts. What she said was true. We felt the restriction when we'd hidden, scurrying home to Hussein's before sunrise.

"They asked me to tell you to move to the campground. It's there," she said, pointing to the location near one of the natural springs at the base of the mountain. "It is halfway between where my father stays and the mountain. That way they don't have to pass by him to see you."

Bad news with a golden cord attached.

Kas said, "Cool! We can use our tent!"

We were so excited we almost forgot to say goodbye and thanks.

We four would not fit into our two-person tent no matter how tightly we spooned but the possibility of greater freedom seduced us. Entirely.

Hussein, like many African people, took hospitality seriously, and his family needed the money from our rent. But we had stayed there three weeks and felt no compunction to stay longer. Kas was tasked with telling him, since I had previously told Pa Sinyani in the Gambia that we would not eat goat. I held onto bargaining chips for occasions like this.

We found Hussein tending his mom's shop alone. No customers and, due to the weekly energy ration, he was slumped on a chair in the dark. A scale sat on the counter. His hands were white from scooping flour and sugar out of large sacks, as though he were weighing his options: stability or sweetness.

"Hussein, Micah and I have news," Kas began. "One of our favorite things to do in Colorado is camp and sleep in tents. That's why we brought one even though it is very heavy and awkward to pack. We have found a campsite near the spring. We want to thank you. We know that we have been staying with your family for long enough." Here, his shoulders almost slumped to his waist. A melting human dough boy.

Kas persevered. "You can come visit us at our campsite. We'll make *you* dinner for a change." Though she was a master of negotiation, Hussein looked insulted. He implacably dumped his sugared hand over. No more sweetness.

"Hussein, you have been a loyal host," I said, "and we hope to welcome you to the United States someday and repay the favor. *Asante sana rafiki.*"

We were at the mercy of adventurous romance. We were twenty. We had already made up our minds.

While we packed, Hussein presented a fair bill which we paid with more money than was owed, and we hustled out, packs on our backs, to the campsite. At the edge of the town, we waved to Everlyn and her infant, standing roadside, a feminine version of Mercury—messenger to the Gods. She gave a subtle nod, not wanting to draw attention to our hasty relocation.

The campsite leaned on the side of Mt. Laku. Like a tuft of hair on a man's back, the only patch of grass in Yangaloi—kelly green and tender as a newborn—poked up through the mud and sucked on the seeping spring water. The camp was off-limits to grazing animals. All the tribes conformed.

We met the campsite guardian, a tall, thin man named Simon with hollows beneath his cheekbones and a rifle hanging unused at his side. We told him whom we planned to entertain and watched for his reaction. He knew them. They were friends. No wonder they had told Everlyn to suggest this site.

I had visions of courtship. I imagined showing Lochili my things, looking through my backpack one item at a time, as we did with the Malian police on the train. Only this showing was to lessen the distances between us, to increase the knowing. Lochili's singing divided me into who I was and someone grander. Everything inessential loosened on the periphery and exposed the core, which now sought to be known.

We leveled ground for our tent and tidied the site, clearing branches and placing logs and stones for seats. We waited. And waited. For days, with impossible patience. We had waited for our warriors so long without contact that I vacillated between desire and indifference, the voice of reason slowly convincing me that Lochili and I were not meant for each other, no matter how briefly. Time would tell. Kas still sparkled at the mere mention of Loiboku's name.

The camp had a lovely shower, a spouting head fastened by a rubber hose to a sun-heated water bladder hanging in a tree. We lit the camp stove and cooked at night—simple meals that, because we had not cooked in a month or more, felt luxurious. From the warrior's *manyatta*, we must have been lit like a stage, our camp lights and stove silhouetting every movement against the blacker outline of the mountain.

We went to bed early, urging the sun to drop and leave us to our darkness—a welcome accomplice. "Nature" was not "outside" in Africa; it was all around. Permeable. Nature inhabited me as much as

I inhabited her. I breathed her dust and leaves and shone her sunlight from my eyes, and sweated her lakes and rivers. Nature and I entangled. Lochili had known her his whole life. I heard her in his song.

Kas ended each night writing in her journal. I preferred to let dreams deepen my experience. Each night, I fell into a fast sleep, and Lochili's raspy voice beckoned. That, and his rough touch shaking my lower leg.

"*Micah, kuja, kuja,*" he said, telling me to come, and not in a tone that banished slumber.

Disoriented, I never looked back when he helped me from my sleep sheet and out of the tent. I was wearing a tank top and a *shuka* that had come undone, and I fumbled trying to tie a knot while the other hand remained in his. I never got this right. I walked everywhere bound like a Geisha because my sheet was strangling with stricture. He noticed my difficulty, stopped, and opened my *shuka*, exposing my underwear. Without so much as a glance, he wrapped the *shuka* and tied it at my waist like a parent dressing a child—the most comfortable *shuka* knot yet, enough room to walk, legs split perfectly.

Lochili's warm hand led me into the night. I wanted to ask questions but knew better than to battle Kiswahili while we were trying to be quiet. I could smell his sweet scent from under his blanket. Kas and Loiboku must have stayed in the tent. I could see the fires of the *manyatta* burning low ahead and the domed houses like the tops of buns rising out of a baking tin. He led me to his mother's, and we ducked inside. The house familiar now, its smells, the feel of the ground, the way walls muffled the wind. Everyone slept, and we lay down on the cow skin, succumbing to the sleeping hour. He gave me his wrap to use as a blanket and pulled me close to him, holding my face in the crux of his veined neck, his arms around my upper back and waist. My face nestled near his throat, the physical origin of his sound, soul sound. We never moved; his erection he neither attempted to hide or encourage.

At dawn Lochili pulled me from sleep again, lifting me from the ground in the low-ceilinged hut. He led me though the dark morning and cool dirt back to the campsite. It all happened so fast. He held me with the tenderness of adoration and respect. When his hand wrapped mine, I felt protected. He squeezed tighter, forcing the warmth of his hands onto mine. I saw desire in his eyes, and sadness. No smile on his face now—just a lustful locking gaze. Such extreme control he showed in waiting to love me, or so I thought.

At the tent, we heard morning voices, long pauses between them. Lochili alerted Loiboku, speaking in low tones through the nylon walls. Kas unzipped the entrance.

"Um, I didn't even know you left until someone else was lying on top of me." She giggled, her hair disheveled.

"I know. I'm sorry. I walked halfway to the *manyatta* unconscious, wondering if I had zipped the tent shut." Lochili listened, and I didn't want him to think we might be speaking poorly of them. I spoke fast enough to ensure he missed most words, but what he read between them was out of my control. I smiled and said his name to reassure him we were not saying unkind things. Then I thanked him. He relaxed, but I still sensed sadness.

"Let's make them chai," Kas said, loving to entertain guests.

"*Karibu chai. Iko saa tosha?*" I invited them, asking in broken Kiswahili if there was enough time.

They responded with their agreeable *ehhh* and sat, at last, around our camp stove.

We had everything Mama used except for the smoky calabash, wood fire, and raw milk. We could offer powdered ginger, however—a true indulgence.

I did not shine in the hostess role. Kas had that honor. Lochili encouraged me by accepting my invitation to sit on a cedar log, tucking his herding stick under his knee. African women esteemed themselves by their domesticity. Tiny girls struggled under the weight of their infant siblings tied to their prepubescent backs, impressing the family with both aptitude and desire to mother. I think Lochili saw the American in me—distracted, self-centered, overeducated—and liked it anyway. Thank God.

I joined him on the log and ran my feet through the soft patch of grass. Loiboku sat in the tent with his feet outstretched from the door, the zippered arch framing his head like a boy in an oversized parka hood. He admired Kas' ability with the stove—this particular skill set of hers won points.

"Chai is finished!" Kas said, handing Loiboku a steaming cup. She walked Lochili's cup to him. I reached for the other two cups—the least I could do was hand hers to her. The chai smelled spicy sweet. The perfect amount of carton milk colored it caramel, not too dark, and creamy.

We sipped the tea in silence, and looked out at the lake, the rocky hill of Moloi. The warriors needed to leave to graze the animals soon. The sun inched above the horizon.

Lochili petted my head tenderly, running his hand down the side of my hair to my cheek as he said goodbye. He had never done that. They thanked us and disappeared into the *manyatta*.


"Loiboku loved the tent, and being together in it alone was great," Kas said. "How was sleeping in the village?" She had lost all her anxieties, a woman well loved, washing out the cups with water from the spring.

"Nothing happened in the hut. Maybe I should take off my underwear? Wave it in the air like a surrender flag," I said, uncertain what was keeping Lochili from sex. Maybe he felt my ambivalence. Maybe you couldn't have sex with your family lying six inches away.

"Loiboku and I will make the walk to the village tonight, friend," Kas said. "I'm sure that's what Lochili is waiting for. A tent is a novelty. He let Loiboku have first dibs."

I hoped he and Loiboku had worked out the details, but the Lokop seemed concerned only with the present and left the future to others, namely Kas and me.


The camp provided basins for laundry and showering. I lost myself in the pleasure of washing jeans, the way my hands and feet glimmered clean. I tossed the rinse water, hung our clothes on the spiny acacia fence, and looked up to see a man—Lochili—walking. His pace was urgent.

Kas watched with me. We walked closer to the fence.

Lochili looked behind him as he walked. I saw no one, but heard the village buzzing in the distance.

"*Micah, supa oleng. Na enda Mt. Laku sahi.*" That same sadness claimed the vigor of his voice as he told me he was leaving for Mt. Laku immediately. He looked again over his shoulder and repeated himself, making sure I understood him. *"Na enda Mt. Laku sahi."*

*"Lochili, sahi? Ta rudi?"* I asked if he meant right now and when he would return, turning my palm over in the air with the question hanging from it, a gesture I saw them use often.

He did not know when or if they would return. He did not know when or if he would see me. Loiboku was also going to the mountain and passed Kas his goodbye via his brother.

Lochili looked again toward the village and said something we did not understand.

"Lochili," I continued in Kiswahili, "we will wait for you and Loiboku. We will wait here for you." I saw his frustration, his sadness, unchanged. They would not return from the mountain as long as we were in Yangaloi.

I reached my hand over the fence to him while tears pooled. He wiped them dry, just as he had cleared my brow of sweat the first time we sat together in his mother's hut. Hands, tears, sweat, heat—he held my hand and stared into my heartbreak. He was so different in this hopelessness, one dark spot on the sun.

With one final squeeze, he released me. He apologized to Kas, whose face was streaked wet. She said Loiboku's name and placed her hand on her heart. Lochili nodded, said my name once more, and turned up the mountain path.

Kas and I remained at the fence until we could no longer see him, tears falling in hot channels. My body wanted to chase after him, but the daydream stopped when I reached him and had nothing to say, no future to offer. To release sadness, I imagined the scene again and again. I ran fast, right to him, but before he saw me, I turned back. I imagined it again, running faster until I no longer had the urge or the ache. No future.

Kas wouldn't have it. "Micah, let's try to find Everlyn. She'll know what the hell is happening."

Everlyn stood at the entrance to a small tobacco shop in town, as if she were expecting us. She gently bounced her baby on her back.

Her smile reminded us to honor the greeting and restrain our Western urge to get to the point.

"*Supa, Everlyn! Habari za asubuhi?*" I greeted her with feigned happiness that concealed the truth.

"I am fine, thank you. How are you?" she replied, her eyes searching deeper.

"We are okay, but a little sad," Kas said. "Your brother came to tell us he would not be in Yangaloi again. He had to travel to the mountain. Do you know about this? Did we do something wrong?" Kas asked without looking away as she fastened her headband.

"Yes, I know," Everlyn said, casually twisting her spine right and left to keep moving and distracting the baby. We walked away from the tobacco store for privacy. "They cannot see you because my father forbade them. He knows they have been spending some days with you." She continued in the same acquiescent manner, the submissive-woman syndrome that frustrated us unendingly.

*Laissez-faire, my fucking American ass*, is what I wanted to yell.

But the profound acceptance in her left us no choice. We had to do the same. The warriors would not return. There was nothing to do. Nothing but ask one last question.

"Did we do something wrong, or is it just because we are not Lokop girls?" I had to know.

Everlyn grinned, looked to her feet, and said, "No, nothing wrong. He knows they will not be ready to work, to move the animals, if you are here. They like you too much. Lochili tried to change him but they went to the elders and the elders decided. They were supposed to leave last night, but they cheated them and stayed. They could be beaten by the elders." She looked at us to see if we had been with the brothers last night. Kas and I betrayed no one, sensing the grave situation.

My heart stuck on one thing: Lochili had chosen not to make love on our last night. Knowing we had no future, had he cast off his desire? Or had his father's dictate caused too much fear? I felt his heat rising and falling against my belly. His enigmatic, unsolvable ways made me even sadder. I would have said more to him that morning if I had known. How could they have that much silence in them, knowing the futility of it all yet not saying anything? My heart wedged between awe and despair.

I wanted to ask Everlyn things but my questions vaporized. Better not to involve or implicate anyone further. I wanted to confess my love for Lochili so she could tell him. I said nothing. We recognized the truth standing there. We would never see her brothers. Reality cut with barbs.

We left Everlyn bouncing her baby on her hip. Without our warriors, Yangaloi suffocated us. They had carried off its charm in their colored beads and face paint. A fly-infested ghost town haunted by lost love, harsh realities, and prejudices remained. It was time to leave for Nairobi.

It took us two days to find a truck going to Lamaresh. Relieved we were going, Hussein alerted us to all possible transport, so we would take with us the constant reminder that Kas had rejected him and chosen a wild Lokop *lmurran* with whom she could not speak—so much for Hussein's civilized, English-speaking education.

Everlyn and a few villagers came to say farewell. Hussein spoke to the driver and made sure we were safe. He blessed our journey—never asked us to write or promised he would, which I admired. He was both kind and authentic, knowing that our friendship had reached its shelf life.

I watched out the top of the truck, as we rolled along, bracing myself against the railing. I searched for villages—circles of domed mounds and acacia fences that my eyes were now able to see. The first trip, the surrounding unfamiliar had absorbed them. I savored the fires burning inside, the smell of the calabash, the smell of dung and animals, and the feel of the splinter-like hair of the cow skins. Perhaps the warriors held us to them in their profound silence. Perhaps they preserved the memory there. Words couldn't do it. I believed I could feel Lochili missing me but would never know for sure.

A torn zipper on my backpack, pushed into the corner of the truck, caught my eye.

When I emptied the pack that morning, had I seen our money belt? My mind reviewed the contents. I had packed and unpacked the bag so many times now, I knew every item and how to turn it just right. No, I definitely had not seen the money belt. It held a thousand dollars.

Ambrose? Hussein?

I looked at Kas, the memory of Loiboku curling her lips and glossing her eyes. I left her there with him. We could not do anything about the money now.

I looked beyond her, beyond what used to be important, and let memory have its way with me.

Maybe silence had fashioned me after all.

The truck bounced over boulders and collapsed into cratered depressions before Lowaa appeared on the horizon. It looked like any abandoned refugee settlement, its outskirts flanked by nomadic huts. We planned to stay one night and assess our resources. Only I knew our financial situation was grim. We chose a hotel with two stories of stacked single rooms boasting hot bucket showers. I asked Kas to pay, as I no longer had money on me—neither Kenyan shilling nor American dollars.

We made our way to the room. I propped my heavy pack against the mosquito-bloodied plaster wall. Lowaa stifled without the blessing of Yangaloi wind.

"Kas, I didn't pack my money belt this morning."

She turned to me.

"I haven't seen it since we left Hussein's to camp. The last time I looked for it was after the wedding. I realized this on the truck." I waited for her reaction. She deserved time to react. It was, after all, *our* money.

Kas stayed silent, choosing whether or not to allow the news to taint her experience. I sighed and sat on the bed. She knew a thousand dollars was in that belt, and we had six more months in Africa. I watched her mental calculations. Her face lightened, and her shoulders gave a shrug. She still had not said anything. I risked speaking.

"Well, we know they need it more than we do. I don't want to know who. I don't care."

Kas said, "It's true. Let's make sure we're right—that we don't have the belt—and then just …. let it go. Maybe we can call our parents for a loan so we can stay as long as we'd planned. I know they miss us. It's not much we need. When we return, we can pay them back."

Then she did something that made me admire and love her even more.

She threw up her hand, letting imaginary bills sift through her fingers. Love still glowed in her heart. Her nonchalance made me laugh. My laughter made her laugh. The laughter so powerful we writhed in fits. We fell on our beds, bellies cramping, and wiped the tears from our eyes. We laughed at the warriors, the insanity of having sex in bushes, following them to a Moloi wedding, almost dying by crocodiles. We laughed at our rich love, despite the barrenness of Yangaloi. We laughed at the treachery of thieves. We laughed because my conscious mind could not deal with the betrayal and the fact that the money belt, which contained one-sixth of the total cash we'd brought, had gone missing. We laughed with hearts so full that our minds went numb. I saw it in Kas, too: no more working and worrying and paying careful attention. And finally, we laughed at our naïveté—our belief that impoverished Africans could afford to like us for who we were and not for our relative wealth.

And then, we cried.

I moved to Kas' bed and held her with one arm, our heads together like bookends.

"I am so sorry, Kas."

She knew my apology was not really for the stolen money but for the greater heartbreak, the inequitable way of things. I apologized for the world. A faith, a philosophy of choice seared into us that night, our youthful mores rearranged. We chose love, to open despite fear, despite the violation of what we cherished far beyond money—the desire to belong, to be friends with Africans.

"You know, when I think of someone taking my belt and finding that absurd amount of money—" I lay across her bed, my legs dangling, "—all I feel is excitement for them." Kas sat up. "And I feel sad that I would never have given it to them. Not knowingly. They had to take it. I would have loved to have seen their face when they saw the amount, though."

"How can we blame them for needing it? We can always get more," she said. "They couldn't make that much if they worked a lifetime. Let's not think about it again. Let's imagine it like a gift we've given."

"Yeah. It was for charity, a write-off, Uncle Sam," I said, winking.

"Fuck it," she said with a smile.

With a belly laugh and a few tears, we had discovered and protected what was vital. My love for Africa grew even more. Africa played host to catalysts, one bittersweet expansion after another.

We decided to call our parents when we reached Nairobi. Seven weeks had passed since they'd last heard from us. The small towns between here and there had no phones, and we had been too preoccupied to write.

Hawo, Habiba, and Mary lived in Lowaa, but to see them so soon after the raw nerves of loss and betrayal risked too much. We needed more distance from Yangaloi.

"We tried to stay within our budget, Mom, but we're having a hard time because East Africa is more expensive than West Africa, or at least Nairobi is expensive," I lied, not wanting to alarm my parents that we had been robbed. It only felt a little bad.

Kas' suggestion worked. Our parents, concerned for our welfare and happy to hear from us after two months without word, each gave five hundred dollars. Their one caveat was that we stay in better touch. They signed off telling us they were grateful for our adventures and our health.

They had no idea!

Our second night in Nairobi, we were robbed again, this time by the police. While we wandered the garbage-littered streets, the police caught a thief rifling through our bags in our hotel room. They apprehended the man and found him with two hundred dollars on his person, which equaled the amount Kas had left behind. The hotel manager told us this with a strict sort of disapproval in his voice, as if the robbery had been planned and executed by us! It was always a toss-up whether the money would be safer on our person, or left at our lodging.

When we reported to the station, the police had changed their story. "We found the man in your room. He entered through the window. But he didn't have anything on him. No money." A navy-blue uniformed officer leaned over the counter and said while mixing his words with cobra venom, "This matter is over. There is no one else for you to speak with." He had a voice so dark and eyes so dangerous, my feet started walking backward over the shiny black-and-white tile. Who was he? Head of brainwashing?

Kas and I never went out after dark again. At night, we tracked the police trucks patrolling the dark alleyways under our window. Covered, slow moving, heavy with diesel smoke and intimidation. We made one friend at the hotel, Rudy, a political refugee from Zaire who lived on our floor. Rudy's light skin and tall frame hinted at his Tutsi origins, and the shadowing around his sunken eyes suggested hardship. He told us those trucks picked up people who were never again heard from. Disappeared.

Refugees knew such things. Ardent, overly cautious, Rudy didn't tell us about his past, or his people's suffering, their scabbed-over trauma, their diminished trust. He kept all of that to himself, in the private vault. From the rooftop, Rudy taught us about which streets to walk on, where to eat for little money, and how to get back to the hotel the quickest way. Our hotel housed the destitute, most of the rooms leased as apartments to refugees, prostitutes, and the unemployed. Kas and I mixed it up with them while we waited for our visas to Zaire.

We showed Rudy the guidebook, the photo of Zaire's mountain gorillas. We had to do something drastic to shake our minds off impossible warrior lovers.

Rudy held the book a long while. His vault opened a crack. However hard his life, he was a survivor. And survivors share their methods of survival—we gave him our friendship, and Rudy gave us contact info for his gorilla-tracking brother in Zaire.

# Twelve | Silver and Gold in the Congo

*God circles a moment, a place, a man, and that which is circled is not Yan-*
*galoi nor is it Lochili. The man is still out of reach, out of my awareness,*
*living another story. Then destinies collide, vast and spinning—rightness*
*aligns and sears a truer path. We are all carried. It works that way for us.*
*God circles places on the map for all of us.*

But I did not know this yet. I was simply tracking gorillas.

Zaire endangered everything. We caught a ride in the back of
a lopsided pickup to the Uganda-Zaire border. The overloaded bed
swung off the steep faces of volcanic rainforest as the truck tires clung
to the narrow shoulder.

Zaire (now called the Democratic Republic of the Congo) sighed
with desperation. Though free from the corruption of Mobutu Sese
Seko—one of Africa's terrifying leaders—the county was not free.
Inflation meant a cup of tea was worth a plastic bag full of tattered
bills, ironically decorated with Seko's face and pictures of a miner-
al-abundant country. The natural jubilance of the people had suffered
years of military-backed terrorism, the rainy season, and bad politics.
Kas and I knew Zaire had declared a state of emergency, and the US
embassy had issued warnings for Americans to make haste and leave.
But Zaire was home to the wondrous mountain gorillas.

In the dry season, villagers walked everywhere. But the rainy season misted the air and delivered downpours the ground could not absorb. The deluge washed out roads so the locals floated through the green countryside in wooden boats, the current steady enough.

Border police allowed everyone in the Ugandan pickup truck to empty into Zaire, except us. Kas and I were routinely escorted into border offices but this one was particularly menacing. Two windows, barred and flecked with grime, obscured the view. Yellow paint sweated in the flickering fluorescent light. The whole place quivered with bad vibes.

Four men in camouflage, roughly thirty or forty years in age, surrounded us. One man leaned against a wall, resting his folded arms on his semiautomatic rifle. He frightened me most, eyeing us like meat. The others asked questions.

I pretended to know almost no French to limit our interaction. These guys had plenty of time to squander and could detain us to stave off boredom. The boss, a short, fierce man, told us to sit, pointing to two chairs. He wanted to see our backpacks and our passports. The five-day visas pasted inside needed stamps. A fatter, seemingly kind man scrutinized the photos and flipped through to previous visas, ignoring the only one in question. None of this mattered. It was clearly a crooked mess.

Kas looked at me to keep her cool. Who appeared most reasonable, least unscrupulous, in this hellish station? The fatter man lacked courage. The others were hardened, not about to relate to us as vulnerable travelers, or even as sisters or daughters. They wanted money, maybe sex too. That we were American might normally deter them but the US embassy in Kinshasa had emptied its office and fled. We were without representation. Who would know if we disappeared? Our parents, but not for a couple of months' time.

"We can answer your questions in English, if you speak English?" I knew they did not.

The one in charge closed his face tight as a fist. He pounded on the desk and asked how we expected to be in a French-speaking country alone if we could not speak the language. I assumed sheer innocence and shrugged my shoulders as though I hadn't caught what he said.

My stomach raised hell with my gamble. I knew he looked for any reason to explode. I feared for Kas, for our fate, and held my ground.

The fat policeman stopped snooping through our passports. He had not stamped them. They lay halfway between us, stacked on the desk. I longed to grab them and run back to Uganda.

The guards glared. Silence crept along the yellowed walls and plunged us deep into mounting fear. The world endured many types of men: good men—like Guy, Lochili, and my father, whose heart was pure even when he drank,—and men like these. The men I had known had cared for and protected me, all my life. Their love could not prepare me for these men.

Kas and I waited without speaking. The border police wanted a bribe but didn't know how to ask in English and weren't yet angry enough to do anything rash. We refused to spark their tempers, looked right at their faces. No cowering, despite our knees shaking under the desk.

The man with the weapon crossed the room and grabbed my left hand. He pinched my ring finger where a wedding band would be if I were married and muttered something in their vernacular. I let my wrist fall limp. He tossed my hand away with disgust and the fumes of last night's liquor. We had to get out of there.

"What do you need from us?" I asked insolently in English as I reached across the table. "If you are finished with our passports, we'll take them."

Kas forced her voice to drop an octave, in strength. "Our visas are valid."

No one stopped us, so we took our passports, placed them in our jacket pockets, and said, "Merci." The only French word we spoke to them.

The boss barked at us as we reached the door. He had a suggestion for a hotel in the nearby town. *Hotel Menace*, I thought. I pretended not to understand him and shrugged apologetically. We left without stamps. A smarter risk than staying to obtain them. The whole country was falling apart. Stamps were the least of our worries. We walked beyond the crossing gate and cattle guard into lush jungle.

Through rain that sliced the sky a thousand diagonal ways we made out a few thatched dwellings.

Kas and I stayed at the first accommodation we found and learned it was the only one. The row house manager was an older man with a sort of crater in his skull. He sloshed in galoshes around the muddy compound. Everything sloped, built on uneven ground. The village had no restaurants. When we asked where we could buy food, he sent a young boy to a family so desperate for money they agreed to make us dinner, which we could eat in the manager's adjacent home.

The row rooms sat empty by day, except for two permanent occupants, we later learned. A deranged woman stayed in one room. We caught only glimpses of her in a torn dress that exposed her right breast, her hair graying and matted with dirt and trauma. A lecherous man roomed in the other. Kas caught him spying when I went to the bathroom—a hole in the ground, disastrously uphill from the cement-block rooms where we slept. We had enough time to shower before the border police, who slept in the vacant rooms next to the lecherous and deranged, returned from the post for the evening. The air, like the rooms, felt heavy with hopelessness.

One American dollar later, however, we were eating the most delicious fire-cooked beans, tomato, and potato casserole, which warmed our bellies. The sun went down, turning the rain-gray sky two shades darker. The hotel scared us. The incline kept the water from flooding our room but created perpetual drainage downstream from the loo! Near the outdoor mud-floor shower, which defeated the purpose of cleaning feet, a wicker cage with pigeons hung quietly. Of course, we had to know—yes, they were for eating.

We arranged for a guide to take us up the volcano to the gorillas early the next day and locked ourselves in for the night. The border police stayed up, loud and possibly drunk. In a downpour, they pounded on our sturdy door. They tried to push it in, hands reaching in underneath first. We saw their dirty fingernails. And then their gun barrels.

"Open the door! We need to see you! You cannot hide in this town. Come out. We have to stamp your passports. Get up, American girls! Come on! Let us *stamp* your passports!" they shouted in French.

Raucous laughter, howls, and demands. We sat up, wide-eyed,

bracing ourselves for the break in. I moved over to Kas' bed and whispered, "Let's get out our Swiss Army knives."

The two iron latch locks jangled as they pounded. Alcohol made a circus of their coordination. Tumbling, stumbling, someone fell into the door and used it to brace his languid weight. We had left that border station unharmed not because we were American or because they remembered their humanity but because they knew they had time. Away from national outposts, we were as vulnerable as the despairing pigeons held captive in the wooden cage. In fact, we were illegal. They had every right to arrest us.

Kas and I stayed vigilant—bodies gripped, with knives open, for hours. Each thudding, drunken stumble broke the possibility of sleep or peace. We waited, hard and tense.

At three in the morning, the men passed out, and by four we vanished like gorillas in the mist, in search of the primate nest with young Jackson.

Jackson was a twelve-year-old boy whose French was poor but whose spirit shone, despite the despair around him. Kas and I shook off the perilous night, ready for adventure. The dark rains engulfed us. Zaire had not been warmed by the sun in weeks. Jackson insisted we wear good shoes. He had included in his fare peanuts, bananas, and French baguettes for the hike. His task was not to track the gorillas—professional guides with guns did that—but he wound through the labyrinth of paths and scattered homes on the steep face of the mountain. We would reach the official trackers near the summit through Jackson's care.

Most tourists with money drove up the backside of the mountain in Uganda. Voila. But Rudy, our refugee friend in Zaire, had alerted us to his brother, the gorilla guide. We took the deep discount tour to see the nearly extinct great apes, which made us enter through Zaire instead of Uganda. We wanted to hike through gorilla environment, laboring up the chancy steeps through the forest. The trek prepped us for seeing the planet's most wonderful creatures. Even if we did not see the gorillas, we felt we had to work for something this grand.

The fertile land grew coffee, tea, banana, papaya, potato, and mango in its red-black soil. We walked with flashlights for two hours, hunting in the dark for the next step, beating down wild grasses with careful steps. As the sun made its way up the eastern range, exposing the highest peak, it warmed the land and dried the covering mist.

We entered a village just waking. Women started fires and men hiked up toward the few bananas that remained untouched by yesterday's foraging. Gorillas liked banana trees, Jackson said, not so much for the fruit as the knotty fiber. They would shred a healthy trunk into strips within minutes. He whispered that the farmers did not like gorillas but wouldn't harm them because it was not their way.

Poachers were the problem. Poachers hunted gorillas at night, sometimes for trophies, sometimes to kidnap the infants and sell them. The farmers turned a blind eye, protecting their families and their crops instead.

Once past the village, I asked Jackson about his family. He said, "My father mines gold in the south. It is dangerous work, like diamonds and copper. Everything stolen by our government. People die. My mother is no longer living. That's why I work for tourists that come to see gorillas, but now we did not expect anyone. It is dangerous in this country."

I had no response. Jackson was a child.

We climbed to a wooden cabin with a porch. Jackson tapped on the door. A hulky tracker in army fatigues and black-soled boots emerged. Philipe, our guide for the remainder of the journey, smiled at us with confidence and the desire to please. Philipe carried a gun, a large knife housed in a case near the top of his hip, and a machete. He was fit and tall and moved effortlessly up the mountain. I glanced once more at my worn Converse sneakers and hesitated over Jackson's warning about good shoes. No matter—I would scrabble up in bare feet for this chance. Jackson stayed safe in the cabin to wait for our return.

Philipe tracked in silence as he sought last night's nest. Gorillas moved continually, spending the night lower in elevation for warmth and climbing higher in the early morning, eating their way up the volcano, descending again in the evening. If we were to find them, it would be just after sunrise, not too far from a sleeping settlement.

The massive silverbacks, weighing three hundred and fifty to four hundred pounds, slept in trees. Philipe stopped us. A question in his eyes. And all the time in the world for us to respond. I looked about and Kas looked, too. He pointed out a big mound of dung at the base of one tree.

Without knowing, we had walked under a nest—it was not last night's but one slept in the night before. Still, the tree hardly appeared touched, the branches folded over one another to form a hammock, a leaf mattress, astonishing us both.

The sun grew hotter, the air thick with humidity and small gnats. Our guide wiped his brow with a bunch of crumpled leaves he picked and shifted the machete into his other hand. He whacked the unmarked trail with cutting, rhythmic strokes.

After hours of hard hiking, and slipping, the bottoms of our pants had soaked through. Our knees were mud. Philipe motioned for us to get low. It was a rule he'd said we had to follow, it could save all our lives. Silverbacks behaved in unpredictable ways. This season, due to political instability and rain, few tourists had visited. The gorillas' tolerance had not been stretched.

We sat motionless, listening to the buzz of unfamiliar insects and bird songs. Philipe cupped his ear. He heard them. They were near. The birds sang out, flashing colors in the trees.

Philipe motioned to crawl toward the lea. As slow as cold honey, we made our way, one arm, one leg at a time. We heard the loud rustling, not far away, and knew the troop may already have spotted us. At the wide expanse of flattened grasses, we squatted, avoiding eye contact. We pretended to take little interest. Each tiny movement we made required caution, giving them plenty of warning if they were watching. Surprising a silverback is a bad idea.

Philipe blocked my view but I heard a hollow knocking sound ahead of him. We moved together deeper into the clearing. He signaled for us to sit and look at the ground while he scooted just opposite us. We crouched, compact and submissive. I could hear them more clearly now. Low belly grunting and loud feeding raced straight to my heart. I was afraid to look but I knew they were seeing us. From my periphery, I stole a glance. Large black mounds of muscled body scattered throughout the green brush. Many! The male silverback remained hidden.

I kept my head low, looked down, and pretended to sort the grass with my fingers. Kas did the same. Then, in a loud and lightning-fast display, the silverback came thrashing and pounding toward us, circling back, pulling the lesser canopy's twelve- and fifteen-foot-high trees to the ground, snapping their trunks like toothpicks. He hollered and beat his chest, turning it upright to the sky. We cowered, looking to Philipe for instruction. He motioned for us to stay still. The rules were: do not run, do not stand, do not look at him even though he is the source of your concern, and never touch a gorilla. Keep at least ten feet away to prevent the passage of infectious disease and minimize provocation.

The silverback set his boundary. The massive powerhouse of black and silver snorted and whooped, stood on two legs, and thrashed rapidly onto four. He ran at us once more, stopped abruptly and grabbed one of the females to mate. She protested briefly then surrendered. Kas and I saw very little of this feral fornication, our eyes stuck to the ground.

Satisfied, the male sat and calmly stripped a tree of its leaves, anchoring the bent branch between his spread legs. My chest heaved. My heart pounded. The gorillas continued grazing, more peaceful now, somehow accepting us, the initiation complete.

And then we met the family.

A baby ambled on its knuckles toward us. Philipe said, *"Bouge pas. Dis rien."* We obeyed his warning to stay put and say nothing. Not wanting to rouse the silverback's fury, I looked away from the baby.

Sudden weight, as its dense body climbed onto my side, settling my right hip deeper into wet earth. The baby stuck thick, warm fingers in my ear and pushed my hair around, trying to rile me but I resisted touching him for fear of alarming the group. The baby's mother moved closer, watched me for harmful body language. I became a frozen, collapsed jungle gym while that kid played, stealing glances under my arm. He had his fun with me and gradually I broke open to his charm. I held my breath and embraced every sound, smell, every sensation, almost as though we merged, this furry baby and me, our hearts desperate to connect.

To the silverback, I appeared indifferent, unchanged, even discouraging. Behind closed eyes, I cried raw love. In so few minutes, this beautiful, brawny primate pulled my heart as deep as anything I had ever loved. The youngster's play was rough and curious. His body smelled like hot fur and dirt. He rested his full weight on my side, toes curling strongly into the creases of my thighs, grabbing grass, then leaning his tender head down to look up into my face. I braced my arms so I would not topple and stayed stone as I silently came undone. He brushed my exposed forearm in slow, tender strokes, cooed and nudged. All I wanted was to touch him back, feel him fully, nuzzle into his wild hair, grasp his rubbery skin and hold onto him forever.

The group had moved closer, keeping a careful watch on their youngest member.

The baby soon tired of his slow playmate and left to climb into his mother's arms. I absorbed our incredible moment. Kas gaped with amazement—we were changed by this. She'd been right next to me, close enough to feel his antics and the trust behind them. I turned slowly so I could see them, the silverback family. The adult gorillas ate, stripping bark, chewing noisily, while baby rambled, seeking someone, anyone to entertain him.

The large male foraged while he kept one eye on us. Sunlight glinted in his silver fur. His brown eyes shone, gentle and intelligent. Philipe came to us. Silverbacks were often shot defending their infants from kidnappers, he said, and the mere thought crushed the breath from my lungs. Kas had tears in her eyes. We felt so far from human, yet so near family.

The band continued farther into thicket. Philipe and Kas and I watched for a few moments, followed them only with prayers, and headed down the mountain stunned with beauty.

That primal beauty was our guard and shield to survive one more evening with drunken, bellicose officers. We gained it from the gorillas and on the ascent and descent of their mountain. Only nature herself bestows this defense.

A purity of instinct and fearlessness had finally found us.

We were at last out of our minds.


The men wandered home to their rooms that night and retired, without the drive or the attention span to harass us again. Kas and I slept as though cradled in the top of a tree, ensconced by branches.

The border opened at six in the morning. We slid through where the gate hung open, leaving troubled Zaire at five, rushing to a vague sense of safety in Uganda's terraced landscape. Once well beyond the border, we breathed easier. Kas sang a little and took a gulp from her water bottle. I walked like no road was too long. The indomitable spirit of the mountain gorilla came with us—an integrated power we could call God. We carried it in our heartbeats, our footprints. For in the gorillas' patient, ebony eyes, God's grace reflected and she reigned.

# Thirteen | COLLISION

*Ukunda, Kenya—Indian Ocean*

KAS AND I wandered through the story of our senses, different countries, one foot- or bus- or boat-length in front of the other, rather lost and rather filthy. For ten months. Satisfied in part by the richness of the journey. Aware of our good fortune in avoiding peril. Feeling lucky. Wanting more than unplanned adventures. Still wanting in. Still savoring Lochili and Loiboku. So we made our way back to Kenya— only this time we headed south out of Nairobi to the coast, a ferry ride from Mombasa to a beach resort named Ukunda. We planned to rest and clean up before making the journey north to Yangaloi once more.

And here it was. The collision. The way in.

The Indian Ocean shimmered light turquoise. Darker shades plunged deeper. A large stretch of sand glittered gold, running with the horizon.

Five Lokop warriors walked toward us, a mirage skimming the sand. Their spears glinted in the sun's afternoon light, crisp red cloth silhouettes against the blue-green of the sea, beads clinking in the breeze.

"Kas, look," I said nodding my head in their direction as discreetly as possible.

"What on Earth are they doing here?"

I could not help myself. Rash excitement prompted me to shout across the sand between us. We had not seen anyone even resembling the Lokop warriors in months, and we had missed them.

"*Supa!*" I strained my voice, shouting against the wind. I rambled on in rapid speech, showing off. "*Serian ake, serian n'gang, serian manyatta?*"

They did not expect a Gutok-speaking tourist with wild copper hair.

They stopped and eyed us. Dressed like kings in warrior regalia, their hair ochre-stained, adornments draping their toned bodies. The unlikely mirage of them collided with their realness, that uncompromising self-possession that made my knees weak and my belly flip.

They made a beeline to us.

"Uh-oh," I murmured, "they're coming."

One warrior strutted with his head high, hair short and tight to his skull, muscled calves bowing out a fraction, but his feet marched in a steady, agile gait. I recovered my Nilotic manners. I asked after their families and villages with a demure smile, regretting my impulsivity.

They answered, clearly annoyed, as if slapping at mosquitoes. Because, after all, tourists were mosquitoes from afar.

And then they waited.

I began in slow English, believing they must know it, to be so far from home. "Um, sorry. We have visited Lokop land and have seen how you live. We wanted to greet you in your mother tongue. We are Americans and have been on safari in Africa for nearly a year."

Two warriors, unimpressed, continued their trek to town. Three remained. They stuck the tips of their spears in the sand. The leader, the agile one, leaned a foot against his calf and shifted his attention to us. His insolent attention. His behavior said that Lokop warriors were really none of our business. As far as they knew, we were just beach-lounging foreigners.

Kas and I propped our heavy baskets, full with pineapple and papaya, against our legs. We mentioned Lochili and Loiboku. The three men did not know them or their clan. The leader watched me, homing in on my level of disappointment.

Tourists passed and stared.

We waited for introductions. Ploote, the leader's cousin, made a start. He had buck teeth so large they seemed fake, and his halo-like smile matched his afro. So friendly. Ploote told us that the handsome man with lighter skin, long pleated hair and a few freckles on his cheeks, Lududuma, spoke neither English nor Kiswahili. Lududuma watched every interaction and waited for translations.

The serious warrior, the leader, took no notice of the tourists craning their necks as they breezed by, yet he had already noted Kas and I were somehow different. The Lokop used to be one tribe with the Sai, who were widely known here. Under colonial rule, the Lokop were pushed north and the Sai south. He said, "What on Earth are you doing here without parents?" I was struck by his paternal instinct and his English—the best we had heard in Africa, thank God. I remembered Lochili and our struggles. But what stayed with me, was the way his voice stood against the waves.

Ploote asked for our names. We gave them. Then, playfully, he said, "Let us carry your fruity baskets and escort you to your hotel." The lilting, clear English drew a big smile from Kas. He reached for her basket, forearms and biceps wrapped with bracelets of leather and metal.

"Do they refuse to cook for you at your expensive hotel?" the leader asked me, peering at our produce. "Or did you buy the student special?"

Then he laughed heartily. The first smile we'd seen.

We laughed, too. The basket clearly stated we were camping at the hostel and could not afford a room, clean sheets, the umbrella drinks, or even beach chair rental.

We shuffled through the hot sand toward an inland stream that divided the far-as-the-eye-can-see beach. Kas and I waded in, small waves tumbling at our feet.

The warriors stopped at the stream and handed us our baskets.

"It's just up here a little further," Kas said, enjoying their chivalry.

"We cannot continue. Beach regulations." The leader smiled at the absurdity but tilted his nicely round head in acquiescence. He was quick with a remedy. "Why don't we take a Coke later. We can come and bring you to the place."

It was not a question.

I saw him as a bridge, a connector who could provide the missing pieces about Lochili, Loiboku, and Lokop culture in general. I had no idea he had already entered my bloodstream. We agreed to meet at seven and thanked them in their language, "*Ashe-na oleng*."

The warriors smiled, turned, and sauntered down the beach with such ease and possession, I forgot this place was not their home.

Shuffling our feet in the glow of a single streetlight, Kas and I waited for our warrior escorts. We enjoyed the feeling of being protected, once again. Of holding things in common. Of promise, plain and simple. We shared English and Gutok and who knew what else.

Promptly at seven, when the sun dipped below the horizon and dusk spread like deep-purple eyeshadow, we were greeted by him, his cousin Ploote, and Lududuma.

Kas and I had showered and changed our clothes. We donned salubrious tans, light-colored tank tops and crisp *shukas*. The warriors were as we had seen them earlier. What would they have changed into anyway? A different set of beads or leather bands? A new sheet? The dressier version? Having two pairs of shoes was excessive for nomads. No, they were just as before, basic and poised.

I brought a mango from our basket as a gift for him. He thanked me and took a bite, holding it with his teeth and me with his dark gleaming eyes. As we climbed into the *matatu*, he paid the tout. He stepped aside to allow Kas and me to enter, carrying the mango in his steady hand. When he took his seat next to me—the second indication of his attraction—he no longer held the mango.

I looked out the window and said, with pluck and mischief, "There's your new mango, rolling in the dirt."

He laughed, and his smile could have lit the whole bus. Dusk itself paused. "Yes, now it's a gift to the Earth. I didn't want you to see it, but you are too clever. I don't eat sweet things. We eat meat, milk, and blood. Did you know that as well as how to greet in my language?" He spoke gently, and then added with charm, "There will be many fruits and vegetables for you when you are with me." I went all wobbly inside. Like that poor mango.

He chatted with the Lokop warriors about how I busted him while he pulled the straggly fruit strands from the bottom gap in his teeth. They laughed when I mimicked how he winced as he bit into the bitter skin through the flesh to the splintering seed.

Kas watched me closely.

Mangoes and love, flesh and splinters. *Keep eating.*

The warriors told us they earned money by two means in Ukunda. They performed nightly dances at the resort hotels, providing the tourists with a sample of their traditional culture, song, and dress. And they sold their beaded leatherwork. There was a third way—male prostitution—but few partook.

The men formed a close-knit community. They had their own village among the coconut groves. Kas and I were happily inducted into the dance troop and followed them like groupies to evening performances, one hotel posher than the next. We were neither guests of the resort nor the Lokop. So we opted for hiding in the grass or the towering bougainvillea bushes backed up to a thirty foot drop to the sea. The few hotels built on hills provided stunning views, worth the risk.

We eavesdropped. We caught most of the warriors' performances, trying to remain still so as not to get caught or tumble. One evening we hid in the dense tropical potted landscape of the venue the warriors preferred. This hotel created a semi-circle around a well-lit amphitheater with high-rise mahogany seating for the guests. The warriors liked the sound jumping feet made against the wooden floor, a sound all new to them. Kas and I had a perfect view. The dance could never conjure emotion like dancing in the village moon with the wild listening, but once we saw him and Lududuma and Ploote enter, we closed our eyes and imagined we were there, pounding the dirt. That night and every night, we entered the dance trance until, finally, the applause resounded and shook us. The warriors passed by and tucked us into the fray. There were twenty or more Lokop *lmurran*, sweaty and fragrant and fine.

"Did you enjoy the dance?" He always asked, like Lochili had.

I thought to myself, *Enjoy is not the right word. More like crave, be haunted by, lose my snooty sense of self—*

Weather permitting, we walked to a restaurant and surrounded ourselves with the joviality of warrior company. They escorted us as near as possible to our hostel campsite. Kas and I crawled into our tent and recounted the day's events before falling asleep, their songs permeating our dreams.

We sensed some ridiculousness in how we spent our time, the unproductive dawdling day in, day out, as groupies, and our friendship with the Lokop *lmurran*, which was so strangely natural and reciprocal. The warriors' hearts were lonely for female friendship, their girlfriends far away. Lududuma clearly found Kas intoxicating, though he could not understand anything she said. Kas and I felt a brother-sister kinship for the group, for the first time in Africa—maybe ever. In return for their humor and guardianship, we gave them our praise and tales about their continent. Fascination compelled us all, and relaxation, and mingled stories, our notion of family extended like baobab limbs. We became our own gorilla band.

Ono soap in the clean sheets, the first night. Rightness has its own strong draw. His woody, candle wax scent both sweet and of the flesh. His *rungu* under the motel bed. The Lokop prayer. The victory whoop. Then he and I enter our first sweet, hard night of lovemaking. *La-la salama, Micah.* This time, in this intimate circle of dance, I am the one to catch him. Time fractures. My lion, my silverback. No one, least of all time, is harmed. No one else exists in that rhapsodic present.

"Today we will go to Mombasa and call your Mamas." He said while shepherding, of all things, seagulls. The small flock of white birds contoured with his switch, toward the waves, away from the waves, weaving. One would occasionally look back to question what this self-possessed human meant by orchestrating their movement; he also orchestrated the call to my family, as promised. I loved that my mother was important to him. I knew what place Mama held in the heart of a nomadic warrior. The gap in his lower front teeth taunted me. I imagined putting my finger, then my tongue in that secret gap.

Why did he smile at me as if he heard my thoughts?

No one sat on the Mombasa ferry; there was no room. The journey was short, the boat, rusted, well-worn. This particular ferry cost almost nothing, the discount vessel used for bringing people to and from work, even on Sunday, or to visit family if they were not working. Kas and I were the only white people on board. He told me to be careful, not to let anyone try to open my small backpack. Then he decided to hold it for me. He strapped it to his body, not unlike my heart.

"Mama!" I shouted happily into a payphone in Mombasa.

Tears sprang to my eyes. It had been a month or more since we had spoken. It was early in the morning in Colorado.

"I want you to say hello to someone," I told her.

He took the phone and cleared his throat. "*Jambo*, Mama. I am here with your lovely daughters, Micah and Kas. Mama Micah, she is safe. Don't worry for her safety anymore. She will come home to you with Kas. I wanted to hear the voice of Mama Micah. Is your life okay there in America? How is there anyway?"

They talked for a few moments. My mom cried and thanked him and told her she felt better. Then he handed the phone to me.

"Micah, what tribe is he? Where are you now? Which country? You know I really needed this call today. How did you know?" She sounded sadly desperate.

"We are happy, Mom. You can relax. We are the safest ever," I assured her. "His tribe is Lokop, but we met on the coast in Kenya. We are there now. I will tell you later. We will be home soon, well almost. Two months."

I paused as he looked at me, a little pained.

"Why are you speaking so slowly to me?" she said, not used to my extreme diction.

"I'm speaking to you so he can understand me as well. If I talk too quickly, I lose them—it's my new habit, I'm always conversing with non-native English speakers."

"Well, don't you speak English to Kas anymore?"

I thought about it and turned to Kas. Then said, "Mom, Kas and I don't need to speak to each other anymore. We always know what the other is thinking." We smiled. It was true. "Telepathy," I said for my mother's sake. And his. "Mom, tell my dad I called."

My mother never forgot this phone call.

She never forgot his voice, or that he knew to call her. That she needed my voice. He was already synced up with her.

On the ferry back to Ukunda, he said, "I think you and Kas would enjoy seeing the village where my family stays. It is far, and we will go by foot. It will be an adventure."

My eyes lit up with the words. *Village. Adventure.* I could never have enough of either one. Just seven days after meeting the warriors on the beach, we took the ferry to Mombasa, where we called our parents once more before traveling to where there was no phone, pole, or wire.

The three warriors put on Western clothes for the journey through Nairobi, aka Danger-ville, different from the days when they traveled everywhere in their red cloths and bare chests. He was strange to my eyes in pants and a button-down shirt. No ochre in his cropped hair. Hidden beads. The awkward way modern clothes looked on him, the straight seams and forced modesty—I would claw them to shreds if I could.

But the warriors were not cowed. The warriors, to a man, still carried spears.


I left him, Ploote, and Lududuma in Lamaresh, reluctant but intent on the promise I'd made to Kas to seek out Loiboku again. I rattled like the sequins on a ball gown climbing up into the truck, so decorated with his beaded gifts. "*Nanyorai*, you must do as you promised. I trust you. But go and come quickly." His voice was kind and full of confidence, his eyes deep with shepherd patience.

Kas looked over the creaking truck side and said, "Thanks, we'll be quick. I can't wait to walk to your village."

We returned to our old stomping grounds, Yangaloi. But could we ever really return?

The town felt different, heat exaggerated the destitution. Nothing was familiar, as though the place had been erased from memory, locked in the past. We stayed three nights and four days and never saw Loiboku or Lochili again. How could a place be so full of heart and then just empty? Kas cried as we boarded the truck heading back to Lowaa.

"Please, Everlyn, tell them we love them and that we will miss them," Kas said.

I told her to remember him the way she saw him last, sitting in our tent drinking her chai as though they were married. "I'm so sorry. I wish you could have said goodbye."

In Lowaa, we went to see our friends Hawo, Mary and Habiba, as we'd promised. The hotel owner's daughter knew the way and walked us to the family home outside of town. They lived on the banks of a dry riverbed. Hawo came running from the kitchen, tying her scarf around her head when she saw us, her flip-flops barely keeping up with her feet.

"My friends, you came! I have been wondering about you." Hawo hugged us both with genuine happiness.

Habiba emerged from the one-room home with no visible signs of the punishment she had suffered upon her return from Yangaloi. But she wore her head scarf and a full-length brown plaid skirt. She came laughing and jumping when she recognized us.

Hawo led us on a walk along the river so we could talk. Stickers clung to the frayed ends of my *shuka*, and the blue sky seemed as if it had never housed a raincloud.

"Tell me what happened after we left," Hawo said. "Did you see the warriors again? You could not have stayed in Yangaloi this whole time, did you?" She wanted every detail and could not take her eyes from Kas, who recounted her love of Loiboku and then the sadness at not seeing him again. Sweet Hawo swung her arms and sucked her bottom lip, so eager to know. Story was everything and ours now spilled out.

As we told them about the new warriors, the Lokop by the sea, Habiba threw her body away from our gathering, yelping as though the love was stinging her with pleasure.

"You miss him. No, you love him!" she declared. Then she howled. It was fair. Habiba and I could see into one another. Her married man, my impossible dream.

Kas only smiled, saying nothing. The trickle of river water and the flat, desolate riverbank stopped me suddenly.

"Hawo, where is Mary?" I asked.

"Mary died. A month ago. She was sick in her lungs," Hawo said, looking to the ground.

Kas and I embraced at the sudden shock. She started to cry and went to Hawo, which made me cry. Lovely Hawo, beyond grief, remained like a stone. No one knew what to say. Habiba twisted away, lost in sorrow.

Kas held Hawo. I said softly, "We are so sorry. You loved Mary; we all loved Mary."

I could barely speak. It was horrible to think it, but even in life, Mary had been so quiet, so reserved, almost lifeless, so different from Hawo and especially different from fiery Habiba.

I asked if we could buy them dinner in town. Hawo deferred. Her father would not allow it. He had been stricter since Habiba's return from Yangaloi. No more access to married men.

We stayed another hour, to lend them more of our traveling freedom.


The emotion, the unclean water, or the *githeri*—a mix of unshelled corn kernels and beans—made me ill for the second time since arriving in Africa. For two full days, I had diarrhea, vomited in spells, and felt cold with fever. My one consolation was that I would be with him soon.

Kas ran to the main road each time a vehicle passed through, trying to find us a ride to Lamaresh.

"It's probably better I don't travel today. Where would I poop on a truck? In a bag?" My joke brought Kas nearly to tears. When I suffered, she suffered too.

We found transport on the third day and paid extra to leave with one less passenger rather than wait for the vehicle to fill. My body refused to recover completely until I was with him. He brought all goodness alive in me.

# BOOK II BODY

"Here in this body are the sacred rivers; here are the sun and moon, as well as all the pilgrimage places. I have not encountered another temple as blissful as my own body."

—*Saraha Doha*

# Fourteen | BODY PILGRIMAGE, MIND PYRE

I SEE HIM first. He whittles a stick in the motel courtyard. He holds his head slightly tilted, his lion-taming patience peeling the kindling layers that surround his feet. And every step to my beloved, every beat of the blood in my body feels downhill. I'm drawn like water falling over the edge. He sees me and stands with a wide smile and open arms waiting to be drenched, so I run and soak him. Our embrace purges everything. It all washes clean. When he grabs me an entire life evaporates leaving us free to revel in this first of reunions.

*Habiba you are right. Oh, how I love him.*


In Lamaresh, we stock up on tea, rice, sugar, beads, and tobacco and load them into our small backpacks already laden with gifts from Nairobi. That afternoon, we book rooms at the Jadana Guest House, a two-story building painted sweetly blue. While the sun still heats the courtyard, I ask to wash my clothes. He brings a basin filled with water and a bar of soap and watches me struggle to get my underwear white after my cycle. I hide the stain from him, folding the underwear into my fist.

I will show you how to get them clean. He extends his hand and says, Give them to me. Don't be ashamed, *Nanyorai*. There is no bad about this body we all have.

Reluctantly I hand over my undies. Without scrutiny, he dips them in the soapy water, puts them between his hands, and rubs vigorously on his knuckles, committed as though his life depends on it. When he is finished, they are white—like niveous spring iris. I look away. So silly. Hadn't I heard that disciples washed their beloved master's feet in servitude and grace? If he wore underwear I would wash them, wash anything. I hand him another pair. He cleanses Western shame, centuries of it, in his earth-strong hands.

We start walking before sunrise. The crisp air stings my bare shoulders. I know they will soon sting with heat, but for now Kas and I feel chilly. The incline out of Lamaresh meanders and traverses like an uphill river. It winds around people's homes of mud and wood. We smell fires and hear women singing as they sweep the red dirt compounds. Naked children play until they see us. They fear warriors but stop to stare at a different animal, this white one who moves like the warriors but is from another place. The warriors do not acknowledge anything but the path.

At first I resist and try to chat with Kas, to occupy my mind, and engage language, but the walking urges me to be quiet. My body speaks another language. Its alphabet comprises sensations, alerts of muscles and impulse, waves of subtle electricity and light. I can see his back, broad shoulders angling in to his waist. Kas and I have fallen behind. They walk purposefully. For me each step is somehow surrender, the sacrifice—of all I find familiar—and the pyre.

We are now in this hot, dry cedar forest—his only home, home to his ancestors' bones and their ancestors'. The trees themselves are ancestors, towering layers of bark and scraggly beard-like branches, twisted tops. We walk through the unmarked burial ground—a pilgrimage, the air full with birdsong, the clanging of distant livestock bells, and shepherd lip whistles. The warriors sing. I walk in silence in my body, deep in the cavernous hollows of corporeal knowledge. Each trancelike step finds Earth, finds time with the warriors' cantillation and their silence.

Far from water or people, my foot lands suddenly in an enormous recessed print. The once-wet soil, dry now with mounded sides and perfect padded toes. An ancient footprint pushed powerfully into Earth like a stamp. I stand incredulous. The largest land mammal walks here? Elephant! He waits for Kas and me, looking back. His eyes watch my face.

Elephant? I whisper in case they may be nearer than the dry mud suggests.

*L'tome*, he says as he nods, smiling.

*Wild wanders here*, I think, staring down at the prints. *Wild uproots cedar trunks and breaks boughs. Right here!*

I look up with big eyes, child to father. He guides me in this world of senses. He teaches me how to call it. *L'tome*. I am an infant, new to smells, sights, hearing, and most subtle of all—my knowing beyond the words.

Eyes back down to Earth, I find more prints. Obsessively delighted, I am following a herd and yet hear nothing. My steps grow cautious. The warriors ahead start singing again. A sonorous warning for resting beasts who may otherwise be surprised by us. For me the song sounds different. Surprising. For me it is a haunting reminder of everything I do not remember, a way of being that is at once so essential and unfamiliar. I listen. Kas listens. Some alchemy. I don't know exactly what is changing, but I feel shifting inside me. It comes sluicing in with this land, cedar forest, elephant breath, and my own silence. I am losing the difference between thinking and speaking, speaking and listening. It all runs together, one large channel of grace.

We are out of the forest cover. A village to the right and one way in the distance to the left. The land swallows people in its vast grassy-tongued mouth. People are red specks of movement now, busy with survival, shepherding. I look at them. The land bakes and cools; it watches, this body of land.

The sun's tireless ambition mesmerizes me. Great sky cogs hoist it up and up, brighter and brighter, almost directly above now. It sings, Praise Me! Heliolatry! Sweat leaves salt circles everywhere. Water. We need water. The warriors already know. He takes my empty bottle from me.

Beside us, where a river once ran, a parched pathway remains, and layers of urine-salted dirt that are thirstier than we.

He says, Cousin come help.

Ploote digs the sand with his hands. The Earth shows a darker hue, and deeper appears damp. They hollow out a basin, stop, and wait. Kas' eyes widen as she watches the invocation for water. There is nothing left in me but a hope that it comes.

In minutes, a slow gurgle of brown water seeps into and pools at the bottom of the hole.

The water is rising, I say. You did it. You found us water!

Lududuma shifts his heavy braids and gathers firewood from the surrounding bramble. He places the wood in a stacked pile ready to ignite. I can see from his eyes that he wonders what my commotion is about, but no one tells him. He lets it go. He rubs one stick with a harder branch. A spark, then smoke, and at last a flame. The heat attracts even more shine from the glowing sun.

Lududuma knows he does not possess Kas. He saw her heart was taken with love long before, maybe even since their initial meeting on the beach, but he tries to care for her nonetheless. And they do sleep together, but he is not Loiboku. Kas rarely says a thing.

Salty-urine tea with camel's milk and sugar, and we walk again.

The straw valley expands beyond vision, leading us to cross over dry beds and double back into the desert labyrinth. The warriors cease singing. He tells me they are listening for elephants. Dung lies wet and steaming, like raked piles of summer grass after rain. Elephants are dangerous in the wild. One stampede could kill us all.

When the sun hovers at the horizon, throwing fiery, sweet streamers, we arrive at Lududuma's village. The homes are sturdier than the ones at Yangaloi, made of branches, animal hides, and a mixture of cow dung and Earth.

Young warrior girls turn to scrutinize our bodies and strangeness. One shoos a white-and-brown-patched goat into a pen, still looking at us, daring and direct. She forces eye contact, which connotes disrespect. I like her ferocity. For a briefness, I forget my intention to kowtow, settling instead on accepting her challenge, merely by the narrowing of my eyes. She grins ever so evenly. A real opponent to my own feisty wiring.

The girls' faces are round, their necks taper beneath rings of red beaded necklaces that prop their chins in exaggerated pride. Their upper bodies are bare, nipples erect, hourglass bellies coated in a thick, greasy red fat. Slender waists accentuated by earth-sweeping leather skirts that come to a decorated point in front and back.

More girls gather to see if not greet us. Some wear exotic head-dresses secured by a copper chain resembling a horse bridle running dramatically under the bottom lip. Their foreheads wrapped with beads and shiny pieces of metal, they hold their heads upright, shoulders pulled back. *Not many women prettier on Earth*, I think. So raw and hardened yet soft enough, mirroring the desert, the red dirt itself.

Kas and I trump them only in our foreignness—exotic by default. We try to minimize our impact. Something between truth and fear causes us to do this; truth because we prefer not to upset the balance, and fear because we are vulnerable. We understand their envy. Two strangers arrive with a pack of strong and attentive warriors, sleep with them way out here in the Kenyan sticks. Because we cannot speak to the girls beyond greeting, we cannot befriend them, or ease the tension. But we can walk humbly.

Kas and I wait as first Lududuma and then my lover place spears outside a hut and enter. We follow at their signal and sit bunched together with them on an elevated bed made of branches and twine that cinches leather hide to the corners. More warriors come in, surround us, and begin the rapture of greeting and laughter.

We are eleven in all. Kas and I sit quietly, waiting our turn, which we allow Lududuma to dictate. We learn that if we talk to each other as they are speaking, they stop to listen even if they do not speak English. They pick up words and sentiment. Deep perception peers into us. Even in near darkness. As the men rally together, they are ever aware of the young Americans who have traveled farther than they have, these masters of travel.

Dusk is meditation's companion. The two drift together in perfect pattern, in the hut this evening, releasing me from day bondage to reflect on spirit. Silence knows my throat and mouth now. It dwelt there for hours. I never knew such silence, nor it me.

The warriors turn their attention back and forth from us to Lududuma, who is the storyteller in his village. My lover never looks at me when we are with others, as though he loves me too dearly to risk drawing attention. His disregard plays with my heart and their curiosity, but they know.

When the talking ceases long after dusk, he breaks the silence with English. The others marvel at his knowledge of this hard language.

They are making you tea with milk, he says. Drink two cups so you get the fat for our travel tomorrow. I nod and smile at him.

We drink black tea with sugar and camel's milk from a calabash. Cured gourd smells of fire ash and is waxy with animal fat. Tea tastes best from it. Once our appetites are satiated we sit in silence, and the warriors begin their evening serenade. Lududuma starts rocking back and forth, bellows to the surrounding night, and others join. Kas and I sway too.

My lover sings for me. I catch his gaze, glinting in the firelight. While singing, no eyes blink. They steady their sight beyond the beyond. The warriors sing for hours, never certain of when the songs end until they do. The end of the last song empties into one of the still gaps.

My lover is the first to speak. He says, We will sleep in this village tonight. There is not enough space in this home for us all, so, Micah, you and Kas will stay here, and we will stay in a home nearby so you don't have to feel fear. Can you be all right here?

I answer him with my unused voice. Yes, Kas and I can stay here.

I look at my friend, who is as content as I am.

Is this Lududuma's mother's home? Kas asks. If it is, please thank her for us.

Lududuma stands, ready for sleep. He smiles when my lover translates Kas' gratitude. It is not unusual his mother has surrendered her hut to us. It is expected. Nomads borrow beds regularly when their long journeys keep them away from their own.

*Ntepere N'kai*, I whisper to my lover as he leaves. Sleep with God. It feels good to say.

*Abakiye, Nanyorai.* He blesses my sleep as I have his.

We have space to lie down, when the warriors retire, though in Lokop there is little regard for sleep. Stories and song rank higher. Waking at odd hours in the night is customary—whenever the pulse of life rises. Sometimes they wake for sex, sometimes for food or to talk. People sleep when they are tired enough. If they are not sleeping, they contribute to the noise, which is punctuated with wide gaps of complete quiet. Not a full eight hours anywhere in this bucolic existence.

Physically I am exhausted, but deeper within me, something comes alive.

This is village.

# FIFTEEN | HARD YIELDS TO SOFT

LIGHT WARMS MY eyelids, streaming in from sliver openings in the walls. Others are stirring. Shepherds take the animals early and sleep in the bush while the animals graze. Kas is up, writing in her journal with her headlamp.

Good morning, I whisper, wiping my eyes.

She says, Cow skins make great mattresses.

I hear women walking past our hut. I peer through a sliver. They walk, jerry cans strapped with fraying twine to their foreheads. They walk briskly, and the dust stirs in through the holes. I smell night clothing, sooted with charcoal. Easy-gaited, tall women—they somehow remind me of the cedar trees they burn. Odes to cedar smoke. Two women pass close. I see rough hands, gritty and dry, hardened by work. They will walk miles for water.

The *manyatta* fires burn hot, the trees have needle thorns, the insects bite and sting, the sun bakes, and the dirt leeches oils from the skin stealing even a baby's suppleness. I feel my own skin, less fatty, more like tanned leather.

Nothing in the world
is as soft and yielding as water.
Yet for dissolving the hard and inflexible,
nothing can surpass it.

The soft overcomes the hard;
the gentle overcomes the rigid.
Everyone knows this is true,
but few can put it into practice.

Even in Lokop land, the *Tao De Ching* reminds me, the soft also dwells. Sunrise. And at dusk when everyone speaks in hushed tones, guiding the animals safely back home. The softness breaks the hard each time a baby is born, a lamb, a calf. Warriors and children walk together hand in hand. The softness breaks the hard when he reaches for me. Softness is breaking the hard in me.

He and Ploote come to find us. We take chai together in the house, but he drinks his quicker than usual, as if he has something on his mind.

He says, I know you are both strong, and I would also like to be in my village, but I think to rest a day can be good for us. We will drink plenty of water here, eat, and stay one more night. We leave early tomorrow. Okay?

Okay, Kas and I say in unison. It is not a king-sized bed or a sea-breeze promise, but it is also not one tired leg in front of the other. That day we stay near, wandering only feet outside of the village, find a trickle of a stream to wash our hands and faces. Kas writes, I fall into no time and follow it willingly. Yesterday, today, tomorrow lose their identities and merge, this one moment, this thin thread running over as few as three rocks.

The next day he prepares us for the journey. We will walk from six in the morning until midnight. A mere eighteen hours. Kas says she'll go find Lududuma, to say goodbye, but he stops her. I don't think it is a must, he says.

She nods and ties a bandana around her head to ward off the scalp-burning sun.

We see Lududuma standing at the edge of the *manyatta*, alone and waving, a remorseful slant to his eyes. The young girls' scorn makes more sense now. Kas and I represent the bright lights of a faraway place and the annihilation of tradition, the loss of their men.

The village disappears behind us. My lover slows to speak with Kas.

I and Lududuma are of the same clan, but we don't walk together. He has a girlfriend here. He never mentioned this girlfriend to me.

It's okay, Kas says. With or without a lover, it's all the same to Kas.

Okay. We forget him, he says in consolation.

Already done, she says, wiping her hands of Lududuma and his braided charms.


We walk in the cool morning but soon noon is upon us. The Earth heats as though its molten core has risen to the surface. I hear two warriors walk up behind us at a fresh, fast pace.

Without turning to see, he says, They will escort us to my village by night.

Kas and I lock eyes. There is so much we are not privy to anymore. As they pass, I greet them. They ignore me.

They're taking this escort thing seriously, I say, nudging her with my elbow.

Kas giggles and says, VIPs in the bush!


The land grows drier. Shrubs replace trees. Shepherds in bright red flash against the horizon, moving mirages of goats, cattle and camels. Lokop are the only people of this land. So hot it bends the heart into dust. Will I adapt with more time? My legs ache. Thorns tear my skirt. My arms darken and scar with lines of drying blood. Frustration builds, bringing me to another edge. Faith alone, I think, faith alone can close the chasm, as the desert takes traces of my blood, skin and skirt. Scant remnants. Bread crumbs. A path that vanishes as we walk it.

Rarely do we see another village. He points to an area where his family once built their homes before the climate grew too dry and the herders had to travel long distances to feed their animals. His family has been at their present village for roughly two years, a long time to occupy the same place for nomadic people, but the rains have been accommodating. The area has a name. *Nanaiiolo*. *Nanaiiolo*, I later learn, means the land that is spotted like a leopard.

In all this heat and shine, his face is both devoted and mischievous, eyes flirting with everything, even the light. He never tastes or smells bad—anywhere. Maybe because he does not eat sugars, except with chai, or because we are always walking. His smooth back muscles ripple with his easy walking cadence.

I remember merely days after we met on the beach, his back looking much as it does now. He stopped then at a small kiosk selling beef sausages. I rolled my eyes in disgust. He turned like a hurricane, blowing furious, voice pointed and said, Is this sausage somehow unsafe for me to eat?

Suddenly ashamed and self-aware, I shook my head.

His eyes, the capillaries filled with blood, he says, Here, where we have the problem of food, we do not make an opinion of what someone chooses to eat. The body tells them what they need and don't need. Micah, you have seen my land, how Lokop live. We are shepherds of cows and goats, camels and sheep. Because I take care of them, those are the animals I eat, nothing more. This man, he points to the kiosk, takes care of his cows. I have seen them with my own eyes. Now, I do not want to be angry with you so please walk in front of me, or behind me, so I am not reminded of your ignorance.

I nodded and said, I'm very sorry. Eat and be healthy.

He walked ahead with Ploote, and I confronted the surge of sensation overwhelming me. He has no fear, not of defending his animals, nor of reprimanding his American girlfriend. The flush of embarrassment, the raw respect I have for this warrior and the line he had drawn in the sand. I wanted only to cross it to be taken into his capable arms.

We have been walking eight or nine hours, I guess by the height of the sun, when Ploote gives him a small bouquet of leaves.

What's that? I ask when I catch up to him.

The two unnamed warriors smirk.

Darly, this is for mens, he says, already knowing I am suspicious.

But what does it do? Why do you chew it like that? I ask.

His eyes are piercing, more intense than usual. The chewing alters him.

My Irish Catholic, addicted genes trigger memories I'd rather forget: family holidays exploding in fistfights, yelling adults, my early teen years abusing hard drugs. It all rushes into my face, my non-wholeness.

Can I tell you a story? I ask him cautiously, so that judgment will not enter my voice, the sausage incident near in memory.

He nods and grabs my hand. We walk in tandem.

You don't drink alcohol, I say, but at home, many people, young and old, drink. My father drank too much, falling down, not sleeping, spending all night where they sell alcohol. He would speak loud and laugh loud.

A desire for control wells up in my eyes.

He chews the green plant.

I shiver with fear, unable to continue.

*Nanyorai*, he says, You have made me to understand. Alcohol makes your dad to be different. *Miraa* makes me to be different. My *Miraa* makes you sad, so I will not chew *Miraa* again. We have no time for troubles or painful memories between us.

I cry in thanks and walk the land that is spotted like a leopard.

He calls Ploote to come. Cousin, take this *Miraa*. Enjoy it. I am finished chewing it.

I reach to hug him. I open beyond my father's alcoholism, my abandonment, my old stories. I laugh. No tears. How simple he makes everything, how soft.


Let's take water here, he says as he points to a copse of toothbrush trees. He breaks a long branch into several and hands them around.

We sit in the rare shade. Rest feels good but pure inertia overtakes me. My hips ache—my whole body aches from hours of warrior pace. I set my pack down and scrape the sticky spit of dry mouth from my teeth. I don't know how we are surviving this trek only on camel milk tea. Perhaps the fact they turn every cup into syrup with heaps of sugar.

The warriors, busy chewing *Miraa*, sit and talk with crazy-eyed energy. The sun presses late afternoon heat around us like a net and I beg for strength. Kas and I are dehydrated. We have water, but we know to conserve. Sip, sip what we have in our bottles.

Maybe someday he and I can chew this leaf together. Maybe the leaves of *Miraa* only *outline* the leopard's spots.

At dusk, we all hear heavy thumps on the ground. Bodies pushing in brief struggle. A startling cry sounds from the brush. Certain death, I feel it. No one stops walking.

Dust from our feet floats in the moon shadows. I itch to look back, sure that predators lurk. Scents come, musky scents, swallowed back into the night air. A faint breeze chills my nervous sweat. Our singing and laughing yield to prayer. We all pray, keeping one another close and alive on this pilgrimage.

Before the sun went down, he'd held my hand, flirting. Now, I carry two heavy stones, one in each hand, and his clear instinct watches over us. He envelops me without touch. The warriors ask us to form a diamond shape for safeguarding Kas and me, surrounded by spears and ancestral whispers.

The higher the moon climbs, the shorter shadows it casts. My imagination shakes free. I see the careful posture of predators everywhere. Every shade, stealthy. Every sound, for me. We walk and entrain, the six of us. Walk as prayer. All instinct. No thought.

As I turn toward a thicket on the left, he steps out of the diamond, out of time, and hurls his *rungu* into the bush. Kas and I throw our rocks. The warriors shout battle cries and jump at the snarl in the shrubs. A large body flees, crashing into branches, breaking them. I crouch. A familiar smell of straw and animal collapses around us. My breathing returns.

Lion, I whisper. I know this is true before he answers.

Yes, darly, we frightened it. I struck it with my *rungu*. Did you hear the sound the *rungu* makes when it strikes muscle? Not bushes? That's how I know. Do you want to see its feet prints? We can see which leg I hit, he says walking over to reclaim his weapon.

Not really, I say.

The warriors laugh at me.

Okay. Lion won't have American girl for dinner tonight, he says.

His humor is a form of protection, I know. Keep the heart light. Keep it playful.

Kas ignores the humor. Do you know if it was a male or female? Kas knows females hunt together.

Yes, female, there are others. Listen for the male in the distance. He goes like this, *ngoohwhoop, ngoohwhoop, ngoohwhoop*—he mimics a male lion's haunting bellow, and I reach to cover his mouth.

Do you like that, *Nanyorai?*

Ask me later, I say, still standing in formation like it is my job.

Okay, we go. There might be others. He walks a few steps, then stops abruptly and asks, Do you hear that?

Shit and shinola—I strain my ears but hear nothing. What do I listen for? More lion? I ask.

Hah! No, that is the sound of my bull camel's bell. No lion. The village is near. Just there, he points into the consuming darkness.

I feel useless.

Kas, can you hear anything? I ask because misery and futility love company.

No, she says.

We tuck into our diamond and listen for the bell. We walk a full five minutes before I hear it. The bell rattles hollow in my chest, opens my throat. My eyes fill as though this sound alone saves us. I feel something in my body, a presence heavier than thought and prayer.

That's the most beautiful thing I've ever heard, I say. That's the sound of your home!

The bull camel bell invokes a hurrying, make-sure-the-muscles-do-not-freeze energy. I walk faster, still moving within the weighted God-ness, the home-ness, exploring them for the first time.

We are close now—the warriors walk so fast we are almost running.

A rare sight spreads below the grassy incline—twenty domed mud-dung huts dot the landscape, a little darker than the surrounding night. The fires from the village huts urge us on, lend strength. Though we have not eaten since morning, I am full on the promise of rattling bull camel bells and the stink of lions. Now there is fire, too. A fence of spiny acacia limbs, about seven feet high, greets us with its shark teeth. Ploote drags open the heavy tree gate. Goat poop pebbles scatter as we pass, four warriors and two strong women. He diligently replaces it, this barrier between safety and the hungry bush.

Most villages are blessed with their own soothsayers. Natiyon, his mother, is one of these. She helps even people from neighboring villages to *see*. Her blindness came from being bitten by one of Africa's most venomous snakes, the green mamba, not just once but three times. Natiyon lacks physical sight but she possesses the art of premonition.

The night we arrive, Lintan cries with joy at the threshold. His mother asks him where his foreign girlfriend is. She has not heard from her son in months. She's had no word of him or his life in Ukunda. Kas and I stand outside the hut waiting to be invited in, and she says *Nalangu*, the word for a person who comes from across big water. She has *seen* us walking together and knows he is bringing me.

I am not surprised by her knowing. It only makes the God-bells resonate harder. Kas and I take our places inside her hut. We drink strong chai. They talk for hours, catching up. We nestle in with Lintan. Natiyon explores my face. Kas drowses and wakes.

He stares into the fire at his ease, then suddenly asks, Are you tired Kas? I think that was enough exercise for you? Kas is strong, likes to hike, and yet she is beyond ready for this invitation to sleep. She laughs at his kind teasing.

We say, *bushed* back home. And I am bushed. Will we all sleep here tonight?

Bushed, he repeats and he clicks his tongue, which is shorthand for *yes*.

I look around the shadows of the small, close hut.

Plenty of room, he says. He moves to an empty spot, farthest away from everyone, and places his *shuka* over the calfskin. Then he looks to me to follow. I ask him, stalling, What do I call your mom?

Call her, *Yeyo*, the word for Mama.

I think of Natiyon's knowing hands on my face. I think of his hands.

His mother pulls the larger coals to the edges of the fire, allowing it to die back, a weak glow. Our fire never dies back.

I remain wide-eyed not sure what to do.

I know his look, that sexy desirous stillness. If I go to him he will want to make love now, here, in his mother's home. He waits, watching as I struggle. I do not move. It feels like a crevasse, a mere eternity, stands between us.

Natiyon speaks to him as she tends to the fire.

Did you understand what my mother said to you? She said this is your home now. No need to fear. *Wou ene*, Micah. He pats the space next to him with a dying glint in his tired, determined eyes.

He has brought me here. He has saved us from lions. He loves his mother and his dear young sister and he loves me. In a village so small I can hurl a stone across it with little effort. I could topple that heavy tree gate and sleep in sharp moon shadows.

I crawl across the crackling dry skins, anxious as a cat. The hut is too low to stand upright, and because I am submitting my will, crawling seems right.

He whispers into my ear, We can love here, it is our custom. You can feel comfortable.

He fumbles with my knotted *shuka*. Every muscle in my body braces. My eyes dart through the dark. Is anyone watching?

He touches my cheek with his lips and says, My mother and Lintan will be pleased to hear such sweet sounds. Don't worry they are already sleeping, he says in a voice loud enough to wake them.

I know better. I know the total circumference of the hut is ten or twelve feet. There is no partition, only a center where our feet meet like gathered spokes of a wheel.

The fire hushes.

Just as all our other nights, he begins by kissing me, a sweet nod to Western ways, then positions himself on top. I bury my face in his neck to muffle my breathing. He is aroused. I am a stone. His mother and sister are within a long arm's length! Kas lies right next to me.

He enters me, thrusting his pelvis more gently than usual, but all friction shifts sound and space.

I listen beside us rather than feel him. I hear the cow skin crinkle.

What are others hearing? What are they thinking? Kas farts, a soft hiss beside me, and I want to clobber her for being asleep.

When I reach the pinnacle of discomfort, he does the unimaginable and whispers to me—sweet nothings no one should hear. I put my hand over his mouth and grow even more rigid. At this, he laughs out loud. He is messing with me! I do not know whether to be furious or laugh. I stay stiff as cardboard, my skin and muscles apparently owned and operated by the U.S.A.

He grips my shoulders and the shame shakes free a little. My fright, my frailty ease. I smile. He is laughing, until he is not. Supremely confident in his skin, in his home, in his land, he turns intense. I try, I do try to control everything but I am coming apart, becoming a part. His warrior heart is unlacing every stitch with his lion whispers, Come on, come on, let us go. Every inhibited stricture loosens at his urging, and I arch my head back, closing my eyes. I yield.

He reaches orgasm. I cannot, but something breaks open. We've whacked a path, and the first time through is always the hardest. Now the way has been cleared. He finishes. I begin. Awe struck at this revelation, this new me. I lie in his arms testing the beauty and heft of this soft glorious way, surrounded by his smell, held in this family circle, feeling him inside me. I listen out for judgment or ridicule and all I hear is the perfect cricket chorus.

The music of quiet all to myself. As tears come gently, innocently, so do I.

# Sixteen | Village Rhythm

I WAKE TO Natiyon's soft tones, his spacious pauses, the fire blazing with a large misshapen pot of tea resting on the side. Natiyon faces me but because she cannot see, it is like I am not here. I spy on him whenever I can. He sits, back to me, *shuka* slung over one shoulder exposing the other. He stares outside the hut opening to the dawn but succumbs entirely to the present, his mother, a slow waking, our new way of being together in the village. Kas is feigning sleep but I know she is awake. She's a light sleeper and the village has begun to stir.

I listen to feet shuffling, cows in the distance, bleating baby goats, birds and people murmuring. This morning light is still the craft of the moon—more reflected than direct.

Suddenly my belly grips upwards to my throat. The nausea is quick and overwhelming. I don't know what is wrong. I search for causes of the energy swell. Is it physical? Emotional?

I realize, half sitting up, that I am afraid to leave, of ever leaving, leaving him and them. I force deeper breaths, saying to myself that everything will be okay, and it all settles. A stillness envelops me, the stillness of this very morning, on the soft skins, within soot-covered walls, the smell of chai, with him and his mother. Energy rises within, and I want to shout out: Good morning everyone! Good morning goats and cows and camels with bells! I am so happy! I am so happy to be here with you. Thank you for this village, this moment—

He turns as though he hears my soul's celebratory greeting and catches the gleam in my eye, part exultation, part overwhelm.

*Ulilala vizuri, ngarayai?* Did you sleep well my baby, he asks with an irreverent twinkle.

*As soon as we are alone he is gonna get it*, I think.

Kas pretends to be waking, too. She smiles at me and says, Well, I sure didn't.

I raise a conciliatory brow to her, and he laughs at me.

When in Rome, she says and sits up, ready for chai.

Natiyon greets us with camel's milk, tea and sugar. He does not take a mug because he is not supposed to ever eat in his mother's home. He told us this on our walk. Even then I did not ask why. I no longer care about trivia, about corners of the intellect. My intellect bows to something greater. The poor thing takes a well-needed rest.

We sit outside Natiyon's home, the shaded side, watching women of all ages bead necklaces, legs extended, ankles crossed. An ant highway crawls over them, flies rest where sweat droplets gather. No one swats or brushes them off. Toddlers dance to young girls' singing, their soft bellies girdled at the waist by jingling bells so they will not be lost. Until death, children wear a necklace from their mother that contains a message by the order and color of beads.

My lover breaks the women's morning ritual. He tells Kas and me to follow Lintan. Lintan practices her English with a vengeance. We hear, *kinttent, kentint*, and laugh. She does not know English nor Kiswahili, never having gone to school, but she attempts the new language with boldness. Content, I say. We are content. Kas nods. Lintan takes up my hand and starts teaching me Gutok. *Tree, branches, huts, baby goats, stones*, anything and everything. The *manyatta* shines in the sun, small ovals of grass show recent rain. People stretch sleep from their bodies, gathering near their homes, brushing teeth and watching us. We say *supa* to everyone and sometimes they say it back but sometimes they look on with shock; waking to two white girls walking amongst their huts. Some shout their questions, their funs, as he calls it, and Lintan replies with the obedience of a village child though she seems to know she is stifled in this adult world and yet smarter, less afraid of the unfamiliar, less afraid of us.

Most of our walk to go bathe, she forces us to learn the names of local plants. She notes the poisonous ones by waving her hand and simultaneously shaking her head. I can barely look around; if she catches me, she gives me my next assignment.

She digs up a root growing where water looks to have recently run. Girls carve beads from it to entice warriors. When the root loses its scent you break off a fresh piece like squeezing a lavender sachet. She wears a chain of amber beads with pieces of this root around her waist, perfuming her belly. She seems too young to want attention from boys but I also seemed too young. We know what we know.

We wade through thickets and dry grass. The sun is picking up its head. An outcropping of giant boulders rises out of the savanna— maybe fifteen or twenty feet high. She climbs one and turns to help us to the top. A large divot has been worn into basaltic rock, a basin that collects rain water. I check to see if the warriors are near. No one in sight. Kas and I quickly undress, use a plastic Nalgene bottle to carry the water away from the hole to splash our faces and underarms and between our thighs, the cool tingle wakes every nerve. Glorious be water. Though we mainly use Lokop toothbrushes, today I want peppermint taste and dip my twig in the bottle. The water still holds its cold from the night, and makes me thirsty. I ask Lintan if I can drink it by bringing a cupped handful to my mouth and saying, okay? She raises her eyebrows and makes a clicking sound. *Yep.* She drinks as well, chatting away happily. I think of the wild that might have quenched its thirst here, leopard paws, this very shimmering pool. Everything is simple. Everything just is.

I know I can learn their language but I also know something will have to shift in me in order to do so. A new pattern in my brain or perhaps a changed heartbeat. Gutok is still an inarticulate jumble. Sign language works without a hitch. Lintan throws a head nod, a signal to dress, and fast. I look but do not see or hear anything.

The warriors appear from behind a cluster of trees. Even he ignores me which prompts us to gather our things and make our way down the rocks. Talking amongst themselves, they climb a higher boulder and begin to remove their weapons.

Lintan does not acknowledge the warriors and leads us back toward the village. On the way, she shows us where we can relieve ourselves. When we do not stop, she is convinced we don't understand. She pretends to have to pee, lifts her leather skirt and squats with a smile. The Lokop do not use toilet paper; it is a luxury sold by merchants. No shops this far from Lamaresh. No luxuries. The ground is littered with bleaching bones, broken branches, animal skins, drying goat and cow dung, not toilet paper and man-made trash. The land resembles a Georgia O'Keefe canvas waiting for the vibrant orchid or fragile lily for contrast. Perhaps it waits for me.

When we return to the village, the hut is empty. Lintan invites younger girls to meet us, four in all, nine-to-twelve years old. Shy at first, they grow comfortable and begin talking, encouraged when they discover we do not speak Gutok. Kas and I sit with pained smiles, understanding nothing the little birds say, out of their rosebud mouths. The ends of their skirts are beaded heavily which causes the leather to hang true. The older girls wear a red cloth over the leather for accent and necklaces so many in number they slash and scar their shoulders above small breasts which glisten with the remains of red grease—not as neatly applied as the girls in Lududuma's village, more like children with smeared lipstick. They are rascally pranksters waiting for inspiration to strike.

Lintan asks rhetorically if I have a baby, pointing at me and pretending to cradle an infant in her arms. When I shake my head, she gets up and lifts my shirt, bringing her mouth near my nipple, pretending to suckle. The girls convulse, crazy with laughter. Kas and I do too. Once my shirt is lifted and I do not seem upset, they take the invitation to gawk. The nipples and the areola are a different color than the surrounding skin? They point, giggling and gasping, no emotion censored, the way a breeze lifts the leaves and then moves on.

Breasts are not particularly private in Lokop culture—most women walk exposed. Breasts are more relevant to child-rearing than sex. Legs are different, legs must be covered to the ankles which is why Kas and I gave away our shorts in West Africa, except the pair for running.

Lintan tells us to remove our shirts permanently. She has already seen our breasts while bathing. She and her girlfriends want us to belong. When I shake my head no, she giggles and removes one of the beaded strands from her neck and gives it to me—as though the strand makes whole all misunderstanding and diversities. I hug her and her stiff body language says she is not accustomed to being embraced but relishes it. I do it again. She is thinking of me as her older sister. I feel her welcome us as completely as our bathing basin holds rain.

We visit with the dear rascals all afternoon, through the quiet time when naps replace activity. The young girls amuse themselves with beads and little imaginings. Two are sleeping. How I miss his voice and smell. Will we remain in the *manyatta* every day, all day, without seeing him? I want to respect his customs but I want him here even more. I am used to getting what I want when I want it. The Ugly American within wrestles my contentment into a headlock and says, Enough already, come find me! Without warning he pokes his perfect head into the hut and all our younger friends rise and flee. Even Lintan bows her head. I blush, wondering if he heard my missing him, my inner complaint.

I see in his calm smile how crucial it is to live in balance. His *sagesse* knocks my selfishness for a loop. People walk on the edge in his desert. Life is truly hard. One mean, unkind sentiment might push hearts out of round. I sense this. Being kind, being smart, being reverent is for them a matter of survival, not nicety. His serious, warrior persona, I honor it. His veneration for his family, I honor it. Even making love in the presence of his family, I honor. It is a tie that binds.

He says, Before we rest, my father has asked me to bring you to see him. He sleeps with his second wife, not my mother, when I am here, so you see him little. Remember to call him *Apaya*.

The elders sit with withered skin and throaty voices, telling us to join them outside. An old acacia tree leans over us all. *Apaya* toys with his beaded tobacco gourd hanging from his neck and asks his son to translate. He begins to speak as the others watch. They nod in agreement, twirling their carved walking canes in the dirt.

This place which is our home is known to us, but for you is like a star that has decided to live in a river. It is not your sky. We can see that your bodies are struggling in this difficult climate. When we struggle, we know which mountain to visit to pray, which animal to slaughter, which rock to listen to, but you have none of this.

My lover asks us, Do you understand the way my father is speaking to you? He uses story. I can help you to understand later but now just say, *eh-na*.

*Apaya* continues, This land grows goats, not rice. Rice needs much water so your body may want too much water. Take chai every morning with camel's milk and sugar. You will then begin the day as we do. The land is thirsty, our bodies are thirsty. My son will eat exactly as you.

I hide my distress. I am sure boiled rice will please my lover less than that one bite of Mombasa mango!

*Apaya* begins to tell us about Lokop creation, how *N'kai* created black, brown and white people after creating everything else, the trees, the rocks and rivers, the animals both domestic and wild, how *N'kai* put himself in each with specific instructions on how to live together. How a cow one day ate the instructions and why Lokop feel honored to eat a cow so they may remember how to belong to this Earth and one another. *Apaya* then made a parallel story and caused the others to become riotous with laughter, adding their own humorous tangents.

My lover says, You see my father is wondering how you know to get along if you do not eat that cow with the instructions in its belly?

Kas and I giggle at their cleverness but we also feel less than brilliant in this meat-eating Mecca. It's such simple genius, food, body and climate, interdependent—wherever we live, we metabolize all. I feel silly bringing rice into this dry area.

We thank the circle and start walking toward the huts. They are still weaving tales.

I say, If you eat my rice, I'll eat your goat.

He grins and says, Goats eat rice.


At our hut, I ask him, Where is the bathroom? I know I will want clarity in the middle of the night. Now seems like a good time, in case he vanishes again.

Lintan showed us where to pee, I say, but I saw no signs of poop. And I don't want to poop in the wrong place, I say smiling.

He laughs at my crassness. And then he reveals the whole desert sanitary system in one word.

Hyenas, he says. Very hungry, dirty animals. They leave nothing behind. You can use the bathroom anywhere outside of the *manyatta*.

It takes me a minute to absorb the profound simplicity of this.

Wake me if it is night because I will go with you into the bush, he says.

Or maybe not so simple—

Hyenas do attack.

I shift my shoulders into a broader frame. Do all the women wake men if they have to go at night? I act tough but he knows I will be tugging on his *shuka*.

He stays with me. Before we sleep, after we make love, in an effort to change my focus, he asks, Which animals have you not seen since being in Africa?

I make a mental list of all we have and come up with hippos. We haven't seen hippos yet, I say.

Mhmm, hippos.

But I am still hung up on the toilet. Beware the lulling village night rhythms or you may find your ass licked by a hyena.

# Seventeen | WHITE GOD DAUGHTERS

I WAKE THE following morning to his low voice. He is not singing, but he and his mother might as well be for the swaying sunlight on their words. I remember the heat of the village dancing last night and the sweetness that came after, and look to Kas who is awake and reading. She elbows me. We snicker.

Voracious, I say, retying my *shuka*. I wish she had someone. But her journal still fills with Loiboku musings and Lududuma only made things worse.

He helps his mother pour the tea and milk into the calabash. I am hungry, losing weight in sweat, dancing, making love.

Having attended to his mother, he acknowledges me. *Ntepere serian Nanyorai?* He asks in his sweet-toned morning voice that reaches always toward the Earth.

Yes, I slept very well. I flirt with his desire to hear me speak Gutok, and sometimes resist for fun.

Before we trekked to his village, I had asked him which body parts of mine he admired. He said with deadpan seriousness that he liked my *ngiok. Ngiok* is the Gutok word for ear. He said this as though it were true of all lovers, all ears, and I yelled with delight. I think my ears even blushed. The ear is common, homely. I know it is a labyrinth, its complexities misunderstood, but a favorite part?

*Serian nteperie ngiok?* I ask him, all sweetness. Natiyon stifles a giggle when I greet him as my ear. She must think I am confused.

He ignores my flirtation and suggests we walk to Ploote's village.

Kas smirks and says, Does it mean anything serious like marriage?

He says not a word. The truth is he would like her to love Ploote. Spiky red afro, immense Adam's apple, gangly gait and all.

We pack for a long day, changing shoes and underwear. Kas takes a flashlight in case we get back after dark.

Natiyon steps out.

Kas stretches her arms sideways in a world-class yawn.

You're lucky he doesn't make love as long as he dances, I say.

Frequency trumps duration, she says. I'd be doing the same thing if Loiboku were here.

You two unstaked a few tents, I say.

But seriously, Micah, how many hours a night does he actually sleep? You two wake up throughout the night, right? I toss her a ChapStick, a cherry peace offering.

I hear the villagers outside speaking to him. They ask him to help them buy goats and camels, believing he has prospered in Mombasa. Now he has a white girlfriend from America. What next? A new car?

I check on my camel before we leave and try to identify it in the baby camel pen. Ploote steps up to assist. He scans the seven young-sters and says, with authority, There, the one with the crinkly hair on its backside. Just then Kas joins us. We all stare at camel butt. Ploote withers a little and drops his arm as though it doesn't belong to him, the arm pointing at my camel's cute *derriere*. Kas smacks her lips, fresh with cherry scent, which makes Ploote jump and shrink simultaneously.

The warriors both bring their spears. We walk east across the sandalwood-dotted land, the trees and brush that we are beginning to know and name.

Kas and Ploote fall into their tales behind us.

*Nanyorai*, he asks me, Do you notice something that all the war-riors wear?

I find his question funny because the warriors' things are all of the tribe, the collective. Spears, *rungu*, adornments, even fanny packs with money, but this last item only while at the beach.

Darly, do you see a certain necklace that is different from the others?

I never correct his English when he calls me darly. Even though, secretly, Kas and I joke because the word does not belong in his mouth. I don't know where he learned it but it is his term of affection, so it grows on me. I look back at Ploote then to my lover, studying their beads, their arm bands, every strand. He breaks my concentration with a quick and undecipherable comment to Ploote. Ploote laughs. I love these games. He often tells stories or gives me challenges, daring to hold the punchline close for weeks.

As retaliation, I speak with Kas in Spanish. He revels in that dare— too clever with language, he mimics our conversation so we are not certain what he understands and what he merely imitates. Sometimes, when he catches me off-guard, drifting to sleep or in a torpor on the beach, he sneaks in some soul-shifting insight. It's uncanny. He says a few words and all prior events make sudden sense, come crashing into my mind with charm and clarity. The punchline truly punches. I have learned that when he involves Ploote, and his cousin laughs, days may pass before he revisits this particular game. I am given just enough time to forget before being enchanted by the grand finale. I swear he savors humor like no one I've ever known.

And since I have no real answer, yet, for his question about warrior regalia, I avoid guessing for now. It may be the baby necklace that every warrior wears, and it may not. I decide to savor his humor. He strings me along like a bright bead. I say nothing, happily tied up with the wonder of us.

Kas and I take the lead, following an unknown path barely discernible from the surrounding dirt. The warriors meander at a leisurely pace behind us. We climb out of a wide valley cresting to a summit and lose them from sight.

At the top of the incline, a tall man walks toward us with a weak but persistent stride, his thin head a little unsteady on his shoulders.

He's alone, I say.

Yeah, weird. We haven't passed a village.

We greet him as we have been taught and maintain our pace.

*Apaya*, we call in our best, highest voices.

He stops, says nothing but follows us turning with wide eyes, turning slowly—the oldest person that we have seen. He then opens his arms. He looks like the *Apaya* of all *Apayas*. White stubble pricks from the deep lines about his aged face, his eyes lightened with cataracts.

I know he's not asking for a hug, but what? We can't embrace him, a stranger on the road, so we keep walking.

I don't know, Kas says to the question I never ask.

We look back after several paces and watch as the old man hails our friends. They stop to have one of their famous greetings.

The sun is high overhead; three tiny black birds chirp happily as they chase one another into some bramble. My T-shirt stifles with trapped humidity. I take a deep breath and try to name the quality of the air so I can recall it someday. Hot and prickly. Dry pine needles. I look out at thorny brush and acacia horizons, the cloudless, sharp sky.

Like buckshot, the warriors rake back their heads and laugh. They laugh convulsively, roaring high, then almost silent, breath caught, then loud again. Knee slapping. Ploote's chin gets caught in his warrior beads. He struggles to free them. The men whoop with glee.

We have already walked for hours. Kas and I wait and drink water, watching for them to catch up. They come straggling toward us. Weak with laughter, working to stand upright, he says, Micah, do you know what that old man thought?

I shake my head at his clumsy joy.

This elder thought he had died and gone to heaven to meet *N'kai*. He thought you and Kas were God, but he could not believe God greeted him like a daughter!

Ploote is panting with laughter, his red halo bobbing.

You know he is one of the oldest Lokop people still walking and he has been in the village the whole of his life. Can you imagine, darly? To see you two—but he cannot finish his sentence, roaring again. I am free-floating in some universe parallel to the life I used to occupy. I am barely here, barely anywhere. Deified with humor. And I am smiling.

The sight of you two would have killed him but he thought he was already dead and God was there greeting him. God was two white daughters!

More laughter.

He was waiting for you to take him, Ploote says bending over, holding his belly, eyes tearing up.

Kas and I had no idea godhood took such a hilarious turn.

I offer them water but they are still convulsing.

Finally, they drink and shake off the mirth.

He says, We are almost there, not too far, as if he's already forgotten the old man, but I carry the crazy misunderstanding with us. It livens my step—God daughters. I sing Doc Watson's version of *Summertime* and *House of the Rising Sun*, and Bill Withers' *Ain't No Sunshine*. I teach them the words. He looks at me especially long and sweetly while I sing. The sexiness of last night's dance lingers. *Ain't No Sunshine* touches a nerve. We both love the present and recoil from the future like we will touch fire when it comes.

The present will have us, if the future will not.

Ploote's village greets us, his mother and father quick to make chai, but the chai is darker than at my lover's village. Less milk. The village is smaller with fewer homes and somber. No one laughs, no Lintan takes our hands to lead us on word adventures. Still Ploote is happy to be home. He delights in introducing Kas.

Kas says, in Gutok, how nice it is to meet everyone. Ploote's mother has welcoming eyes. Kas asks to take her photo which gives Ploote so much pleasure.

We stay only long enough for tea. The merry adventurers must head back since the sun sets early each night. Living near to the equator means that we will walk for hours in darkness. I no longer fear this, I love it. Time disappears. We need nothing more than song, story, silence and walking rhythm. We walk, walk, walk breathing in dusk, amidst scant flora, which bodes well for us and not for predators.

When night falls, we are still hours from home. He asks if we want to pick up stones like before. I already have one. He discovers it and boasts how clever I am, his darly. Kas must be fighting not to roll her eyes! She has two, and no one notices.

We see home, which looks new to me from this approach, like it has turned its back on us. He holds my hand as we cross the bush-fence threshold. We greet a sleepy Natiyon. Lintan does not stir. I say goodnight to Ploote, Kas, and my lover. Ploote thanks Kas with the shyest smile.

I curl up on the calfskin, and he stays awake to recount the day to Natiyon, bringing news to her of Ploote's family, I imagine. I decide never to ask what he and she speak about. I leave that their mystery. I do not want to take Natiyon's son from her. I am learning how to make space for others. Like any deity worth her salt.

# Eighteen | THE TROUBLE WITH THINKING

I WAKE EARLY but he is gone. This is the first morning he has not greeted me, after the first night we did not make love. Doubt enters my body like a sneaky teenager. I replay the previous day, the walk, the intensity with which he looked at me. I want to trust everything is okay.

Kas still sleeps. I watch her. She is truly beautiful, her thick black lashes and peach-fuzz cheeks.

She has never seen me in love like this. I've had many boyfriends. I started young—most would say too young. At twelve, I was capable of a sexual enthusiasm most seventeen-year-olds possess. No one taught me. I was not raped or coerced. It was something I innately knew. I chose a boy a year older than me and we fell into one another. I saw desire everywhere after that, the secret sort, the unspoken draw between strangers, in the way men looked at my mom, even in the way they looked at me. Older men. Desire, lust, passion created the world, of that I was certain. I felt relieved when I learned my astrological sign. We Scorpios are sexual. And so are nomads.

I trusted boys. But something happened when my dad left. The alcohol. The abandonment. We all have dragons to slay, fathers do too, but I didn't know that then. I pretended not to care, for him or my boyfriends, which felt safe. I allowed no possibility of being left behind. I just moved on when emotions demanded too much of me. The dragons of love and loss had too much power. Kas witnessed heartbreak after heartbreak. Not mine. Theirs. I said to them, *I don't think the dynamic is right*, or *how can we explain chemistry?* And with that it was over. My checkered past stirs quite the dust storm in the sparse nomadic hut, and it isn't even full sunrise.

In Lokop land, there is one type of toothbrush from one perfect tree—not hard bristles or soft, blue-handled or purple, electric or manual. And you never own it here. Is my love for him like that, perfect and simple? Just what I have been looking for? I may vanquish my dragon this time—not by running scared but by following him all the way into his dung-layered lair.


Lintan arrives to escort us to the shower rocks. She grabs my hand and leads Kas and me via a new path. Some of the plants are not familiar and she uses this to teach us. She talks the entire way. It works, her tireless repetition. The cadence of the language starts to untangle. I still want to see it on a page, break it down, categorize. Instead I let go and listen like I am falling asleep, more receptive. We walk today without chai. Natiyon was away. Lintan tells us we will have breakfast later. It is the only way the Lokop distinguish present tense from future. They tag *later* at the tail end of a sentence. Otherwise *now* is all there is. This manner of theirs both inspires and frightens me, preoccupied as I am with thoughts of commitment and becoming a Lokop wife.

Dear Lintan draws me back to the present by picking a tight bundle of leaves and rubbing them all around her body. I lean my nose in to smell but they lack scent—some type of insect repellant, we understand by her imitation of buzzing and shooing.

At the rocks, a group of warriors are leaving, hair propped dryly up with sticks, red cloths tied off to wash their legs. I scan the group for my lover or Ploote. Disappointment has a thick taste. We have our morning ritual. Why not today?

We bathe, brush our teeth and wash our hair which has grown long. It is a real chore heaving the wet, knotted mess around. Lintan's head is shaved. Her brother's is too. His hair used to be very long. First the primary school in Gabaroi forced him to cut it, and then he shaved it to the quick when his cousin died of malaria. Lokop erase the records of tragedy from the roots.

I watch the fresh-bathed warriors leave, stricken with jealousy. My lover told me *lmurran* gather and primp after bathing. They braid one another's hair, apply charcoal liner to their eyes, and orange and red ochre to their faces, and mend necklaces. Though the women and men bathe separately, *lmurran*'s lovers often join them after, adorning themselves as well.

Someone will apply his paint when I am no longer here. Maybe someone is doing that now. I dwell a moment in the stark, unsettled state of the future.

Christ, I can barely breathe there.

I climb down and find a stick. I break the end like flower petals— he loves me, he loves me not, he loves me. I try asking Lintan. She understands but does not know where her brother is, so I let it go. My urgency? An old dragon, sizzling.

Kas gathers our few bathing items. Lintan hands me another stick to break apart. I practice divination as we walk, snapping off the end, tossing it like a six-year-old girl.

The village offers no respite. No warriors present. The *Apayas* play *ndotoi* under the big tree. They slip their stones over the dimpled wooden board like backgammon pieces. Women are not allowed to play. Like I care to. It needles me how much I don't care and how I obsess.

His mother dishes up *uji* for us, a rich cream of wheat made from United States' relief-wheat spiced with sugar and fatty camel's milk. I take a sip, my belly rumbles and I run for the brush. I make several ass-chapping trips, miserable and sick with diarrhea. Lintan wants to escort me but I stop her. *Mbaya*, I say. *Bad*, rubbing my belly. I won't subject her to the indignity. I imagine shepherds stopping to view the white girl's camel bum as I squat, staring down at the prickly broken grasses. The day drops into misery.

When I crawl into the hut, back from my fifth trip, pasty with depletion, Natiyon takes my hands. She closes her eyes and begins chanting. I pull back when she spits on my face. She holds my hands tighter and spits twice more. Droplets sprinkle my eyes, nose, the ridge of my lip. Kas stifles a laugh. My stomach heaves. I close my eyes and mouth, purse my face and allow Natiyon to continue. Three more times. She says *God, God, God* and urges me to lie down.

The air blazes. My fever burns to ashes in my joints. I try to find soft spots on the calf skin, shifting onto one hip, then the other. I sleep all day into evening. Anything but think of or taste or smell *uji*. When I wake, a small boy crouches near me smelling something he has pulled from the fire. He holds it close to his nose, closes his eyes. He is in heaven. He sees me and runs, clutching the lavender-scented towelette I had tossed into the flame earlier.

I am not sure if he's real or I dream him.

I make one last call to the bush with Kas accompanying. It is dark. Natiyon stokes the fire and asks Lintan to give me tea, which she serves black and bitter.

I am angry with him for the first time.

In the fever-dizzying night, I wake to his face floating above me, wild-eyed, painted, fresh from ritual. His forceful kisses wet my cheeks and throat as I twist from under him, waking to full anger. He reaches around my skirt and pulls the knot free. I shove him away but he grips me and climbs on. Heavy strength. The moon leans through the slats in the hut walls.

He whispers in Gutok, a type of foreplay I taught him. I coil inward with his kisses, and push away to teach him a lesson, the way a child strikes out mid-nightmare. But his heat infects my legs and belly. My fever joins his. And with this slightest surrender, he pushes inside me. My body lets him in. We sway together back and forth on the rough hide, breathing one another like air. I cry, and the fever releases a little. He holds tight like we are one body, pulls into me deeper, rubs his face on my hot skin, smearing paint and despair away. He is fire. Raised by fire. Pure igneous. I want to punish him. I want to devour him.

He whispers, *Nanyorai* I am sorry you were sick today. I missed you. I know you said *no* to me at first but I needed you.

I grip his waist. I ask, Where were you?

I was doing ceremony with *lmurran* and preparing them for our journey back to Ukunda.

Journey back? I do not understand. We have only been in the

village two weeks and already we are going back? Kas and I are too much trouble? He detests eating our diet?

He interrupts the turmoil. I will tell you all tomorrow but now let's sleep. I need you to be better. He settles beside me.

Will you be here in the morning? I have to ask it.

*Nanyorai*, I will be wherever you need me. You must try to trust this.

I spoon him. I say, Do you bury each other when you die?

Shhh … He lightly covers my mouth and says, Darly that is too big question for this time of night. You will not die here, and if you did, I will know what to do with your body. *Ttssk*, he clicks his tongue and says, How will I now sleep with such thoughts?

I burrow close, his skin the perfect temperature. His ash scent stays on my body, even the next day. How many days does scent remain?


Ritual. May all mornings begin the same. He sits with his back to me, his cloth draping one shoulder, the other exposed. That bare shoulder is mine to trace—my eyes climb and conquer it again and again. Gray light streams into the domed entrance. I never hear him wake. His mother is here but they are quiet today. I listen to the movement between them. He is deep in thought, rocking a little. I watch, and the day comes clear.

My belly is empty and tender but my fever has gone cool. Natiyon stirs tea leaves and the smell makes me hungry. Steaming chai from the pot mixed with sugar, milk and something new. Ginger!

His eyelashes flutter. He knows I am awake.

*Ntepere serian, ngejuai?* he asks, looking over his muscled shoulder.

Why he refers to me as his leg this morning, I do not know.

Though she is always within feet of us, his mother gives us privacy by keeping to herself. She becomes a foundation of our union. We are connected to one another through her, her fire tending.

Kas wakes with the smell of chai and the sounds of my slurping. He hands her a cup.

Natiyon's spit or his lovemaking, I don't know what did it but I feel whole again.

Ooh, ginger, Kas says.

I tell her we may be leaving a little earlier than planned.

He stands and leaves once he sees we have our chai. Kas and I are still thought of as small children. We have not been circumcised but because he has been, he is not allowed to take chai in his mother's home. I somehow forget this every single morning.

A young boy appears, wearing a dirty cloth covering his genitals. He greets us all. He is about ten, still wearing his mother's green beads around his waist and the packet of healing herbs stuffed into a leather pouch around his neck. The Lokop are a superstitious people.

The young boy speaks in quiet tones with Natiyon, solemn but purposeful. Something is not right. Natiyon opens a rusted metal chest that is tucked where she sleeps. She removes a white cord rope and begins striking her palm with it, not hard, the cord snaps and whips through the air. Kas and I fade into the background. We learn the most when we are out of focus, forgotten. Natiyon says a few words to the boy. He turns hurriedly and leaves saying a reverent *thank you*. Natiyon coils her rope and packs it away in the chest.

My lover speaks to us through the hut walls. I find it funny, chatting into the thin grid. There's no privacy in nomad land, not even the walls as boundary. He says the young boy lost a baby camel and fears for it, so he came to find out if the camel is still living and where.

Can we help find the baby camel? Kas asks, always ready for a hike.

No, let him go and redeem his own problem. He will learn not to let the animals stray.

Lions, hyenas—I see my lover suddenly as he was the day he lost his calf, a shaking, frightened boy. He interrupts my vision saying, Mmm-hmmm, and then he ducks his head inside. Darly, are you remembering me as a young boy? Those days are far now. He smiles.

I cannot handle any more of his magic.

Later, we see the boy with his baby camel. The boy prances, lifting his head high, fully in control now.

Did your mom know the camel was alive? I ask, leaning into him. Did she direct that boy to where it was lost?

She knew the exact place. The rope tells her. She is very powerful in our village and has helped many warriors to locate their animals. Sometimes people lose their childrens. We call her *Liboni*, which I think for you is like witch doctor, he says, as he twists a partly broken branch from a tree, staring into the distance. Then he asks me, *Nanyorai*, which word do you hear us using most in Lokop?

I barely have to think about it. I hear it all through the day and night. I say, The word for God, *N'kai*. That is what I hear most.

He says, Yes, that is how the rope knows to show my mother. We believe *N'kai* is everywhere.

I reflect on Natiyon's gift. I want to know what the rope would say of our future. I do not want to know which hyenas wait for me at home.

My mother told me I had premonitions as a girl. I would ask her about specific presents that she had, as yet, only intended to buy. I told her about presents she had hidden up high, too far up for a four-year-old's reach. I predicted accidents and said spooky things which made adults uneasy. In adolescence, the seeing stopped.

Here in Lokop land, everyone is capable of listening beyond words to a cosmic intelligence, a sacred murmur. He pulls me in close. He says, You know, my leg, we have no word for *thinking* in my language. We never used to do this thinking thing. You want to try it? Not thinking?

Right now, I am thinking about not thinking and it is making my brain hurt, I say.

Yes, if you stay with me longer you will learn, he says.

Is that how you hear my thoughts, because you are not thinking?

I don't know. The answer would require thinking.

# NINETEEN | REFLECTION

HE SITS WITH Kas and me under the lacy acacia tree at the village center. He wants to talk with us both. It has a blessed spirit, this tree. It has heard so many stories, watched so many elders play so many games, witnessed grievances resolve and love bonds form.

We will leave my village and go to Ukunda and that big water again, he says.

So soon, I think. But I don't object, we ask no questions.

My father told me we must leave. He is worried not about your food but about your safety. Ejocho warriors raided cattle in the neighboring village. The warriors lost their lives.

This deep in Lokop? Kas says. That's daring and stupid.

I will never let anything happen to you as long as I'm alive, he says and chuckles at the thought of his own death. My father says you are like his own daughters now. But you are not familiar with our livestock-raiding.

Of course, the village would prefer to keep a lead warrior like my lover at home, with the possibility of another raid, but it forfeits him so he may escort the helpless back to their umbrella beach. Kas and I were strangers to *Apaya* and to the village, just weeks ago, and now they accept responsibility for our lives. They risk their animals. They petition for our care. Father risks son.

You must stay alive for many reasons, I tell him. Please thank *Apaya*. He is so wise and kind.


He touches my hip from his seat near the fire. It is still dark.

I whisper, Good morning. Is it time to go?

Yes, wake Kas. We will make it in a long day because we do not go by way of Lududuma's village—but we walk with the same speed as the wind, he says and winks.

We don't take chai. Kas and I say silent goodbyes to this hut, Natiyon's fire, animal skins and sooty dung-cedar walls. Natiyon and Lintan are out already milking the camels for our journey.

The sun sleeps below the horizon while the villagers gather to give their goodbyes and blessings. Many walk us to the acacia fence, some keep walking as though they will come along. Lintan amongst them. The older women call our names over and over invoking with repetition knowledge of the path back; back to them, back to this spotted leopard village, *Nanaiiolo*. Can they know how far we will go from their idyllic lives, across the ocean? Do they know how we will disappear into the distance, into this gray light? They don't know the word *Atlantic*, yet they seem to by the ardor and permanence of their goodbye. Young girls weep, Lintan clutches her brother's arm, folding over with rank sadness. I already miss her bright spirit, her glee. She brushes away tears but more stream. I cry. Kas cries. The family does not know when they will see their beloved son again. Ukunda is so far. But he tells me this farewell is for Kas and me.

Natiyon grabs my arm. Her eyes reflect first light. She leans in and spits on my face as she recants prayers to the divine. He tells me to follow her prayers with, *N'kai, N'kai, N'kai*. I do. Other villagers join. I turn, looking for my *Apaya*. He steps out from behind a group of elders, puts his hand high in the dawn light.

I shout, *Apaya*, and put my hand up, too.

He says with a tinge of woe, *Ditai*.

Lintan grabs my hand. Her brother kisses her head for the first time in her life. Sweetly shocked, she laughs now as she cries. He sends her back and she immediately obeys by wiping her tears and turning toward the huts.

We have our backpacks, Nalgene water bottles full with water, and one with camel's milk. Wait, I say, I'll be back. I run toward the village, calling after Lintan. She comes running. We hug like two strong saplings, planted close, and I hand her my water bottle. Share this with Natiyon, dear sister! She says, *Ashe oleng ganeshyie.* Thank you, sister. And something about *ntarasi*, about keeping the bottle forever. I say, quick as tears come, You will take care of my camel? I point to the curly-headed baby who is looking right at me. My *Ntarasi*? I say it with so much love, I kiss her cheek, and smell the anise ChapStick Kas gave her last night. Each time they fill the water bottle or smell the ChapStick—will they think of us, in this present-saturated, dry remoteness, this land that is both a perfect fossil and without a past?

It starts me crying all over again. I kiss Lintan's soft cheek again and turn.

He smiles. He says, We can make it with one less bottle. They will use that each and every day, and I will cup water in my hands for you on this journey, if you need. He knows I need more water than he ever will.

The dawn silence absorbs us. He and Ploote follow closely behind, their pace pushing ours. The sun feigns weakness but we know its tricks. Soon it will glow, center stage.

He shouts to us, after an hour, Cousin and I have an idea. From Lamaresh, we can make a small safari to Nakuru. There is a lake with pink birds. I think you will enjoy and it is on the way to Nairobi. We don't need to hurry to that beach in Mombasa, do we?

Kas says, We want to continue this adventure with you right to the plane! And a lake sounds great.

Ploote jumps in place, so fond of her. Best friends, he says. We are best friends from totally different worlds. We have to show you the all of this one.

We laugh and push the coming departure from our hearts.

Ahead, young Lokop girls gather. They have dug a large hole for fetching water and fill their tin cans and calabashes. One is down the hole, hoisting the vessels up to the others. My lover greets them and keeps walking.

Can Kas and I sit with them for a few minutes? I ask.

He shouts to them to tell them we are coming. They nod in agreement, so pretty.

One takes my water bottle which is still nearly full. The others make space for us around the hole. I have a thorn in the sole of my Converse. A girl grabs my shoe and breaks the thorn off. The others laugh at her gruffness, while she smirks. But the tip of the thorn still pokes through the fabric inside. I take out my mirror, reflecting the sun's light deep into the throat of the high-top. They all gasp and move closer, pushing Kas aside in their haste. The thorn-breaker grabs for the mirror and stares at her image—for the very first time? Lokop region does not host reflections. Only those on the rare surface of pooling water.

She gives a shout. She jiggles her red beads, examines the stain on her chin, her round face turning to see all angles. Another girl takes the mirror and opens her mouth to see her teeth and tongue. The girls cry out to *N'kai*, astonished by their beauty, giggling, praising their creator. A slender girl with crossed eyes smiles with delight. One after the other, they hold the mirror and glow.

My lover hears the commotion. He leaves Ploote and the shade tree to join us.

He asks for the mirror. They hand it to him and grow quiet. He raises his eyebrows in a playful gesture, admiring his own handsomeness. They bust out laughing. Then he returns the compact to me and says, We must go, darly. I think you enjoyed your visit?

They are even more beautiful than this mirror shows, I say. Please tell them.

They giggle at his praise and resume bathing. I hold the mirror slantwise, find the tip of the thorn, push it through and put my shoe back on.

The sun blazes. We now follow my lover and Ploote who move fast.

I think of the mirror tucked in its dark pocket. I think of beauty without thinking at all.


Micah, Kas asks, slowing down, can you do me a big favor?

She rarely calls me by my name. She rarely slows down. We have hiked for hours without speaking.

I need to borrow your mirror to look at my crotch, she says, pointing down as though I might not know where her crotch is. Something isn't right, she says.

I shout to the guys, We need privacy. Can you keep walking ahead?

Kas squats in the shade of a thicket and lifts her skirt. I hand her the mirror, but its face is too small. She angles it forward and back, and just before she hurls the darn thing into the bushes I say, Kas, I can be your mirror.

She frowns and heaves a resistant sigh.

I've been pushing off your feet for weeks, having sex. I'll look for you.

She hands the mirror over with a slant on her mouth.

I squat, and instant empathy overtakes me. Her labia are crimson red and swollen.

I'm so sorry. When did you start to feel this? Fuck, it looks painful.

We squat knee to knee like tribeswomen. We steady ourselves with our palms in the dirt.

After we left Lududuma, she says. It came on slowly but now it's really shit. Those poor village girls.

My emotions flush instantly though I try to keep cool, raging red as her labia. That bastard! Maybe the Lokop have herbs, I say. I'm sure it's just a yeast infection that's out of control—

Yeah, like a bakery! she says and stands up.

When we catch them, I ask him to walk with me. I do my best to describe the problem.

Our womens have some herbs, yes, but we are too far now. Better we look for a treatment when we arrive in Lamaresh. Lududuma is a scavenger like a hyena, he says with heat. Ploote pretends not to be listening. Kas walks beside him saying nothing. My lover spits and says, Kas that stupid warrior has no honor even thinking your name. He is bringing everything from Mombasa like a suitcase. The selfish one.

I watch his eyes go empty. To him, Lududuma no longer exists.

I watch Ploote take up worry.

Are you okay for this long walking, my lover asks Kas, or do you need rest?

Kas looks vulnerable. She keeps walking. I admire her courage.

Neither one of us has ever contracted anything. I can't do much but try to keep her mind off her swollen vagina.

I stomp the ground and say, I want a fresh spinach salad like nobody's business! I know the leafy greens make her happy.

She cracks a smile, my sturdy buddy, and he asks us, What is fresh spinage sald?

I say, It's Spanish, winking at Kas.

She laughs weakly and takes my hand.

We walk day into darkness. How nice a bed will feel after weeks on the hard skins and this incessant feet-to-earth march. The scattered hues of Lamaresh light the sky. We welcome the buildings and surrounding forest as old friends. I take Kas' pack as she leads the way into the hotel courtyard. The same hotel. The manager delights to see us. He asks about our experience in the village with dubious eyes. We pay for the night and request hot water. I set Kas' daypack on the concrete floor in the whitewashed room. Ploote walks off to his room.

I lie in his arms and pretend I see the careful shadows of Natiyon's body, hear Lintan's soft breathing. I miss the crackle of fire, the skins. He holds me tighter. I know Kas misses far more.

Kas? I whisper. She is usually last to fall asleep and has much on her mind.

Did the warm bath help?

I'm not about to complain, she says. About anything. Ever again. This, too, is village.

# TWENTY | MARY CHRISTMAS

THE NEXT DAY, everyone feels better. We take a *matatu* to Nakuru to see the lake. Nakuru is a bigger town than Lamaresh, with a large vegetable market, two hours from Nairobi. This breaks up the long trip to Ukunda. Kas and I want the vegetables as much as the ponds and pink flamingos.

We hire a man with a baseball cap to oar us out to the middle of the large, quiet lake. Green wooden boat, candle-flame pink flamingos, late sun, swirls of birds and a flurry of squawking. The grassy bank drifts into the distance.

My lover holds my hand and kisses my cheek.

From the deep, a bull hippo rises to our right, his snout rippling the water. I smile at the striking show, but my lover stands, braces his arm against my body and shouts to the captain, Watch out! Then says to me, eyes only on the water, I wanted you to see these animals but this close is very dangerous. Very.

The captain frowns, widens his stance and braces, trying to steer around the mass but more emerge. More sodden, gray backs and nub ears and small eyes. No room to navigate; hippo mines everywhere. Hippos are responsible for more human deaths in Africa than lions. We learn this later. They are territorial and temperamental. They are also fast, on both land and water.

Darly, watch your side, he says as he leans over the shaky stern, straining to see into the murky water. I cannot see anything and wonder how he knows the hippos' presence before even the captain.

There. And there, he says pointing. Kas and I lean in opposition to keep the boat steady. Gray boulder giants pop up slowly, snorting water from their nostrils that flare in distress. Some stretch their cavernous mouths, speckled pink, brown, and gray. Backhoe rakes. Their massive square teeth look like backhoe rakes and their huge tongues draw me down the gulley of their throats at least forty times, there are so many of them.

Ploote clutches the side of the old boat and leans into the middle, away from terror. He doesn't know this beast, and he cannot swim.

The captain oars as though through tar, gently, gently nudging giants off the bow.

Hah! my lover says, This boat driver needs to go where the water is not so deep, then they cannot hide. I am telling him but he drives like a scared man.

Ploote looks plenty scared. Hippos surround us on all sides. Kas and I keep breathing and balancing, breathing and balancing the boat.

Standing tall, he says, We are just trying to be lucky now. Hold the side of the boat like Cousin. Do not let yourselves fall in.

I think he is actually enjoying the thrill, and luck has nothing to do with it. He stands on this watery seesaw, trying to outsmart giants. And he loves surprises.

Ploote says, Micah, do these hippos eat mens?

No, I say. But they will kill us in the water because they do not like anyone else, and they can flip our boat.

Concern flashes on his face. Ploote and the Loch Ness monsters. I quickly realize my mistake and say, We'll be at shore soon.

We lean and search, doing our damnedest to avoid the agitated hot-pink jowls. Finally, the driver eases our way into shallower water and the gray backs stop rising. Behind us, beady eyes, too-small ears, and long whiskered snouts slink back into the deep. We have now seen hippos, plenty of them.

We drift parallel to the bank. Once on shore, my fearless lover scolds the captain. If you knew there were hippos so near, you should not have taken us! The captain shoves his ball cap down tighter and apologizes. Before leaving, we take a group photo, laughing at our fortune, feeling certain we are invincible when together. Even the captain flashes his rident mug, all in one piece and a few shillings richer.

On the walk back to town I ask my lover how he knew where the hippos were. He says, My skin tells me. He takes my hand and his touch sends even more current through my body after this.

In the late afternoon, after the hippo hooplah, my darly tells Kas and Cousin that we are taking a nap. Kas takes a book and asks Ploote for company downstairs in the restaurant. I pretend I am not aware, modest as a schoolgirl. *Afternoon nap* or book and cafe? I am pleased with his choice but feel suddenly self-conscious, making love out of the hut and village. Middle of the day and all.

We crawl into our single bed and each other. Float the outrageous lake of love beyond all control. Questions flow back and forth in waves without words—how will this be between us, me in my country, you in yours? Is there any way around the pain? Departure is mere weeks away. I kiss wet spots on his shoulders. I open and rise. He hushes me with promises. We tear the day and mend it all, in flames. Then he gazes up at the ceiling, not close but far, letting his mind drift where it is unaccustomed; the imminent separation. He lingers only a moment, then asks, Micah, you remember I was telling you about something to notice on me, a necklace?

I glance down under his shoulder to the beads resting on his body. He is about to wrap up the story that he started while walking to Ploote's village, to fold me into another surprise.

I remember, yes, I say.

A thin strand stands out now. It seems older, well worn. The beads uncharacteristic in color—yellow, white, midnight blue, lime green, even clear.

Yes, that one, he urges. Do you understand the importance of this necklace? He rolls toward me onto his side.

I shake my head *no* even though I might. I want to hear him tell it.

My mother made this for me when I was a boy. I have been wearing it for all those years. It is the only thing I keep from before circumcision.

When I have become sure I have found a girl, I give this to her and it becomes our marriage bond.

I swallow, a pause for a quiet *yes*. I love bridges, any handmade bridge between him and me.

He takes the single strand and inches it over his head. This is for you, he says. You take it to Mama Jolie and Papa Duane and ask them if you can marry me. They have to agree. My mother and father also know.

He shimmies the necklace over my head, pulling a little harder over my feral hair. I am raw with tears. They stream down my face into the creases of a smile.

I will ask them, I whisper, But I already know that what I want, they also want. *Ashe oleng*. Thank you. I will wear this until I come back to you. I will wear it like my skin, to eat, to sleep, to bathe.

Yes, there are two worlds, Micahai, the one we see and the one we do not see. Our love has to shine like the moon and sun in both.

We kiss our promises to one another and he wraps the necklace around his index finger drawing my neck and face nearer to his chest—holding my body, the necklace, and his body in a nuptial tether. We make love again, sexier. He has one leg off the bed for leverage, standing like a flamingo. I do not even think of birth control anymore, it's all so right.

We don't shower. We hurry down to meet Kas and Ploote. Kas sees the necklace right away.

I just got engaged! I roar.

She giggles and closes her book. Really? It seems right.

Ploote blushes and his shoulders open out. Strong wings. No one feels the need to ask about logistics. There's no desire for logic at all. I love that they don't press for answers. They are as much a part of our dream as we are.

Over our chapati, rice and beans, I touch my new necklace often. The strand falls, contouring with and against my shoulders, tickling, catching in the tiny hairs at my neck.

Just as I ask Kas what she wants for dessert, semen seeps between my legs.

I am sitting next to her, across from him, and suddenly the

dam bursts. I contract my muscles but the vinyl seat slicks wet. His sperm soak through my underwear and thin, dark-colored *shuka*. I cross my legs, paralyzed with humility, not knowing how I will stand up.

Let's ask for fried plantain and honey, Kas says.

Shit, Kas! I cry, His cum is running out of me. What should I do?

Kas' eyes pop wide. My lover sees and leans across the table to us. I turn, humiliated. Sometimes his protection leaves me no space.

Kas says, with raised eyebrows and playful scorn, Micah is wet from your *nap* earlier. She can't get up.

Oh, darly! I look to know whether he is laughing or sympathetic. He is both. I will bring your jacket to tie around you. I am sorry for my mess.

I flush red. Meanwhile, Ploote turns from the table as if he is deaf, not for his comfort but for mine. He excuses himself to accompany my lover to the coats. How I wish a flotilla of hippos would swallow me up just now—the moments before so wonderful and now a wet lap and a busy gawking restaurant.

When they return, I quickly tie the jacket around my waist.

Ploote smiles his big, buck-toothed smile. Though it never bothers him, even my candor is forgiven in his grin.

I follow the others upstairs, and slink into the bathroom to shower, stripped except for the vow that now dangles from my neck.

When I come out of the bathroom, Western shame still a thin residue on my skin, Ploote is teaching Kas a shepherd's whistle and my lover is wearing my skirt and headscarf! When he sees me we giggle, and all comes clean. An acceptance, so complete, carries its peace all the way in.


We leave chilly Nakuru by *matatu* for Nairobi early the next morning. I say to Kas, Let's hope we don't have any more *poussez* problems.

In Nairobi, we wait and rest in an empty dirt lot littered with brightly colored foils, biscuit and sweets wrappers. My lover sits against a rock with my head on his lap. Kas and Ploote each prop their heads on a backpack. The village exists like a dream. Diesel fumes replace the smell of fire, traffic honks out the heart-breaking serenity of morning, Western polo shirts and trousers stand stiffly next to the memory of leather skirts, nipples and beads. Trash overwhelms the raw detritus of the living and dying. I am not ready for this glimpse of home. We wait two hours and thirty minutes for the bus to Mombasa, then take the ferry to Ukunda.

Once there, we move back into *lmurran's* coconut grove, we fall gratefully back into beach walks, storytelling through the hottest hours, and warrior dances in the evening. My lover becomes quiet, not with me so much, but with others. He allows the warriors to entertain me and occupies his mind with beading.

Since it is December, I try to explain Christmas, sitting under a wind-tossed baobab tree. Sledding and sleighs resist all description, even snow. The warriors' eyes never leave my face. I try to give him something worth savoring. I say, We are not really Christians like the missionaries, but we do celebrate the holiday with food and singing. I recall the thin carols and fat feasts. And the half-hearted way I participated in my own celebrations. I shudder and abandon it all.

I ask about his beading, his newly disciplined manner. You have to make many things now to sell to the tourists because we were away for a long time, right?

He looks at me, his smile taciturn.

That evening, a Christmas parade interrupts my sleep. I am dreaming in his arms when a stinging pain wakes me.

I scream, Wake up! I slap at the dark spots on the bed, barely able to see. Something's biting me! Oh, Jesus.

He jumps up and lights the lantern. A line of war-red, African ants streams in under the door. Blood stains the bed. I pull clenching, gripping pincers from my labia and realize the blood is not from their bites, it's menstrual blood. The ants smelled it?

He pours kerosene on the line, preparing to light it on fire. I can't protest. I feel too vulnerable and the well-coordinated army keeps marching toward my thighs.

He stands naked with the oil and says, You couldn't wait for Christmas dinner, and now you will pay the consequences. He strikes a match and mocks them, saying they did not receive an invitation. He drops the match and the line trembles with fire. Most of the ants are intelligent enough to escape. But some burn.

I ask, Does this happen in the village, when women bleed?

No, we always have a fire and the ants are like mosquitoes. They don't like smoke. I am sorry, darly. Those bites hurt terribly. Are you okay?

I cry. He pulls my head into his chest. I cry not because I have been bitten or because I am embarrassed. Establishing a modicum of comfort with the untamable wildness of Africa has taken me time. Once I return home it will require a thickening of my skin to ever come back, to return to this man and his biting ants. I might not ever be truly at home here. Or anywhere. I bleed too much, have more fat on my body, drink too much water, eat fruit and vegetables, seek comfort in movies, bubble baths, books, and watered-down ritual. One foot in his sacralized wild and one foot in opulence. Is that what I want? For the rest of my life? Can I go wholly native? I finger the beads around my neck, sensing I come too late to this question.

He rocks me. He believes my tears are a response to tattered labia, and that I am emotional because of my cycle. I keep quiet. So much sadness as the fire line dies down. I look in his eyes and hear his words to the ants about Christmas dinner. It is the eve. I laugh out loud. He looks confused, the way men do amid women's storms, but still he walks me to the toilet and waits while I splash cool water on my sore skin.

I sympathize with Lokop women. It sucks having my period here. It actually sucks having a vagina, here. In this moment, I am looking forward to private toilets, sanitary napkins, running water and houses without insects. Then I think of Lintan, when she will bleed. She will use a bit of cloth, secured with twine around her waist—all that is necessary when the diet is as clean and restricted as theirs, and the total cycle lasts but a long day, maybe two.

We walk back and fall asleep but not before I ask the darkness how much courage I possess and how deep it runs.

I wake to swishing against the concrete floor. He flings the charred ants outside with a broom.

Happy Christmas, *Nanyorai*. My sweet leg, my sweetest ear. He greets me with a jubilance that makes the ants and midnight desperation disappear.

I sit up and cover the blood-stained bottom sheet with the other. I say, It's merry Christmas. We say merry Christmas.

Like Mary, Joseph, and the little Jesus?

I pause to give his matriarchal slant on Christmas a whirl. Mary Christmas. Mary Christmas. What a different world this would be if Westerners had let the mothers rule.

Merry means happy, I say as he sweeps my feet with the broom. Happy Christmas, just as you said it. I hop around and think, *just as I am with you.*

## Twenty-One | Every Forest Has Its Sound

We have eight days until the plane leaves for the United States.

He and Ploote go shopping in town, and Kas and I join the women at the well behind our coconut compound to do laundry, as if this is any ordinary day. And it is. The women are animated, slopping their feet in the mud and daring their friends to join them. They endanger the laundry and giggle like kids. Kas and I wash and dry his sheets, our clothes. We offer clothes to the women, clean and wrung dry. Surprised, they nod thanks and examine their gifts with delight. Merry Christmas, we say to ourselves.

We return to find him boiling up dinner in a pot. He has figured out how to use our stove and is stirring something that smells delicious, earthy and sweet. Tomato-red broth, potatoes bobbing, greens and yams.

I am making you and Kas Christmas vegetable soup. We have to make a celebration for our American friends who are away from their families during a big time for families and Jesus.

I reach around his back to hold his chest, saying, Is this the dinner the ants aren't invited to? I kiss the back of his neck. This causes him to ripple—a surge pulses up and down his body.

He shouts, Hah-ah! If you distract this chef, no one will be having Christmas soup. He puts down the spoon, carries me to the bed and kisses me. And goes straight back to his cooking.

We slurp soup and dunk chapati, sitting together on the floor, wondering why we haven't thought to fire up our camp stove in the one room before. Kas starts with a story about Christmas at home, the lights on trees, the icicles, the snowy treetops. She assures Ploote there are no hippos in the woods. I sing *Silent Night* and try to recall the verses from *The Little Drummer Boy*. The singing echoes off the concrete walls and summons other warriors to chant.

The warm broth made by his hands may be contributing, but somehow that chanting and the warriors' living strength drive into my body. Christmas soup hands, faraway Jesus hands. I only know Jesus' hands healed people, and the fearful drove nails into his palms for it. Unforgiving nails in his two palms. Impossible to break. Impossible Jesus.

When we are alone, I say, I feel scared to go back, knowing that your traditions mean more to me than my own. I twist his necklace in my fingers. I search for words. True words. My love for you, I say, makes me question everything.

Don't be scared, *Nanyorai*. We will see one another again physically if God wishes it.

The *if* makes my belly rise. Americans rally against this kind of surrender. How does he hold that much trust?

You can have Lokop celebration each and every time you come. My family already thinks of you as their white daughter. You are half Lokop girl, at least. He smiles.

*Half African, half American*, I think. *Fully conflicted.*

And maybe one day, he says, I will see your trees.

With that tender hope, my world caves in. I cannot imagine him in the United States. It will not be. I know this as surely as I breathe, and it wrenches open a chasm. Everything except him falls in. He is preserved on the edge of the crater. The essential remains in his words, his culture, his way. He is essential.

Eight days to liftoff. One more day here in Ukunda. The hurt runs deeper than his words can reach.


On our last day in Ukunda, Kas takes pictures of us on the beach. He surprises me by admitting he has never been in this ocean, only his feet. Shepherds don't know oceans. He starts to wade out, his beads shifting with his weight as he braces against the heavy cerulean water and looks back to me. I hurry to untie the knot in my *shuka*. He has never seen me in my swimsuit, in this water, the path he carves into the blue. I follow him as far out as I dare, feeling afraid of the unseen, the currents and creatures, until he picks me up. And keeps going.

We dry on the beach. His face is clearer than usual. My eyes focus only on him. I take in as much as I can stand and then look away, and his beauty compels me back. The length of his lashes, the smoothness of his skin, and the way sea salt dusts and lightens the blackness in places, the sweetness of his lips. The clarity hurts. I feel desperate and pray that heart pictures never fade.

He pays me no attention. Mr. Present Tense sticks his finger into his mouth, wetting it, then scoops up sand. Mouth full of seashore, he rubs the abrasive pebbles on the inner and outer surfaces of his shining ivory teeth with his index finger.

This is how he polishes them so white? He has never shown me this. What else have I not seen, what more is there to him? What moments will he live, be part of, that I will not?

I panic.

He spits vigorously and slides his finger around his mouth, watching the sea insouciantly. The sound of my coming tears interrupts him. Without pause he reaches for me, lays me across his lap, cradling my head in his other arm, scoops another finger full of sand, and softly opens my mouth. He barely rubs while he stares at me with that intensity that is only his.

I cling like a baby.

I cannot cry with a mouth full of finger and sand.

When he finishes the simple ritual, he sits me up and hands me the water bottle to rinse. My tongue slips over my teeth.

He sips and clears the polishing sand from his mouth.

He says, Cousin and I will escort you and Kas to the airport, *Nanyorai*. We must see you all the way, to keep you safe. You will not see tears come from my eyes. We say a warrior will spill blood but never tears. Return to your lovely family and tell them about you and me.

I know for sure I will die without his rough devotion.

As he tells me, it happens. One morning we travel to Nairobi. We take rooms.

It is finally here, this impossible day.

We make love once more in the squalid Nairobi hotel, but even that is painful. I do not know how to be this tender and still breathe, my nerves exposed to a fire that threatens to burn them numb. Other hotel guests bump the walls and a tap drips, horns blare outside, and body confusion numbs everything.

I feel it too, *Nanyorai*. It is like I am hearing you now and at the same time missing your voice—he touches my breast, he touches my heart—like a young baby misses its mother's milk while it drinks.

I only say, I will miss our village.

Every forest has its sound, he says. Try to remember these sounds from the village, those birds and special wind. Or the way I speak with my mother in the early morning. You are leaving to come back.


It is time. The blades of our airplane churn the warm January air. Kas goes first. The woman in stark blue with red neckerchief takes her ticket. Her eyes widen when she sees my tears and snot. She wants to say something to me but sees him and does not. My breath sticks in my chest. I gasp. I do not look at him again. I cannot.

I take the first step of many, too many, away from him.

# BOOK III SPIRIT

"When a shepherd comes home in peace, the milk is sweet."

*~African Proverb*

OUR STARK INDEPENDENCE returned first through our biology. Somewhere between Africa and Europe, Kas started bleeding. Our bodies had been as exposed to the environment as Lokop huts; we bled every twenty-eight days, with the full moon. We began and ended our cycles no more than hours apart. But unlike Kas, my period did not come.

We landed in Denver and still no menses. Jet lag, processed plane food, and emotions delayed it, I told myself. Kas and I no longer needed to sleep side by side, protect each other, travel together, bleed together. My body was already calibrating, lungs squeezing, heart aching.

After a home-coming celebration at the airport, my mom and stepfather drove me to our huge home nestled in the high desert mountains, a four-tiered stucco castle made from the surrounding dirt. Satisfied, duty done, my stepfather retired to bed. Mom glowed. She tucked me into a wooly afghan on the couch, her Spanish cheekbones full of motherly pride—one of her daughters was home safely. Desi's year in Argentina ended soon. Two daughters, then, in a mansion of her love. A mansion made spotless for my homecoming. I wept alone in the oversized bed and lay awake from three until the sun shepherded forward my first day without him. I hiked in the pine and cedar forest, sat in my favorite red cave, the dirt floor littered by the bones from mountain lion kills.

*Every forest has its sound.* I was deaf to this forest.

I tried to imagine the words I could send to him as substitutes for flesh, anguish and longing. I asked the expansive view; I pled for some quick metamorphosis. My sorrow climbed the silent cave walls. Words and bones, suddenly so alike to me. One line from a Rumi poem became my go to maxim: *We have ways within each other that will never be said by anyone.*

I imagined living in this cave. How could four walls, straight lines or linear thinking ever sustain me again? Even a sentence, especially a sentence, required governing and stricture. Before meeting him, I used to strive for those rules in language, in behavior, even if only to break them. But I had cut loose the confines of conditioning, and language, spoken or thought. The world of words not only lacked allure, it lacked silence. By definition, language lacked silence. I needed silence. I had been unsaid, and my family and friends wanted to talk about it.

Even our love was reduced to words.

I spent two weeks in my parents' home, writing letter after letter. I wrote him even more when I returned to Boulder to finish my degrees, pushed along the path with so many. I found a waitress job and shared a bedroom in a large Victorian home with Kas. I put on boots and gloves. The garish Pearl Street performers with dollars in their hats—it seemed a winter circus had moved to town to mock me. I might have detested them, but I was still clinging to the adventurous possibility of bringing him here. If Candide was the eternal optimist, I matched him step for step.

When his first letter arrived, I read it aloud, smelled it, scrutinized the paper.

*Baby I am writing this letter here in the beach under the big tree where we used to stay and tell stories. Your golden and precious letters met me. I read your letters very keenly and understand every part. They are my libraries that I read under the tree and before bed every day. My palpitating heart made me not to reply fastest time possible since I didn't have words to express myself and even difficult to hold my pen. I am missing you like when you*

*miss your only child. The whole world to me is like I am nothing and val-*
*ueless and no ground to stand on just because of missing you like a sickness.*
*To relax a little I pray to N'kai to let me meet my Micah again either here*
*in Kenya or America. I pray because many friends and people claims that*
*I am now crazy because I have now a tendency of walking alone. I don't*
*want anybody, even Cousin, but he just don't want to leave me. I never*
*sleep without saying your name and praying for your blessings in this life.*
*Please keep me busy with your letters. I miss you so much, so much, so much.*

The single blurred spot of ink on *Please* broke me.
Who taught him *palpitating?* I laughed. I longed to know.

"Micah, we are talking about the importance of cash crops to the
African economy. Do you have anything to add?" The skinny oaf of a
man wore a Patagonia climbing shirt and two hundred dollar jeans.
What on Earth could I add to my international economics professor's
world-view? It was all sewn up and shiny as tinfoil. I looked up to
see his eyes behind the tight glasses. I wanted to tell him cash crops
destabilized economies in Africa. People grew coffee in countries with
limited soil, sacrificing more nutritious plants that could help with
hunger and illness.

"No," I said. Let him suss it out himself.

I had joined the semester late. Classes meant exactly nothing to me.
If I could have run into the bush to hide from my education, I would
have. I could not concentrate, not even enough to care about failing
classes. There was some disconnect between what was required of me
and my present ability. I would rather have walked in forests with
elephant queens and kings than follow our matriarchs and patriarchs
of academia anywhere.

Two weeks prior, on a snowy day in early February, I had positive
results for a more vital test. The intern nurse stuck the needle in my
arm's hollow and all I could think of was goat blood, pooling in the
torn skin. Seven weeks confirmed. I told no one but him, hurrying to
the post office. I whispered to our baby. Our baby. Our future.

A letter arrived days later—too soon for him to have heard the
news from me.

I dashed into a bookstore and sat with my back to the crowd.

*My mother knows you left Kenya with my baby in your body. My nalangu, because we cannot be together to make decisions I trust you and our Creator. I don't want you to be in pain. I gathered herbs my mother suggested to end the pregnancy if you decide. Take them nine days after you receive this letter, not big amount. You are more sensitive than Lokop girls who use them. On the eighth day my mother plus women elders will pray for you to lose our baby naturally. This is why you must wait. I am sorry my lovely one. We will have time for family later.*

Hands shaking, I unwrapped the herbs and smelled them. Icicles hung from the bookstore eave. The herbs smelled like everything there—smoky and hot. And like wisdom. If right timing had a smell, the whole village reeked of it. Still, his cells grew in my body, good timing or not. Blur of happy shoppers. I held my belly with new life. A bus honked, and two students fell against the window, laughing. When had I last laughed? Girlfriends traipsed down College Avenue in their Uggs. I called Kas from a payphone and cried. She cried.

Kas and I had given each other lots of space to get used to Boulder. Living as closely as we had for a full year, it felt crushingly hard to let go of her. Only Kas knew the village. Only Kas knew him.

*We will have time for family later.* We never used birth control because a whole village waited to catch our baby, and me. But here I walked alone. I avoided the sound of my voice, lost in the physical yearning for we, for us. Crossing streets, oblivious to traffic, I envisioned for our baby the domed huts, Natiyon's face, grazing animals. Him. Images consoled me.

My people asked too many clever questions. "He never eats vegetables?" "What about AIDS?" "What was it like being with a black tribesman?"

I believed in him, and if he said we would be together later, the optimist in me agreed. She forced a deeper doubt out of sight. I believed in us. I only had *us* now.

I sat on my bed and listened to the snowflakes' gentle pinging against the window. Alone with the decision. Even the walls waited. In the silent walk home, I had made up my mind, but not my body. The body clings. *We will have time for family later.* We had to have another chance. Not now. Not this baby. But please, God, do not make me take the herbs. I could not endure the ultimate say. How could I poison the last real part of him and lose him a second time?

His next letter drowned in concern. How was I feeling? What did I want to eat? Was I tired? Were there any pains?

Then, in a long, detailed letter he urged me to file papers with the INS asking for a tourist visit so he could come to Boulder. The Kenyan government did not recognize him as a citizen because of the nomadic peoples' lack of representation and thus would not grant him a passport. Like the Tuareg on the train. He told me he would find a way and bribe an official for an illegal passport. He wanted to help me and hold me. He wanted to see the Colorado trees. Had it been possible, had it been easier, he would have come to help me have this baby.

Three days passed. I wrote daily, sometimes twice. I couldn't find any consolation, so I sent skeletons out onto the page, my sadness, the logistical impossibilities, money. An army of sadness and obstacles, and no money at all. I deflated like a tired balloon. He remained strong and determined and nine thousand miles away.

On day six, he asked the strangest thing. "Please baby buy me this book." *Unlimited Power* by Tony Robbins, the popular empowerment guru. That was all the letter said. I feared doing anything that would give us false hope, and my heartache told me Tony was just the man to give it to us. The strong, white beast. I ignored the request.

On the eighth day, I went to wait tables at the Walnut—my day job—which smelled a certain greasy, all its own. Nine weeks along in my very first pregnancy, I reeled at the fumes. My face paled, my breasts bobbed and ached, and my rubber soles squeaked on spilt beer. Management made us wear a bolo tie. A fucking bolo tie made from half a walnut shell. I carried two Cokes to the soft-handed Boulder businessmen who ordered chicken-fried steak and nachos. They looked at me, raccoon-eyed with sunglass tans from skiing. They tucked the starched napkins into their collars. *Stuff a little cherry pie down that hole, too,* I thought.

One man grimaced, shifting his weight.

*Is that booth too hard on your rich, coddled ass? You don't know discomfort. You don't know hunger. Not for food, not for flesh, not for love. Damn you and your wholesome, whitewashed life.*

"Will that be all?" I asked and slipped the oversized brownie and the bill onto the table. Before they could open their mouths, my inner thighs went weak. I turned away. My body began to cramp. Nervy jolts from my uterus sent me packing, pulling myself along the polished brass fixtures, straight to the bathroom to vomit. In the large, steel-walled stall, I did not vomit. I miscarried. No herbs, thank you, *N'kai.* Alone in that echoing stall, I imagined them in a circle on the ground, elder Lokop women around a fire, witch-like prayers. I looked between my legs into the bowl of red water. Could *Yeyo* see me? Could he feel our baby letting go?

*Apaya? Ditai!*

*Please, God, let us have another chance. I can do this. With the women in circle and the village fathers shouting* Ditai, *I can.*

My rough, lovely village. I still belonged, without circumcision, without ceremony, but conceiving and miscarrying a warrior's baby counted for something. Only now and here, with our child lost and my uterus strangling, could I say that I felt like a woman, strong enough to conceive and lose. I braced my arms against the cold steel for the next wave. They don't tell you that to miscarry, you still pant through contractions, just not the crowning. I thought of my mother, and his. Stabs to the abdomen, cold sweat beading. Natiyon with her rope, telling the end of this story.

Her power reached over an ocean. Her wisdom severed one more connection to her son. The distance between us spread like constellations. It felt that huge and cold and inclusive. I grabbed onto *N'Kai* and wept. I held the whole village in my prayers. Me, losing. Me, embracing. Me, praying.

He loved me. He taught me higher power. He gave me *N'Kai.*

When the heaviest bleeding stopped, I bought a sanitary pad from the vending machine, tipped the bartender, and carefully walked my bike home, detesting all things *sanitary.*

Yellow, white, midnight blue, lime green, even clear, the necklace rose with my breathing. Made by his mother. Worn by him. Worn against my sun-starved winter skin in February. The drafty windows rattled. I could not warm myself. Clutching our marriage vow, sobbing, surrounded by trinkets from Africa, I struggled to find the words to send him. Solace returned as I realized I didn't need them. Not between us, not with this love. Not where our baby was now.

Still, I found a pen and told him I was safe. Shivering, I wrote, "I lost our baby without herbs." I thanked his mother for her prayers; I was so proud my body could receive them. This strange, new love stretched beyond optimism; it pulled me to my knees, still tethered to *N'kai*, to spirit, baby or no baby. I had never had this knowing. Touching but not reading his few letters, I lay in bed, dehydrated, and I surrendered.

Nothing separated us. We would have another chance. Maybe even soon.

Wind raked the windows. A fever started in. Deer picked fine paths uphill through the snow out back. Kas must have come in very late. I slept until morning.

Kas and I dissolved our friendship slowly, like a sugar cube in tea. Our beds lay as far apart as the room allowed. Kas jumped into her studies, her workouts, her life. I mourned literally everything. My fever lasted only a few days. When my body healed, we went running together up the Mount Sanitas trail, but things had changed. Our way of living together created more loneliness than companionship. I moved out of the skylit room and into a studio apartment where I stored books in my refrigerator. I pushed Kas away. I only had energy for silence and him.

Starving. He always filled both sides of the page plus the margins because he knew I was starving. He wrote often. While waiting for a new letter, I read through each old one, sometimes three more times, putting them in order by stamp date.

*My dear, I'm sorry, very very sorry. I wrote twelve letters and I send them all only to know that you have received two. Pole sana Nanyorai. You remember when we were in Nairobi and we bought roasted maize and we put pili-pili and we bought some chapatis near the conference center?*

*You remember the way we walked through the very thick forest to Nanaiiolo and I was showing you elephant prints and explaining they are very dangerous because of poachers? Baby, you remember how the sun appears in the morning at Nanaiiolo when my Mama and Lintan woke to milk the camels? I am 100% missing you. There is no change, when I come to bed, when I go to the beach, Ukunda, or Nanaiiolo. At the Digo restaurant, even Cousin knew that I like now to sit on the chair that you are using when we were together. I will love you forever. My baby camel. Kachem ntarasi.*

In this city of achievement and prowess, of wealth and glitter and health, I congealed into clay. I was not innovative. I had spent my savings in Africa and on the passport bribe he attempted and failed in Nairobi. There was my rent in Boulder, the tuition at CU, everyday expenses, and my paralysis. I mastered living simply, which meant marginally. I worked, attended some classes, went numb and hurried home to his letters. Mostly I preferred sleep to waking life. I hardly recognized myself, the enthusiasm all frozen through.

He continued to believe. He believed in us and he believed in the United States of America. One letter read, "Please call one of the lovely ladies who sits in immigration and tell her about us, talking some sense to her. Maybe she will see that we belong together and she can find a way for me to get a passport." I pulsated between hope and despair. For a short time, I borrowed his view because it felt good, innocent and unadulterated, like snuggling with a baby bunny.

The Boulder snows melted and filled the creeks and curbs. Spring came whether I noticed or not. When I managed to call the INS, sitting on the edge of my futon, rolling hairballs on the carpet, I waited hours to speak with someone.

"He is not recognized by his government because he is nomadic. Is there any way for him to visit without a passport?" I pleaded with the agents, one after the other, each more stringent than the previous, as if they'd read a notation on my account: "Just tell her no."

I surrendered. Man with no country. Tuareg on the train. If he could not come to the US, I would return to Kenya. I would return to Kenya, but with what funds? How could I afford plane fare when I couldn't even buy a half-dozen bagels? I saw that years, even decades might pass before I found my way back to him.

Believe me, time does not heal all wounds. Time shoves us along its compelling, linear illusion. Time is Western. I kicked and screamed over the loss, initially, the staggering separation. Then, with time's fucking arrow in full flight, I succumbed. I began to notice I was hungry for food, I liked feeling the sun on my face. I noticed men were attracted to me and I to them.

In April, I wrote to him. No reply. Gaps between letters grew. As long as he was in Ukunda, I could reach him but when he returned to his family in Nanaiiolo, I lost him to that vast, quiet land.

In the hottest days of July, I made a ninety-minute cassette tape of music. I wrote the lyrics to each song, twelve handwritten pages. I made prints of hundreds of photos Kas had taken, organized them chronologically by country and incident and wrote descriptions on the back. Then I placed a *Nat Geo* map of Africa on top with a letter. The project took a little over two weeks. The letter, like the package, wrote my love for him in bright, last language.

I placed it in the postman's hands and left satisfied.

The shoebox, insured and certified, was stolen at the Nairobi post office and never recovered.

I don't shatter easily. It takes a good pounding, and more than one blow. My Spanish and Irish ancestors did not go to therapy. They drank hard or shuffled rosary beads, sometimes both. I couldn't do either.


"Why do you feel you are here today?" she asked me from the oversized, velour chair, her pen tapping her notepad lightly as yellow leaves blew by the window.

"I feel desperate." The plush furnishings, the Zen clock, and shades of purple everywhere—I had reached the pinnacle of white loss. In Boulder, soul searching was a full-fledged industry. "I don't understand anyone here anymore, my life. I don't understand what we are supposed to be doing. Whether we are part of each other or separate."

"Where here? Boulder?" She asked defensively with a squint. What could possibly be missing from Boulder?

"I've lost him, the village, a baby, and even Kas," I said, with tears welling.

"What is your current relationship with Kas?"

"I think you would say healthier, less codependent. It feels worse though. Empty."

"What was his name?" she asked with fugacious curiosity. I swear her interest read thin as that notepaper. No one who was not related by blood learned his name.

I deflected her attention. I told the truth. "It's not just him. I want to be a villager, a nomad. I want to feel the plants and animals, to know my place in the tribe."

She smiled strangely. It made me bitter.

"I want to want to belong here," I said. Though I did not. Her foreign art, her Persian rugs. I knew how she spent her time, and I attacked her for it. Slyly. She wanted a luxurious, unchallenged life, and I wanted his hand over my mouth and nose, his knee on my lungs like that still goat. If not to die, then to be fucked feverishly. And then awaken to the strands of sunlight and dense smoke of *Yeyo's* fire.


Our sessions offered something. They did help me see that I suffered the grief of a lone survivor. Everyone died in the tragedy but me, well, part of me. The part that stayed in Africa. In Boulder, stuffed with cake, we asked for more. Cake with too much frosting—the luxury of having too much—food, natural beauty, healthy good-looking people, incessant chatter. Few Americans, boiled in luxury, realize that wildness cannot breathe from underneath the *too much*.

I walked everywhere. I even dumped my bike. As long as I had my feet on the ground, I imagined him next to me. A slow, persistent amble. I remembered his voice when he walked behind me or the feel of his hand. I stopped therapy because I could not stand the jolting of the bus, and she lived too far to walk it.

Eight months after I returned from Kenya, I slept with a man. A kind man. I gave my body, nothing more. He lifted my hair off my cheek and said, "I'm afraid if I fall asleep, I'm going to wake up and find half of your face paralyzed, like you've had a stroke." Not exactly sweet nothings from this guy. "There's part of you that is … disconnected, uncirculated." I stopped seeing him.

Every day, I waited for the mail. Every day, the necklace walked with me. Letters still arrived despite my betrayal.

"Micah, *ngejuai*, I know you are very attractive to gents. The way you walk, the way you talk, and your golden waves of hair. Just remember there is a man who loves you, and he is waiting. He is strong enough."

I felt little surprise at his knowing. I asked to speak to him by phone. We arranged a day two-and-a-half months in the future. November came, two months shy of a year since we parted. When I heard his voice, his clear, low voice, it came like a stab. A relentless series of stabs. While crying, I told him about the other man.

"If you need a man it's okay. Keep part of your heart for me. And let's keep praying to see one another again. You did not do wrong, my melodious. Don't cry. *Nanyorai*, it's easy to be confused with this fucking distance."

"Please find a woman," I said. "If not a tourist, a Lokop girl. You are too lovely to be alone. And tell your parents so they are not waiting for me to return to marry you. We don't know, and I want them to know the truth."

"Okay. But you will always, always be my wife in my heart. We will always be."

His tone was certain, undoubting. I gripped the phone and thanked him without words. *We will always be.* Beyond marriage, beyond strength, stronger than this physical Earth and our sexual desires. Neither of us would ever let go.

But we did. Me first, again.

We wrote for eight years. We kept a moderate faith for our immoderate love. I left school, began a yoga practice, moved back to Carbondale, lived on a ranch, and started a landscaping business with my mom. He fled a civil war in Ukunda; the Digo were attempting ethnic genocide. All warriors left the beach. Big gap in correspondence. He was attacked by a lion. I sent money to help with the medical bills. I realized I couldn't work for the rich and famous in Aspen any longer and returned to Boulder to finish my degrees. Now, I could actually take the courses online, which suited me better. But I could not bridge the chasm of our lives. It tore me apart.

What kept my body moving when the pulse of true life had gone out? Momentum? Inertia? Habit? I cannot explain it. And yet I lived it, if we can call *that* forward stumble living.

The last correspondence came in 2000. He sent a cassette tape. In full voice, he chanted songs with *Imurran*. I could hear fire in the background, sometimes the sea. I could see his face and smell him. He spoke to Kas and my family, greeted them and told them his dream of meeting them one day. He ended, saying he would return to his village, where he was happiest and safest. I knew this meant he would not be writing. The space between our letters had spread so wide lifetimes erupted in between, and the possibility of life together closed.

One day, not so many months after hearing him sing, the nomad in me packed up her wisdom and walked on. A blossom would emerge from the African idyll. I knew it would. Eventually. But for now, those roots curled up in quiet dormancy.

First, a black-and-gold feral cat I named Tigre saved me—her hardiness and survival instinct, being close to another warm heart. She never gave up. A persistent, independent, heat-seeking missile. Tigre let me know I needed to keep trying. One morning, as she purred me awake, my pale body glinted like a rainbow-sprinkled cupcake. Our necklace had broken.

I didn't get out of bed for a while. When I did, I gathered each seed bead. Lintan chattered like a songbird, Natiyon stoked embers, *Apaya* rested or played games with other elders. Every bead a memory.

After Tigre, the Peace Corps lent a hand to my recovery. I met a director while tending bar. He invited me to lead a group abroad. I accepted and waited for my assignment with hope renewed. Then I tore a ligament in my knee, playing soccer. I limped for months, no longer a Peace Corps candidate. But I'd been roused. Some needling need had reawakened in me. I hobbled out to Los Angeles to study with an ill-reputed yogi named Bikram Choudhury. He of hot yoga fame. Despite his character, the yoga practice compressed and extended the sadness from my cells. That was rescue mission number two. I had always done yoga but now it felt like yoga did me.

My sister, Desi, and I opened a yoga studio in Denver. Desi excels in understanding nuanced physicality and teaching it as if no teaching has occurred. I began to love our students, loved watching their complicated bodies figure out how to unwind. My life took root in Denver. I confided in my mom and Desi but otherwise, I kept my African lover to myself, his story unspoken, his life unknown. In 2004, nine years after my trip, Desi and I ventured to Kenya to look for him. We asked every red-sheet-wearing warrior on the beach. No one knew him. Nothing was as before. A grand hotel cut the beach in half, and the makeshift warrior village had been taken over by Digo people. I cried in my little sister's lap. We did not find him or his family.

But Africa did influence our style of yoga. We took the curvy, dynamic strength of tribal dance rhythms back with us. We called it the Bowspring. An homage to the springiness and strength of spine. Where did we learn this? From our hearts, from their bodies, in Africa. We decided the masculine lineage of yoga could use a little more feminine fluidity. Butts were meant to mound. Bodies were meant to move. The physical alignment we admired in athletes, in Africans, in indigenous populations everywhere—we decided to wake up and join *that* human race.

Yoga means "union." I managed to yoke together the fragments of my loves: an African village, lions, fires, camels and their bells, the Colorado Mountains, my family, Tigre, good stories, ecstatic poetry, teaching, meditation, moving my body and breath, travel, the sea, my husband, and him.

I did marry. James and I met in a yoga class. He became my first meditation teacher, and, man, did he have his work cut out for him. His cornflower-blue eyes held such compassion. Every morning when the five o'clock alarm rang, I moaned with resistance. He knew the best way to love me was not to indulge me with chocolate or flowers. To love me was to love what I loved. Yoga. And meditation—eventually. Adventure. Africa. Even my lover. James's devotion to meditation allowed such spaciousness. He accepted the whole me.

Strenuous daily practice. Teaching and learning. Open-ended, long walks with our dog. Evenings of cooking and burning things, when I cooked, and laughter. In time, I started to feel grounded and calm.

Desi and I welcomed all who entered the doors of our jewel-purple exercise palace. I exorcised guilt, betrayal, lack of conviction, and my abandonment of the best part of me, while the Bowspring grew internationally and continued to transform lives.

*The sun streams in his mother's house. Sticks and dung, chanting and clapping. The Apayas call a male lion with their prayers. Scent answers. Scent comes. Tribal sacrifice. Quivering pulse in throat, in groin. Musk, Earth, male.*

*The beast pauses and tilts his mouth to the air. The clapping quickens. The cries quicken as the body strides slowly downhill toward me, raising dust. Naked, caged on the dirt floor, I pace a circle. He comes for me. Desperate to leave, I cannot escape, cowering in the dark corner as his massive head breaks through the opening. His hide sweats red, his eyes two gold-green suns. I smell him and want him and gasp.*

James pulled me closer, parting the blankets. "Shhh," he whispered, "another lion nightmare. Try and sleep some more, okay?"

My heart looped like a nimbus, like the curtains billowing out from the French doors. Whispers and strong thighs and boxer shorts would not give me what I needed. The oblivion of sleep and fine cotton sheets suffocated me more than my lion.

I got up to look at the moon. Nine thousand miles. Hundreds of letters, most lost to the wind. Fifteen -and-a -half years after I left him in Nairobi, I slipped off my nightgown and bathed in moonlight, warm as the veldt, vast as my longing for Nanaiiolo. If Natiyon could hear my inmost hidden moan, somehow my suffering would count.

James listened, which helped the years pass. I told him about the long treks and the warrior ochre and wild dancing. We shared the stories delicately. Objects on Micah's favorite shelf. We admired them and kept them safe but never picked them up. One evening, my strong, supple body suffered an asthma attack. I lay gasping on the bungalow floor. I could not breathe and could not die without knowing Nanaiiolo's fate.

James carried me to bed and spooned me when my breathing normalized.

Before sleeping, I whispered, "James, I have to go."

"I know."

Travel plans absorbed my every hour. I had no idea if he was alive. I had no idea just where he lived. I daydreamed about what he would look like, how he would look at me when I told him how I had healed so many relationships, with men, especially with my father, because of him. My ears wanted to be full on his language, his voice, my eyes on the land, animals, and people I still carried within. If he had a wife, I would love her. And if he were dead, well, I could not grieve his death in America. I had to let my tears fall into the dry, cracked body of land he called home.

But I knew he was alive. I could feel him since I'd decided to return. I had always remembered him, cherished him, but something was different now. Maybe our old portal had broken open again.

There was another thing—I wanted to experience the harshness of Kenyan nomads, the drought, the effects of climate change, the dangerous wilderness and cattle raids. I wanted to scrape the hideous frosting off my sweet-ass cake of a life and get real.

Terrified as I was, I trusted Kenya to do just that. I missed her terribly.

I spread every one of his letters in a semi-circle, arranged by date, and found the most recent, which was still seven-year-old news. His brothers had moved away except for two, neither of whom spoke English. I assumed his parents were no longer living, but held out hope for Lintan. She would be married now. I had two short sentences to go on: "Lintan has asked me to choose her husband. His name is Lalesho, and they live in Lamaresh."

When Desi and I had looked for him in 2004, we'd focused on Ukunda. The beach, the baobab tree, the new warrior dance clan—all empty of him. I hadn't considered Lamaresh. Daunted by the impossible trek to the village alone, we had stopped there. This time, I had to get closer. Even if I couldn't make it all the way to Nanaiiolo, I could search for Lintan in Lamaresh. I gave myself a month and a half. James only sighed.

Plan A: Fly to Nairobi, take a *matatu* along the perilous Lamaresh road and struggle with the language and all of the strangers there until I acquired some information. When I knew Lintan last, she did not speak Kiswahili. *Dear Lintan.* What then?

When I last saw her, she was ten. It might be awkward if she did not remember me. We were so warm together. I kissed her head, she lifted my shirt. I wished for that special intimacy again. The thought of her turning away from our closeness triggered a storm of fear. Fears flew even as I welcomed the challenges ahead. How would I manage the walk to the village? How could I find the village without a guide? Maybe his wife or family would reject me. Maybe he would be angry that I came back. What would I eat now? My yoga diet would definitely suffer. And yet I longed to taste ashy camel milk again. With ginger, in chai, piping hot.

Plan B: If I could not find Lintan in Lamaresh—and here my heart actually ached at the imagined loss—I would hire someone to walk with me to Nanaiiolo. A stranger. Among lions. Who did not hold me dear. *No, please.*

Plan C: No traces of anyone. No paths back to him. I would retreat somewhere, sulk and write. Maybe go on a traditional Kenyan safari for diversion, to admire the wilderness. No matter what you planned, Africa undid the plans and dreamed up adventure. Risky adventures, over and over.

Before leaving, I asked Desi to repair our necklace. It now had stout string and a modern clasp. I would offer it to his wife, if he had one, or return it to Natiyon, if she lived. I imagined looping it over Lintan's neck, if her mother was gone. Until then, I wore it.

James packed a large box of cereals, dried fruit, cans of tuna fish, roasted nuts, and cacao protein bars to mail ahead of my arrival in Nairobi. Something about his hands, the way he carefully folded the cardboard, let me know I had sacrificed my marriage. We did not speak about it then. Unlike my cassette and photos, James' food package would arrive. Never mind that most of its contents would be eaten or at least sampled. Kenya's drought had been the headliner for years, and people were desperate.

I will hand it to James: he did not think like a lovelorn college girl prancing about on a shoestring budget; that would be me and my planning. He'd read about the Somali bandits who hid and shot out *matatu* tires on the road from Nairobi to Lamaresh and then robbed or kidnapped the passengers. I admit, the kidnapping and the Nairobi *matatu* station scared me most. Navigating the harassing touts with my heavy backpack and rusty Kiswahili would not be easy, nor would it be a snap convincing an entire bus of people to save one seat for a gun.

With his sandy brown hair slicked back, ready for work, James said, more than a little annoyed, "Honey, you are not twenty, a student or broke. Why are you traveling like one? Let's hire a car to pick you up from the airport and drive you all the way to the village. Forget that crazy bus station. We'll get a guy with a gun."

The extravagance silenced me. The sheer difference then to now. The remote no longer remote at all?

"I know there's no road but if you can walk there, a Land Cruiser can manage."

A Land Cruiser trailing dust and scaring elephants all the way to Nanaiiolo? It felt beyond reason. But because this solved so many unknowns, I fell into it like soft wool. And I fell into what I loved most in James—his rise to be the protector, rough African terrain thousands of miles away notwithstanding. More than a little relieved, I said, "Thank you."

Via Skype, I hired a car and two drivers—one fluent in Gutok from the Sai tribe. Both knew we were headed into rough terrain as well as bandit country.

James had made one more request. I rented a satellite phone so that no matter how remote the village now was, I could stay in touch. Who knew the phone was the size of the satellite it used to communicate my whereabouts? My African lover's surname translated into: *people who like to live without neighbors.* What about Land Cruisers pulling up to the acacia fence? What about hired guns? What about eavesdropping from the heavens? As though the Atlantic was not far enough from his village—how about the stars?

On the plane, I read a letter I'd brought with me, a safety net, a paper talisman.

He wrote, "Because of the fighting and the danger of being outside the compound, I will not be able to send you a letter so we will have to communicate in the traditional way which I know you are aware. This is how I communicate with my family in the village to let them know I am coming."

I let him know. *I am coming.* I repeated. *I am coming.*

What does a satellite phone have on telepathy? I held the letter to my heart, took a deep breath, and felt ready. Courage leapt with me into the many unknowns.

Jet lag takes prisoners. I gave myself a day to recover from the twenty-five hour travel day in a Nairobi hotel. My window framed a leafless tree in the Jevangee Gardens. Stark beauty in this filthy city. The tree's bare branches reached out to clusters of purple flowers like fingertips, tiny trumpets, paper thin prayers for water. A warm Nairobi breeze rustled them.

I visited the tree. I forced myself to stay awake, walking the gardens, stepping over trash. I told myself, *Once someone knows the name of this tree, I can sleep.* I asked every person who passed, male and female, young and old. I circled it, this leafless fulcrum of my universe, pointing up to it. People shook their heads. Some ignored me, some laughed. I walked for over an hour until the sun set and the darkness made sight difficult.

He would have known the name.

Mulu and Landa arrived in the morning. Young Mulu was of the Kamba tribe, a relation to the Nairobi-dominant Kikuyu. Landa spoke Gutok. His big belly pulled his striped knit shirt, dimpling at his navel. His head was shaved—typical of elder Sai. I drew them into the room, to help with my bags, and asked, "Before we go, what is the name of this tree?"

Without pause Landa looked out and said, "It's called Jacaranda, in English." The Sai, like the Lokop, named the entire natural world; the name itself not important, but the unspoken prayer which followed, very.

They escorted me to the olive-green Land Cruiser/chariot. Capacity: eight (large) people. I felt tiny in the back by myself, hopping side to side for the best view. When the city fell behind us, far behind, and the pavement finally ended, I started to feel symphonic. This was the agrarian south, fields, Kenya's greenhouse, fertile people of the seed. I was here and the sky had no end, and we seemed unstoppable, although the potholes slowed us some and tossed me around that huge backseat like a miniature poodle.

Landa drove north, toward Nanaiiolo.

I tried all six seats like Goldilocks, and Mulu laughed. He seemed ready for anything. Fit, muscular, and talkative, Mulu was the metaphoric *gun*. We would stop nearer the final stretch to Lamaresh to hire the real guns. I'd chosen well via Skype, judging by Mulu's biceps and his grin. This guy had eaten the breakfast of champions today and every other day. He jammed his arms on the seat and asked me what we were after.

"I'm looking for a nomadic family, Lokop. I haven't seen them in sixteen years. I was—I am in love with their son."

They cocked their heads and looked dubious: *another crazy white person.* Mulu shut the binoculars into the glovebox with a thud. Landa said, "So, no bird watching? We are Kenyan, but we have never been to this far place. It's rough. And you say you stayed in those villages? Those animal beds? Hah!" He shot Mulu a glance and rolled up his sleeves.

But I knew better than to believe his theatrics. The Sai and Lokop were like one tribe, Gutok a derivation of Maa, Landa's native tongue. If he knew Jacaranda, he knew cow skins. He may not have been to Nanaiiolo, but he knew their ways like his own.

I had paid for three days' driving; one to drive north, one to bulldoze to the village, and one long return day—but the return to Nairobi would either be with or without me. I cannot say why I picked three. Maybe because it is a triumvirate: one stubborn white American, two modern Kenyans, and a moon-dancing village from antiquity. What could go wrong?

We had a nine-hour drive to Lamaresh, if all went well. I gripped the armrest and felt a pang. Was I endangering these guys' lives? Would the village even receive them? Tribal issues were real. I recited a spell under my breath, one of few biblical verses I knew, "Wherever two or three are gathered in my name, there I am ..." *Okay, Jesus, now's your time.*

The road to Lamaresh cut through the venerable Rift Valley, the cradle of civilization, and rose with the escarpment to a breathtaking overlook.

The green hills behind us, the edge of the Sahel in the distance. Cool air invigorating as it spun into the sky and floated down to the valley floor. Mulu was eating roasted maize from a vendor and taking in the view. Landa stood, speaking to the wind. The Sai were once the only human inhabitants for thousands of miles, running with elephants and lions, feet treading over the bones of all our ancestors in the ground vault. Every single time I had journeyed to and from Lamaresh, we had stopped here to pay homage. The Leakys and others are still unearthing those bone families. This place, the beginning of all story.

In time, I welcomed the rise of low-spreading acacias, icons of the East African safari. With needle-tipped, thorny branches and yellow pom flowers, they meant dryness, savanna, the end of agriculture. The land of walking, roaming shepherds. Wisdom keepers. My keepers. Mulu, from an agrarian culture, shifted his weight and gawked like a tourist. "Look at that thirsty lake," he said, pointing.

Lake Nakuru. *I once got engaged there,* I thought, and rotated the necklace clasp on my wrist. I loved secrets. I wore his beads there, not on my neck, out of respect for James and him. How could I sashay in and meet his wife, after sixteen years, wearing our necklace for all to see. *That* was thirsty!

The lake had forfeited its boundaries to drought. Flamingos still made for an uneven blanket of pink, but the hippos we had bumped into from the dhow, years ago, had lost their habitat. Mulu gaped and I mourned. I knew those flaring nostrils, the slow groupings and sudden assaults, their need for sneaky submersion.

Landa leaned into the wheel and hunched his shoulders. He said, "It will be even drier where we are going. You will see the land change to the north, and you will not see water even where there were rivers. It is a terrible drought. Are you ready?"

My mom likes to ask me this. *Are you ready?* I may have all the right shit with me, but, no, I am never ready to watch animals and people die because of climate, because of choices I have made and continue to make. The savanna had clearly suffered. If my lover was all twisted up in this drought, so was I.

Mulu turned to me and answered Landa, "She has no choice. Ready or not."

I pressed my face to the window and forced myself to be devastated, to not look away.

Ready or not, I had once dived off a rickety railroad bridge, two hundred feet up. The sharp approach of the rocks below and the suspended mystery of whether the bungee cord would retract in time—well, that "once" became many times. I dove often. I courted and allayed fear like a warrioress on a string.

A flash of faces from the car window brought me back. Two skinny kids in school uniforms stopped beside us, excited by the Cruiser. I waved at them. They wanted candy and pens, just like sixteen years ago. I opened my window and managed a few words in Kiswahili. I shared my energy bars with them. They laughed with suns in their cheeks. My heart rose.

*Ready or not, here I come.*

We pulled into the dirt parking lot at Nyahururu Falls. Not much had changed. Touts approached to sell me things, but when I declined swiftly in Kiswahili, they backed down. I hadn't spent a year in Africa to be intimidated by people trying to sell me stuff.

The waterfalls ran in thinning strands so slim, I grabbed Mulu's hand and sat. Baboons bathed and groomed at the muddy base. They looked up, wide-eyed, almost worried. Or were they imitating what they saw in us? Nyahururu means *the sound of cascading water*—this sound was a whisper. I stared at the whisper. Water, the source of life, nearly a memory here. I refused to grow nostalgic. While they fueled the car, I hiked down and opened my fingers to the trickle. Terrifyingly warm. I said a quick apology to the baboons. I felt no wrath and no bravery. *She has no choice.*

We stopped a final time at a small post, two hours outside of Lamaresh. Landa helped hire two armed policemen, or rather police boys. *Finally, someone in the backseat with me,* I thought. But mission seriousness pursed their lips tight. They hardly looked at me, hands wrapped around their semi-automatic rifles. In total silence, mile after mile, I appreciated their dedication. To be kidnapped, raped, and killed by bandits was no karmic fate for this do-gooder yogi, fingers crossed. The younger boy fell asleep on the washboard roads, the barrel pointed at the soft hollow under his chin. Mulu giggled with me in the rearview mirror, reached back and shifted the barrel to one side. Landa *tssked.*

The closer we came to Lamaresh, the more the road broke apart with thirst. The infrastructures of the centralized Kenyan government stopped long before Lokop territory, leaving the spear-wielding wise ones to fend for themselves—Kenya's version of our Wild West. The Cruiser hit raised mounds of Earth the size of small camel's humps. Mulu took his turn driving now. He swerved to miss the more damaging domes and depressions. Red dust lifted from the bottom of the truck and settled on our faces. The soldiers sat alert. I kept steady but I was a wreck inside. All the vivacity my first trip elicited came plowing through. Mulu continued gripping the dusty wheel without complaint.

Thirty minutes from Lamaresh, the first large animals appeared. Not as I had remembered them. Gaunt giraffes towered over barren tree tops. A mixed herd of zebras and impalas sorted gravel, from habit, no food in sight. Two red-sheeted shepherds walked alone across the savanna. My breathing grew jagged. The years of lion dreams came back, that cellular haunting, that danger. This time, I knew the danger was me. I saw through all the years of frustrated concern for him and his family, that it was my family, my country—the biting hesitation I lived with turning on a tap, taking a bath, driving a car—our cataclysmic choices had penetrated this piece of idyllic Earth and fucked her desolate.

So much self-conscious disgust partnered up in the backseat that I could barely breathe. *She has no choice. She is here to make amends, make love, or make a mess. Only* N'kai *knows. She has no choice because she still loves him.* Deeper than the disgust ran the undeniable and persistent need to be held by him and him alone.

I took off my wedding band.

Landa slowed the car as a lone bull elephant crossed. The vexed male turned his head toward us. His tusks outsized the Cruiser. His wrinkled hide had outsmarted poachers and hunters and rivals. Lack of water had yet to weaken his resolve, but I feared it was coming. The men in the car sat silent. We waited for the bull to pass. I bowed down in my heart to all elephants, magnanimous family of mine. The young bull stomped in a feint attack and dashed into the brush. Dirt rose skyward. Every live body here, also part ghost.

Nanaiiolo would be a prairie of kindling, primed for Shiva's fire.

When at last I saw Lamaresh, adrenaline tore through my body. We stopped briefly to let the hired guns out, clear of bandit territory. The tire roundabouts, red *shukas*, dusty market lot, fluent cadences. I had my windows down. I had more desire to see him than I knew existed. My eyes kept tearing, underarms sweating. My yogic equipoise threw in the towel, vanquished by racing fear and desire. I would know soon. Undeniable then. Soon.

Landa, ever the responsible guide, broke my spell. "Write all the names for me, and I will look for an elder to ask." *Oh, God, we are ready to ask.* My hand wavered. I wrote in order of hopefulness: My lover, his parents, Lintan and her husband. I also jotted down his brothers' names. From the Land Cruiser window, Landa leaned out and greeted an elder, a man in his seventies, sunken cheeks and faded baseball cap, who politely refused to help us. The hired guns got out and walked on. Mission accomplished for them.

Landa told my story. The old man softened, looked directly at me, and said he did not know my lover. He did know Nanaiiolo. In Gutok, blessed Gutok, he tried to convince us we could not make it there, not even in this car. I listened to the energy. I needed no translation. I grew excited hearing their language. Then I heard my lover's surname—its resonance shot through my body, and these few words came in a whisper: *My ear, my sweet ear, I am near.*

I was not sure if they were mine or his.

The elder asked again who we sought. He did not know my lover's father but he recognized the family name. I pleaded with a smile.

*Wait*, his eyes said. He did know of Lalesho, the husband, married to, *yes*, a girl from Nanaiiolo.

My heart raced. He knew Lintan! The muscles in my cheeks tightened. I wanted to grab on and hug this slow-talking, slope-shouldered old man.

Lalesho was an elected politician, he said, a representative from the Lokop people to Nairobi. And then, the trail cooled. He talked with Landa of other things, as if the branches of a tall, communal tree spread over them, these elders with their tales and gossip.

I asked Mulu why we couldn't learn more about where Lalesho might be.

Mulu rubbed his fingers on his thumb, the universal sign of money.

I smacked Landa's shoulder from the backseat, with a little jabbing kindness, and said, "What does he want?"

Landa grinned very slowly and turned to me. "The old man wants a beer."

This moment, this long-imagined reunion that rushed my blood and agitated all peace for a mere sixteen years, this reunion that kept me alive and broke me with longing, was it worth a single beer?

"Hell, yes!" I said and reached for the shilling and a tip.

The rail-thin elder climbed into the front next to Mulu. Apparently, this white tourist needed the entire back to herself. As tears filled my eyes, the *Apaya* reached his wrinkled hand back, without turning. I grabbed on.

*Apaya?*

*Ditai!*

Still able to hear the sacred voice of the universe, I wept.

We drove south of Lamaresh for a handful of minutes, passed shepherds grazing skinny cattle and goats feeding on what little green lifted its head on the soccer field. Lamaresh, bordered by cedar forest, always kept the most water.

"Yes, he is the town counselor, Lalesho. Lalesho married this girl, Lintan," the old man repeated, quite proud of his assistance. He pointed to a curving dirt road. Mulu watched me in the mirror as tears streaked my face and the dust of Africa once again coated my eyelashes.

We pulled into the huge compound enclosed not by acacia fence or concrete wall but by the radiant green spires of poisonous cacti native only to Lamaresh. I adored these trees. Neptune trees, I called them, for their forked staffs. They stood so thorny and tall, only the camels ate them, and each night shepherds pulled cactus spines from the camels' tender muzzles, even their eyes. To love the taste of something so much you risked splintering your nerve-rich face! I felt kinship. I felt a ridiculous, unhinged love for those camels.

Lalesho and Lintan's home stood solidly before us. Un-milled posts, straight from the forest, stacked upright, linked with white concrete. Two small windows and the front door, trimmed in chipped, sky-blue paint. It was Sunday, about four in the afternoon. I had never been so aware of breathing.

Landa said, "Your counselor is a rich man," and shot a glance at the green Land Rover parked outside.

To my American eyes, the vehicle looked in disrepair and might not even run, but yes, to own a vehicle here, a lot of money was required. We got out of the car, stopping short of the house. Two children played a dusty game of chase, naked as turtles. Three dogs howled, and a cat that resembled my Tigre frisked by. A man with a pit bull build, in camouflage pants and a button-down shirt, emerged. He had an intensity about him, a fearlessness locked in his eyes. Though short, his posture and the way he approached us said *tall*. Everyone gathered to hear our business, people and animals. I waited for Landa to explain, my face stone still. The man scrutinized me. He was modern—in his dress, his style of home, his desires. I had pictured someone more connected to tradition but I understood why my lover would have chosen him for his sister. Lintan would want for little. Lalesho appeared my same age, relatively young for politics or a car. Ambitious.

I could feel her in him.

The elder, ragged by anyone's standards, backed down the driveway at sight of him. I missed how these nomads wandered with nary a word. They kept vanishing into their land, maybe this one, in search of beer.

Lalesho turned to me and said in good English, "I am the one you are looking for. I am the husband to Lintan."

I gasped. "Is she here? Is Lintan here now?" I fumbled with how to say this in Gutok, in Kiswahili, in French, Spanish or silence, longing to get his reply.

"Yes, she is just inside. *Karibu*."

He led and I followed him in. My eyes struggled with the darkness. Twenty or more people looked at me, some traditionally dressed, some not. Overwhelm struck me like a blast of wind. Not like this. Not after so long. I walked rudely backward, without a word. I waited for her in the sunlight, the breeze brushing my cheek. At our last embrace, Lintan's pretty face had twisted with parting, those sweet eyes closed with grief. I could hear her raspy voice, singing, crying when she embraced her brother, teaching us the names of plants.

Lalesho led her out by the hand, telling her who had come to visit, but before he could finish, she saw me. "*Micahai?*"

"Lintan!" I cried. She made an astonished sound, mixed with rapid speech. A burnished, T-shirt- and skirt-wearing woman with enormous, wet brown eyes and wild hair rushed to grab my hand. She led me roughly to the side of the house. We needed to be alone with our hearts torn wide and our strained communication, our memories and the empty years. She hugged me so tightly our bodies lost distinction. Emotion cycled from me to her and back. She ran her hands over me, held my face, touched my hair and pulled me into her breast only to push me away to see me again. She nuzzled her head into my neck, soaking me with tears. We alternately cried and named each other, which was the truest language we knew. It was almost deafening, what the few words carried.

"Oh, Lintan!"

"*Eyah yah yah*, Micah, *N'kai!*"

"Lintan. *Oye* Lintan!"

"*Oye, oye Micahai!*"

Then my beloved sister turned away, collapsed onto her home, placed her head on a window ledge, and convulsed with agonizing wails.

*Oh, God, no!*

I hurried to her, held her, and said, "It's okay. It's okay," but I knew I had no right to say this.

Lalesho had followed us, full of concern. "We have a lot of people in the home. They are doing some preaching. It is Sunday." My heart iced a little; was his concern for Lintan or for his guests' opinions of her anguished cries?

"I came to see this family only. I came to see Lintan and her brother. I have not heard from him for eight years. I must know. Is he alive?"

"I tried very hard for that man. I really tried," he said.

I turned my full attention on Lalesho's every word. What did he mean by trying?

"I stayed with him for many months in Lamba District Hospital."

My heart stammered, *No, not an airport, not a hospital. Why? Why not his village?*

"Before that, he stayed in our home." He looked at me to see if he should continue. He vetted the details. "I don't know what, some sickness, some cancer in the leg that started in his foot and moved up his body to his chest."

*Which fucking beautiful leg?* "No, no, no," I said. I looked at the ground, the sky. *Take them back, please! Take the words back.* I shook and my breath caught, then panted, held back and rushed like some live animal trapped in the dark.

Lintan reached for me.

"No, no, no," I whispered.

I sobbed, and he kept talking. I held Lintan. I stopped hearing. He kept talking because there was nothing left to do with this awkward, emotional white woman who could not say anything but *no.*

"It has been some time, maybe five or six years at least." *Nomads and their no-time. If it were four years, I was here with Desi looking for him.* But this thought was a cactus thorn to my heart. I stayed away. *I knew Lalesho truly did not even know the year.*

"I really struggled with that man. Be strong, please." He put his hand on my shoulder to quiet me but my body quaked, all but undone. Lintan yelped. Her brother had been her joy all those years, how she must have cried when he—

She collapsed, and we fell together onto the cedar house and wept. Those fragrant, scraggly trees took us in, always strong, always a part of us.

No *us.* No longer any *us.*

I could not stand up by myself. I leaned into the cedars.

Lintan wiped her eyes on her sleeve.

I asked the stranger, the pious African counselor who owned this house, "Where are his wife and children?"

Lalesho winced with distaste. "He never loved again. You were the only woman he brought to his village." His curt words brought ravaging burn. "He told me you were his wife."

I turned from them. I turned from Lintan's longing and Lalesho's strict, ordered world to the truth. My lover dead, without wife or child, leg cancer that had raged up into his chest, and my inconstancy as clear as his loyalty. Where was the refuge from that? That perfect man, my lion, my warrior, gone. Never together in Natiyon's smoky hut, with morning's softness slung over his shoulder. Nothing would ever exist with that exacting beauty again. My son of god, son of *N'kai,* sun of this vast desert, gone.

Such was the purity of death.

*Let me die, too.*

I walked a few steps toward the cactus trees, needing a quiet place to myself. Even that need crumbled. I saw the sister I wanted to protect, the man in military fatigues urging me to be strong, two guides from Nairobi eager to hear the news, and I heard the strains of an awkward hymn coming from a congregation of preaching strangers. Such hideous imperfection he left.

I forced the tears back.

*He is gone?*

His family had already grieved. How could I ask them to witness my grief? All the regret, all the prayers to be unraveled would have to wait. As the afternoon sun weakened, I held Lintan and stroked her hair. I asked Lalesho about her brothers. He confirmed they were alive, looking after animals far from the village. I resisted asking about her parents. Enough ghosts traveled with me.

He said, with eyes flashing, reading my heart, "The parents of Lintan are still living. They are in the village."

"*Yeyai* and *Apayai!*"

He broke off a thorn and used it as a toothpick, impressed I knew how to call them.

I watched the thorn crease his dry lips. I had to trust him.

"Can you take me to them? Tomorrow? We can drive the car I have hired. They will drive."

"I will send my brother Luca. He knows the way. He is *Imurran*." I knew this meant that Luca spoke no English but Landa would translate and I needed few words. It would all be okay. I could see them. I could see them for their son.

Lalesho gestured for us to move inside.

Before he brought me into the *Praise the lord!* house, I distracted him. I asked him to take me shopping and asked what the family might need. To show up after sixteen years without gifts would be unforgivable, and in this drought, even perilous.

"I am happy you are thinking about this," he said. "They are suffering too much. Three years, no rain."

"Can Lintan come to the village with us?" I felt Lintan's hand in mine grip tighter. I squeezed back.

"No, she has too many shildrens," he said with a Cheshire smile across his face. The first I had seen from him, a father's smile.

Before I let Lintan's hand go, I said, "Shildrens? I want to meet them all." I kissed her head. I still stood a little taller than my sister.

Landa and Mulu agreed to meet at Lalesho's home at eight in the morning. They made sure I had a place to sleep. Once they'd unloaded my pack from the Land Cruiser, Landa quieted his huffing breath. He touched his eye as if ash had fallen into it. He said, "I am sorry, Micah. This news has made you very sad, even me. Are you sure you feel safe here?"

"Thank you for everything. They will find me a home for the night. Tomorrow we will fill this car with supplies for the village. Yes?"

Mulu stood beside him, gazing up at the cacti, growing to the stars.

"Yes," Landa said kindly, and my two guides left.

Lalesho took pity on my agonized traveler bones. "Micah, I know a lodging, away from this *kelele*," which means noise. I was so tired I could have slept propped against his cactus fence during an African drumming circle. "But first we go shopping." He lugged my pack into their home. It was funny. His head wobbled ever so slightly as he walked, like he was dodging something. His senses were that keen.

I had a few minutes to myself. With the news. With Lintan's tears still on my neck. Many of his letters had recalled our walking pilgrimage. The pleasures and dangers we had shared. I felt the pleasure he would have experienced by my return. I was in shock, but something stirred—something other than my own organs and heartbeat moved. Maybe it was trauma. But it felt like grace. Grief and grace sitting together on the open savanna, in my raw heart.

Lalesho drove us to town before the close of business. Tape covered the Land Rover's back window completely. The shocks were bad but the engine roared with gusto. Seven minutes flew by with intermittent stops, picking up elderly women and their belongings, dropping children at the intersection of their homes. Everyone caught up on the day's news. I may have been part of that news, I don't know. The cultural whims didn't make an impression. I do not remember how we arrived into town. I simply rode my regret. Grief demanded all of me.

"Buy as much as we can carry," I told him. "Buy whatever they usually eat. Buy a lot. I have the money. Buy something for Lintan and your children, too." I waited in the car while he did the shopping.

I waited with no expectations.

Large bags of relief maize, rice, and sugar tested the shocks. Then tea, tobacco, cooking fat, water, and milk landed in back. Lalesho had many animals at home. I saw the fenced-in pens that allowed for freedom—shepherds may leave their remote village, but they rarely leave shepherding. Tallow bars of pink soap mixed up with sweets for the children. Lastly, Lalesho handed in ornate new clothes for his parents. He asked me to feel the fabric. He handled all negotiations. He tipped the men loading the car and smiled at me, at this generous lift to his people, whom I had never met.

He smiled and the Rover roared. "When a shepherd comes home in peace, the milk is sweet."

Lintan's five children stared at the strange white woman, the bandana and sunglasses on her head, the bare arms and quick-dry safari pants. Well, four of them stared, and ducked their chins shyly. The fifth, a month-old baby, only cooed. How the oldest, Kitinta, must have loved her uncle. *They would have had a fifteen-year-old cousin,* I thought, too raw to engage the kids. I looked at them, one to the next. I thought the oldest son had a smile like his, a slight rise to his fine eyebrows that reminded me of my lover. Lalesho made introductions all around, mercifully brief. The Christians were gone now. I went to Lintan.

She stood outside in a trance. She clutched my shoulders and said my name several times. My heart reminisced when she smiled. She buried her head in my neck, both sides, hurriedly smelling me. She absorbed the body aromas, a type of storytelling for the senses. Was she, like her mother, subtly, infinitesimally aware? What had washed over me in sixteen years, leaving its scent as tracks to follow? Lintan touched the necklace, wrapped on my wrist, and stared at it lovingly, out of all time. When she was satiated, Lintan spoke. She asked Lalesho to translate.

"You are my family, my sister, and I never forgot about you, even though I was a child. This time how long can we stay together? When will you leave?" I wish I hadn't seen the desperation in her eyes but I did. It would take some time to get to the bottom of her life, and I quickly took up the responsibility, like a good sister-in-law.

"I will visit *kila siku*," I said, asking Lalesho to translate. "Every day. I came only to find your family. That is why I am in Africa. I can stay, Lintan. We will have time now."

She smiled, and I saw my lover's smile. They shared features, roundness, light. She had always laughed more, of course, but I saw his same humor in her, the same effect it had on others. Their likeness enchanted me and pained me. Like camels and the word *forever*.


At the Erayy Camel Club, Lalesho requested the "resident price," which I appreciated since I hoped to use it as my base camp for nearly six weeks. The Club had large gardens, grassy fields and lots of camels. Although the plants needed water, like everything, the gardener did his best. Fifteen dark, wooden cottages called *bandas*, bordered the grounds. Kas and I had skipped passed Erayy because of our budget. The swanky joint cost twelve dollars a night then. But Lalesho negotiated with Doris, the jovial manager, whose crude humor felt like Vaporub on my chest. I picked up a piece of honeycomb outside the office within earshot of the haggling. Erayy was perfect—a ten-minute walk from Lintan and forty minutes into town, which insulated me from random visitors. I felt blessed. Such an ideal place for grieving privately, yet I would not be completely alone.

Doris gave me my pick of the vacant *bandas*. I scanned the dry patches of lawn between them and the restaurant and chose number eight. From my porch, I had a view of the pool hall and buckets of raspberry-red bougainvillea, flowering acacias, light pink roses, and red geranium. Defiant blossoms amid all the barrenness.

The room seduced me. I felt instantly at home, mostly because I was alone. I did not have to share the two single beds with traditional blue and red checked quilts. Windows let in enough light to summon me from the dark cavern of grief. I would eventually need to move my sadness with words. Under one of the windows, with a perfect view of Nirisia Forest, sat a desk. In black permanent marker, someone had written on the shower wall, "Hot Water!" I should have written next to it: *Fat Chance*.

I hurried Lalesho out. I locked myself in and prepared the space for mourning. I used one desk to create an altar with my lover's photo in the center—a photo of him, bounding, mid-air, beads suspended, dancing—our marriage necklace, a candle James had sent with me, a miniature silver Ganesha statue, the honeycomb I found, and a feather that fell from a dove when I first arrived. Oh, and a dried marigold, mostly closed, edged in true orange. It seemed to me that orange defied gravity.

I unknotted the mosquito netting, took a brief (freezing) shower, changed clothes and brushed my teeth. It was only six in the evening but I climbed under the net into bed. A chill rushed my body. Lamaresh was colder at night like most desert climates. But what was this? A deep, deep cold. I could not warm myself. Dehydrated from travel and crying, my muscles seized. It was subtle at first. I couldn't get water down yet my body withered with dry chill. The core of my bones ached. My skin felt bruised. A headache pummeled and throbbed, inside out. Within an hour, disabled with fever, I lost track of the onslaught of symptoms.

Sometime between dusk and dawn, it came to me. The female anopheles bite at night. Tireless mosquitoes. I scrambled out of the net to my first-aid kit and downed the homeopathic remedy for malaria.

I took a breath and closed my eyes and felt the malaria, the burning virus, penetrate everything. Hot skin, hot desire, chilly bones, camel herds the color of dust, dead rivers, animal hides, sweaty sheets, sweaty airport security, too many smells in that Nairobi airport.

I saw him, waving goodbye. At the Nairobi airport with hope collapsing all around us. Why didn't I look once more? Just once. Return to him. Hold him once more.

Dreaming or awake? Either way, I now saw him.

"You must stay alive for many reasons—" I say, refusing the long corridor, the ticket to America, the goodbye. Warriors do not cry, but Ploote wrote and told me, "Cousin bled from his nose in the taxi. The pressure of you leaving too much."

*Do you know what those words are doing to me now?*

Tears wrack my slack body. Exhausted convulsions.

Then those beautiful salted waves of a beach pull him into cerulean blue. A refuge.

My arms reach for him.

I try to bargain with the waves, I plunge out to him and grasp his back. We take steps together washed with blue. I feel him smile. *Why a smile?* the fever asks. *Why now? Where are we? Where have you gone?* But he is not gone, my arm cinches him to me like dawn to the sun. He turns. We turn in the wave. He smiles across the sky, so big, the smile lifts all suffering and I feel—giddy. Scatterbrained and sweet. Silly as a girl.

*Oh, you think malaria's funny?* I say, disbelieving.

At that, we both crack up.

*No thinking, no thinking at all, my ear, my leg, my darly.*

And then, dry sky. I see him try with earnest ease to convince a magnificent celestial counsel to let me come to him. Beads drape their chests. Ochre paints their faces. But like the mighty INS, we have no control of these things. The elders belch as they listen to his plea. I giggle so hard I return to pure fever. I burn so bright. Every sensation as painful and true as loving him.

*It is possible to die before we die, my darly.* A hostage of heartbreak, I died that night. Surrendered all before my last exhale. I died on an in-breath. I danced with the pain in goofy rapture, releasing sensations as quickly and easily as stacking dishes at a yard sale. Bye dishes, bye love, bye life decisions. Neighbors, please take all. My body writhed as my soul galloped with glee to the end. Hips screaming. Head pounding. Nauseous. He brought ecstasy. Spitty-mouthed, burning up and ecstatic.

Riding his shoulders, lifting me into the reflected light bouncing off those waves and sweet Kas taking pictures.

*Let's keep walking into that blue, deeper yet, carry me.*

Long before dawn, he sent me living gifts. On the flimsy sheen of the net, crawling up with strong, slight legs—an ant, a fiery red African ant that had eluded the barricade of Erayy Camel Club walls. It kept company with wealthy tourists, lowly herders, and cherished specters alike. Through tears, I smiled at the intruder who belonged and rescued me.

I watched its delicate ascent. The memory of my labia swollen and stung with ant pincers. His ant-burning Christmas trail. Our laughter. Surely, he was here.

I touched my hot breasts. *He* was the ant, he was the presence. The everyday hum of him that familiar. I sobbed and ran my hands over my body, my shaky belly, my vagina. When the ant reached the apex of the tent, it vanished in the folds. I vanished in climax. Then, silence. No hum. He dwelled in silence now. I could live there with him, too.

I turned and sighed and drifted deliriously between waking and fever stories.

When I sat up, dark of night, the big red ant marched sideways at eye level. I slithered from bed, trapped it in a glass, examined it when it fell to the bottom, and raced to the door before it climbed out. My breathing quickened, sweaty with the exhilaration of play.

Bumping toward the door, I thanked him. I asked him never to stop.

The light of the quarter moon showed me the second gift. A black feather, glistening at my feet. A wet feather, though the night was utterly dry. Not one wisp out of line, all flowing together, ready to fly. *Volant as he.* I slid the ant gently out. I picked up my feather and tickled my neck with its soft tips, and moaned. Sough in cedars. I went to the shrine and laid it beside the other devotions. The candle burned orange-blue. I crawled back in bed, mosquitoes trailing. A whole highway of them, maybe.

He sent an ant and a feather. Maybe he sent malaria, too—a pretty word when it is not tormenting your body. Instead of leaving me to the seductive path of self-important grief, he sent spirit wisdom, a night of fever-induced cockamamie joy. No one can reach you locked in grief. Malaria reached me plenty. *Malarial Micah.* The name curled me into a fit of laughter. It hurt so much to laugh that hard. We, great human-kind, the bearers of so much history, conquest, creation, colonization, could not even put an end to mosquitoes. Malaria reigned. Ants stayed in camel lodges without checking in, rent-free. And departed lovers could travel anywhere. Was anything more ridiculous?

Humans. Silly two-leggeds. Will we ever learn to surrender to true love's grandeur?

He had. He laughed somewhere. I smiled like a bride.

Dawn entered the room. I drank a full liter of water, put wet tissues on my eyelids and tried to sleep because, apparently, I was not going to die.

When sunlight pushed the long night to the other side of the world, I tore my body from the bed. I found clothes, lightweight but long-sleeved for protection. Where the clothing touched my skin, nerves singed. I was so ill. But I had to make it to Nanaiiolo. He walked beside me, as I prepared to leave, funny and clear. Everything felt different. I swayed between devastation and ridiculousness. I let him help me pack for the trip. The fever had diminished and left a new absurd me. I tucked his photo into the pack. I wrapped our necklace around my wrist to give to Natiyon. We passed through the gate at Erayy. We walked a while, the gentle rhythm of walking felt good. Feet on the ground where they belonged.

The car appeared. Lalesho, not his brother, Luca, rode in back. I greeted everyone. I could feel my body's aches returning as we drove into town, but I prayed my way through them. I smiled at Lalesho. I thanked Landa for driving. I only cared to speak with my lover, so I stayed quiet. I waited for his lead. The hum, I don't know how else to call it, was where I found him, where he found me. This hum, the same desert-sand-through-fingers feeling, accompanied me when I had the asthma attack, even into James's arms.

Lamaresh fell behind us, the shops both old and new, and the hotel we'd spent the night in, where he washed my underwear. East of town, a rugged road climbed through the red dirt hills. Wild dogs crossed the road in a pack. For us, not for them, the water shortage was actually a blessing. Rain would have washed the road into a river and made the trip with supplies impossible.

Lalesho said, "My wife greets you. She could not sleep for the love she has for you." I would let Lintan know he was still with us. Everyone should see with the clarity of fever. I would find a way to comfort her. "I see you have suffered much," he said, softening. "I will do the best translation for you. Remember not to say his name to them. You know we do not say those names of dead. And you can leave the photo of him in the car. Both those things will cause much grieving."

I slipped the photo into my pack, not knowing exactly why I'd brought it, removed our necklace from my hot wrist and put it in my pants pocket. Lalesho was too quick. He noted it but said nothing. I did not need the warnings. I could not bear to say his name aloud. It belonged somewhere else now. It belonged in desert smells, in distant views, in lion manes and elephant memory. In a spear's point, in chanting and clattering beads. The red Earth and blue sky were now his name. And it was hallowed, to me.

"Drink this water, or I might have to start collecting your tears for you to drink. Your lips are dry," Lalesho said, handing me my bottle.

I wanted to say, *You should see my bones*, but the humor required too much follow through.

I sat in back, holding his hand. Tears and laughter alternated within as the road stretched long.

Landa said, "You really traveled those years ago? This road is very long and difficult even with a car."

"There was no road to Nanaiiolo," Lalesho told them. "She walked in the wild bush, like a warrior. The road is only five years old." They both turned to look at me with new regard.

The bush grew dense, denser than when I had traveled it with him, the land now clothed by a few drought-hardy plants. Even they showed stress, the leaves crackled and curled inward. We passed people, gaunt and thirsty, struggling to keep their livestock going, weak with hunger, striving for balance. My silliness succumbed to presence. I felt everything. Every living thing I saw had buried its head to bear the worst. I told Lalesho they still looked happier than most Americans. As we drove by, they slowed to smile or wave.

My heart leapt at their kindness. An awkward vision arose. Americans after Thanksgiving dinner, barely able to say farewell to their host, let alone to greet a stranger. "We don't wave to strangers," I said. "Even when we are full of food."

Lalesho heaved a sigh. He forced his body upright, having learned

I was a yoga teacher. He said, "They are too tired to complain. We know this life. Why not greet one another?" And his eyes flashed with hard-won wisdom that silenced me again.

The cattle were gone. Their corpses dried and bleached off the road. The nomads we passed came from harsh conditions—making one last attempt to find water and save their camels.

"And when the camels die?" I asked.

Lalesho shook his head with defeated laughter. He said he was awed that people so close to starvation were still moving. Nomads often laughed in the face of death. They still died. And when they died, they still laughed.

Goats and sheep straggled past the window. They had fared better in the drought. They ate anything and required less water. But even they were thin, just ribcages with legs, bumping from the road as the Land Cruiser herded them to the sides. Dik-diks, a tiny antelope with large bunny ears, scampered away from us, always in twos.

Mulu told us that his people, the Kamba, were famous for their hunting skill—their prowess in bringing down pairs.

Lalesho said, "Only our young boys hunt dik-dik."

Mulu balked and pulled the field glasses from the glove box, training them on things far away.

Catching my gaze, Lalesho added, "When one dies, the other will often commit suicide." The fire he carried! I felt the warrior behind the button-down shirt. My lover had also told me about those loyal mates. Salt in a wound, the sting still led me to love. All love. Only love. Even Lalesho, especially Lalesho, was a form of the world's tangled-up love.

When we rolled up and over the Nirisia Forest, home of the elephant prints I once saw, miles east of Lamaresh, I recognized the mounded boulders that anchor Lududuma's village. I thought of Kas. My distant friend. I would have to tell Kas.

I felt a little zing, a tingle as we passed his village. My lover had written off Lududuma's friendship. But now he winked. I felt it. He did not stop to judge, he just kept moving. His black, strong legs, his muscular feet that never tired of walking, of heading home—no indication that he might incur disease there, that he might die of anything from those clean, sturdy legs.

But as the boulders faded into dust haze, words of his came to me. Once in a letter he told me, "I am tired of walking."

My walking warrior. I wanted to rub my face on his feet.

"Kenya has nothing for me now," he wrote. Years and letters and dissipated love inhabited those words. Cancer and loss had walked with him instead of me. Now, he did not walk or hold grudges. He floated, unbound from country, from diseased body, even from me.

Lalesho patted the cushion next to him and pointed outside. "We need to use these all seats. Collect those two boys. They are walking a long distance to school." Landa stopped. Two boys respectfully greeted their elders, glanced quickly at me, the malaria-gray woman, and took the seats.

"That's kind," I said, preoccupied with our approach to Nanaiiolo and the crashing waves of sickness that kept coming.

"I attend Christian church," he said. "We must support our shildrens."

I got the feeling Lalesho was testing my religious zeal. I would have rathered he genuflect in savanna straw and cease handing humaneness to the Christians. But each of us had to find our own way. God knows mine was messy.

I rehearsed greeting the family, forced myself to a little distance through repetition. But distance and repetition brought the stifled tears rolling down my face. I wanted my room, my single red ant, my shrine, my griever's sanctum.

Lalesho handed me water.

Landa said, "Micah, we are nearing seventy kilometers! You really walked a long way."

Distance meant little when we had walked together. Every tree knot, each broken reed had enchanted me when it was the object at the end of his finger, his laughing eyes.

The past blasted me like a simoom sandstorm. Missing him took so much courage.

I leaned into the seat back's soft cushion. The beads in my pocket coiled. "We—" I said, "we walked it together."

Near the end of our four-hour journey, Lalesho showed me a school the government had built to integrate the Lokop into educated culture. The blocky school sat vacant, the few windows broken. I snickered like a clever hyena inside. *Their books are the animals, rocks, and plants. Their exam is their ability to endure. They are the professors of the essential—respect for nature, a return to balance and a life without plastic and oils.* But since I now enjoyed personal escort, thousands of miles from my home, in a fuel-guzzling Land Cruiser, I just chewed on my inner cheek. My soap box currently lacked the surface area of a Ritz cracker. Still, I itched, I physically longed to strap on a megaphone and shout Lokop superiority at those hideous gray cement brick walls. Given half a chance, I would have still tiptoed up onto that box—old preachy habits die hard—but the environs of Nanaiiolo came in sight.

I recognized the hills first. Then I spotted the boulders where Lintan took us to bathe. Thank God for the unchanging, seeming permanence of granite and basalt. Thank Goddess for the varying rates at which we dissolve, plant, animal, rock and human. When our beloveds breathed no longer, the rocks remembered hands dipped there into basins, to wash, to raise water from dust. Rocks remembered those prayerful hands.

The Land Crusier slowed and turned right as Lalesho pointed left. "There's her home—my mother-in-law, and the old man is sleeping under that tree."

The shape of Natiyon's hut. I clung to the window.

My *Apaya, Apayai,* curled and resting in the dappled shade.

The acacia fence torn and rattled.

No one else outside, not even children. A perilous, abandoned feeling held the whole village in silence. From sickness? The malaria suddenly burned my body, squeezed my head, and made seeing his parents even more dire.

*Apaya* rose and dusted himself at the sound of the car engine. He wrapped his red blanket about his chest and waist. Lalesho warned me, "They are old and fragile, too hungry. Let me explain slowly who you are so they will not fall down." I felt gratitude for his seriousness, his care.

Mulu and Landa watched us from behind the red-dirt caked windshield.

Lalesho walked to his father-in-law who tottered forward. I stayed hidden behind Lalesho's back until he finished greeting. My body knew to stay behind but my disobedient tears did not wait. I peeked out from behind him at the first pause in their speaking.

*Apaya* said my name in wonder. "*Micahai, ooh, oh oh, n'gareyai, que supat N'kai!*" He whooped with celebration, thanking God for how splendid God was for returning his daughter. My heart leapt at his words, the way he quietly possessed me by adding the sound *ai* to the end of my name. He took my hands in his, looking to the sky. The famine enfeebled his voice but his natural strength coursed between us, all father.

"*Apaya?*" I cried.

"*Ditai!*" His voice broke, shouting incantations and prayers. Our blended ruckus beckoned people from their noon slumbers. In all, Nanaiiolo had only a half-dozen homes left, and a smattering of goats. No camels at all. No *forever* camels. Natiyon, came from the dark archway of her home. Lalesho told *Apaya* a short, quick version of my return, and we all headed into the *manyatta* toward *Yeyai*, my Mama.

My mother came one step nervously forward, not quite sure what had started her husband praise-whooping. I stayed behind Lalesho's wet cotton back. But it became too much, as we all moved nearer, and I ran from behind him. With both hands I reached to hold her—to touch her after so many years.

"*Yeyai,*" I said softly, my voice quaking. The shock, the recognition, the grief literally moved her from me. She spun and ducked into her home, head down.

Lalesho slung his arm around my shoulder and assured me, "She's crying, it's okay. She knows you. Come this way."

In one rapid burst, I saw and lost sight of her face. I felt abandoned. I felt shame. *Patience*, the land said, *she sees more than you know. Apaya* urged us under the tree where we could talk. He busied himself bending and rising to gather wooden stools from the surrounding homes for everyone, so fragile. The last, he brought for Landa and Mulu, who blended into the moment.

Mulu reassured me with a hand on my shoulder, "She's really happy to see you, Micah. She'll come soon."

More villagers came to the shaded assembly. "Will you help him get chairs?" I asked him, motioning to *Apaya*. He kindly did so.

The sun-struck villagers, fully awake, called my name in repetition. I saw no babies, which seemed a mercy in this drought. I remembered several faces, some light in the eyes still shining like long before. Though taxed by years of lack and depletion, the villagers rejoiced. They welcomed us in. *Apaya* stood tall. He thanked *N'kai*. My lover canopied the scene like the acacia shade and held us all tight.

Lalesho told my story. I drank in their faces and the vast, blank hills behind. *Thank God he died before witnessing this devastation.* Everyone took turns, asking questions, studying my face for indications of my life apart from them. Over the big ocean. Despite our efforts to avoid his name, he perched in the center of all of us and our love. We did not say him, but every story intermingled with his bravery, his humor and provisions of care—all stories dead-ended with his large, godly, handsome self. How do you not say that?

Natiyon came out. Lalesho guided her to us. Salty half-moons flaked under her eyes. Her dress was midnight blue. Cotton. I marveled at it. When had the change come to this woman of skins and hides? Her own skin pulled in limp ripples across her shoulder blades. Her breasts hung down. She kept her dry hands folded one within the other.

Lalesho assured her she did not have to tell me the bad news, that he had already done so. "Micah has come to find you, not to locate your son."

She accepted the consolation, although she must have known the truth. Her eyes had regained some sight, the green mamba venom, a neurotoxin, taking years to leave her body. She looked shyly at me, off and on, so different then when she'd read my face with her strong, rough hands. That fire she'd stoked between us burned for merging, for earlier times. Now, she had to let it cool. I think the grief had erased her. She struggled to find a place for me, a spoke without our beloved wheel.

Landa and Mulu unloaded the supplies into her home.

*"Ndaa,"* I said. *Food.*

I wanted to tell her how well I believed he was, still so wonderfully clever, coming to me. Hands on my body, whispers in my mind. So I spoke to her with my heart.

Those without seats squatted. The villagers insisted I take a stool. Several times, I gave my stool away and just as often someone placed a seat under my butt, right next to a fresh mound of caprine poop pellets. The goats, fighting for little patches of shade, resembled pets rather than livestock. They were so few, dependent on any scraps they found. The village children, urged by their parents, came to thank me for the provisions. They did not dance and play as Lintan had. They came languidly, clinging to their mothers' skinny legs. Drought diminished every confidence. Every confidence but *Apaya's*. *Apaya* pranced with boyish levity, trying to locate ingredients for chai, which he obviously did not have—but found in the new supplies. Natiyon asked Lalesho to bring her some sweets. She doled out one piece of candy per child, some with mouths so small they could not fit the whole thing in. Saliva syrup ran down their distended bellies. Watching their older siblings, I wondered how our child would have fared. Despite everything, I found myself thinking about how long that syrup would take to come clean. Water here being as low as energy and morale.

Then *Apaya* and *Yeyo* sought private conversation under a nearby tree. They returned and Lalesho edited as needed, as he saw fit.

*Apaya* began. "Praise be to *N'kai* that I am able to see you again in my lifetime. Praise be to *N'kai* for bringing you here to us, our white daughter, our child. You have come in a drought and seeing you brings us much joy and some sadness. We don't have a goat healthy enough to slaughter for your honor and I have lost six children, one of whom you loved and who loved you. *N'kai* is mysterious. Perhaps it is better you have come now, bringing this food, you have saved us. Thank you so much child. Please greet your family. Please greet your mother and father and sister and everyone there in America which is so far from this place you have traveled to see us before we die."

Then *Yeyo*. "We have known a good past together but it is important for us all to move forward from this time, in a new relationship, and praise *N'kai* for allowing us to see one another again. You have given us gifts. I am getting old, and as you know my eyes are not good, which makes getting old more challenging. I would need a small operation to have my eyes fixed." Then she stopped and asked Lalesho something. He did not translate but I knew it was about my current condition. She saw the state of my health. Thinner. Weaker. Burning. Ever the healer, Natiyon asked a woman to make me the bitter malaria tea.

My turn. "I am honored to care for you both in any way you need, whether food, water, surgery. You are my family and I am happy you never forgot me. I have remembered you always, even though life and *N'kai* had other ideas and kept me from you for so long. I will pray for rain and for your sons, daughters, and livestock. I will try to come to Nanaiiolo again to see you before returning to America."

I drank two cups of malaria tea. I stood awhile at the acacia fence, remembering how Kas accompanied me when I was sick. How she stood up to the bullies in the field in Bamako, knowing no French. And how her spicy ChapStick made Lintan so very happy. How can we lose friends like that? I wished to share with her this new sense of purpose I felt, his encouraging hands on my back, guiding me forward into generosity.

I wrapped my arms around the village, many thanks to my husband's wallet, and assumed my lover's responsibility for his family. The malaria had a hard time keeping up with the speed of my heart.

Before Lalesho and I left, my African parents blessed us and blessed my family. No gap between us to bridge at all. For five long minutes, we stood in the heat, Natiyon's hands holding mine, singing out to *N'kai*. She spit on me, calling all angels. I held on tight. They both blessed my travels, my health, my name, my courage. They strengthened our reunion by saying, *"Ngang nabo," one family*, held together with generous and unbroken trust.

*Ngang nabo*—

A sweet breeze shook the acacia, and I laughed along with him. I touched *Apaya's* hands. I waved several times more. Mulu and Landa sat silently. I encircled my family and their village with a hopeful prayer and climbed into the car.

Driving back through spotted leopard land, the malaria symptoms worsened. Pain stole consciousness. I didn't care. We'd spent so long not saying his name I had to chant it loud, and out loud, and that benevolent act could only take place in Lamaresh, alone in my *banda*. The hours cut in and out like mirages, engine heat and the late fire of the sun, and finally, the roundabout that took me home.

When we arrived in Lamaresh I thanked the drivers, paid them and said to Lalesho, "I am going to my room. I do not want company. As long as this door is closed, I need privacy. It may take several days."

I dragged myself to my bed and called James with the oversized satellite phone, which I barely had the strength to hold. Nearly eight hours in a jouncing car, the reunion, the fever—I was all but undone. His voice sounded real and strong. He let me cry to him. He wanted to know everything. I could feel the gloss of delirium on my eyes. I did not tell him about the malaria.

"I will never be able to tell you what this means to me, James, your trust, your support. The way you see me. Life is so much more beautiful than I imagined." I ended the call and collapsed on my pillow. I cried and laughed until three or four in the morning, clutching my lover's memory to my body. He enveloped me, held me, and grieved with me as spirit does. I rocked and moaned and before the moon bowed to the sun, I saw another blessed ant in the same location, this time *under* the mosquito netting. I laughed aloud. I put the ant outside the window and said to the darkness, "Fine. Bite me." In the morning, three honey bees had gathered near his photo—a complete mystery how they got in, or why they were so quiet and still.

"Thank you," I said aloud. "Don't stop sending your gifts. I'm not ready to let go of you." I scooted the bees through the window. Three, a propitious number, a buzzy trio. They were back in the afternoon, same location, wandering drunkenly, weaving around the marigolds, honeycomb, and Ganesha statue. I watched them for several minutes, full of wonder, and then opened the window to free them once more. The more I saved and freed, the more life called me in.

It was easy to play with him here, play with all his displays of affection, under his sky, giant and blue, reigning over the red hills of Lokop land. "Let's just keep playing," I said. I loved his body. Why not love him in spirit? I felt afraid to lose our unbodied connection. The camel compound was our haven. Our playground. But then I knew that I could break all over again, I could do it just as I broke into being a woman when I had lost our child. Warrior strong, this love. I could play with my dead lover's spirit, however taboo that might be. It was nobody's business but ours.

I called this "the miracle." I shivered with fever. In broad daylight in this small room, I lost things, my one and only pen, my hand salve. He said, after watching me turn the *banda* inside out, *Check under your pillow.* They were both there, as awkward as ants. At night, I sang to the candle, and it fizzled back, clear as a voice. I crept out into the night garden and clipped flowers. I thanked him by enhancing his altar. And by loving every scrap of this Earth. By understanding, even requiring the dangerous beauty of his Africa. By sweating malaria and holding his parents close. And by healing.

*Ngang nabo—my leg.*
*Apaya?*
*Ditai!*


When I emerged from the *banda*, Lalesho waited for me with the security guard and gardener at Erayy. They had placed lawn chairs in front of my room, holding vigil, playing cards. I had not opened the door to daylight or eaten for three days. The fever burned all impurities, and my skin glowed with renewal, my eyes clear.

Honey bees followed me everywhere. They never stung, but they did a lot of mellifluous humming. People noticed, which earned me the nickname *Naisho,* or honey, in Gutok. My two-legged friends in Lokop land would not leave me, either, fearful I might sulk.

I saved my mornings for me and walked to spend every afternoon with Lintan and the children. I brought honey, which won over the kids, but what their mother wanted was my cacao protein bars. We hid from the children and stuffed our faces with those nutty, chewy treats. Laughing, I taught her how to say, "I could use a protein bar about now"—more for my enjoyment than hers. Lalesho and others looked at her so quizzically when she muttered the phrase, strange words trundling out of her beautiful, Gutok-speaking mouth. She wasn't altogether certain what it meant, but she appreciated the attention, the momentary panic it induced in men, and the fact we shared a secret.

I walked the children home from school, helped Lintan with laundry, and wrangled the mama goats and sheep for milking. African ranchers, Lintan and I were. Country cowpokes with breasts and cacao bars.

Whatever I could find to buy the family, I did. New mattresses, furniture Lintan had her heart set on, clothing, school supplies, cooking supplies, and new mosquito nets. She listened to my iPod for hours, a most American ear my dear Lintan had. Of all the songs, she favored *House of the Rising Sun* and *Ain't No Sunshine*, and I knew he was listening through her. I made her sing her Lokop songs. We said so much through our eyes. Mischief returned to Lintan's face. Her *shildrens* saw her as I had, joyful and bright. The world was a far better place for our coming together, unless the world sought a protein bar.

Lalesho visited often, distracted me with adventures, whether looking for big animals or locating the right battery for his Land Rover. Political work, in Africa, is very hands-on. He delivered jerry cans of water to villages. Sometimes I went along. I saw a few wells that used solar power to pump the water, otherwise people were forced to pay for diesel, extravagantly expensive and hard to lug home. These concerns preoccupied me, in a new way: they squelched any notion of self, myself, yourself. Nomads, like yogis, really got the whole "we are all one" concept. One suffers, we all do. One laughs, we all can.

One day, Lalesho invited me on a five-day journey. I protested, initially. I could not bear to leave my lover. But Lalesho said one word. Elephants. They had moved to water. He picked me up two days later, the car loaded with fuel and mattresses, four jerry cans full of water and a spare change of clothes. I climbed into the front and let my eyes drift over the open road, no telephone pole or electricity wires to interrupt the gaze, like looking out to sea—dry, golden sea.

Warring with washboards through dusty villages to Lokop National Park would take half a day. Because of the noisy ride, we spoke seldom. When I could hear, I shouted, my voice strange to my ears. "Lalesho—if you—could—live anywhere—in the world—where would it be?"

I wanted to know if he made peace with his life by imagining less difficult scenarios. Many of us did. Lalesho ignored me but such was his nature—if I wanted to know something, I almost always had to ask two or three times.

I said, "Why didn't you answer?"

Without taking his hands off the wheel, he said, "I did not answer because I have never had such a thought."

Good answer. Nomadic presence. Maybe my lover too, did not pine for greener pastures as often as I had imagined, but then again he loved a *Nalangu*, a foreign girl, who had pierced his present-mindedness and beckoned him elsewhere. *So many roads without end, my leg*.

I focused on the washboard and shut up.

We slept in a large tent on the banks of what was once a flowing river, elephant dung and cheetah prints as neighbors. In an effort to save both animals and tourism, the government piped water from Mt. Kenya to the park. Many animals had left in search of water and died; the distance too great to a viable source. Their hunger and thirst, my heartache—so much distance from viable sources. Normally death traumatized me. But with my sadness quota full, all I saw there was beauty.

The first evening baboons pried open the side car window and ate our food. They sprayed boxed milk throughout the car and then sprayed urine. The interior of Lalesho's pride and joy, a sticky Jackson Pollock painting. We used my credit card and dined at the posh Lokop Lodge. We grinned in our beat-up road clothes when the clean-shaven, cologne-smelling tourists arrived to eat.

A man in a crisp embroidered shirt serenaded us with sappy Swahili songs. I never liked those tourist welcomes. The airport in Nairobi rang with them. I ignored him, leaned my head over the open railing to watch the gazelles and giraffes nervously drinking the piped-in water. British bird watchers chatted. Wealthy retirees shook with delight at the easy views of wild animals. I suddenly wanted to hurl them all off the balcony. I fell into hot despair. Dressed in yesterday's filthy safari gear, with a bandana concealing my ratted nest of hair, I wanted to clean the temple. None of this should continue: the piped-in water, the drought, the opulent dining, the frivolous chatter, the disrespectful manner in which we gawked at animal souls, clinging, on the brink of survival.

I couldn't eat. I felt so lonely for him.

Our Swahili guitarist jammed a few hard chords and bellowed out *House of the Rising Sun*. A complete musical about-face. I spun to scrutinize the singer—were there signs of spirit-possession? Why this absurdly dark rambling-man tune when *Summertime* would have pleased the crowd? Why? Because in evidence of his continued love of surprises, my swift-footed king rambled from town to town, making me giggle. And Mr. Swahili belted out the lyrics of American miseries, ending in death and the eternal sun, which to me, knotted up his embroidery.

People chatted. I heard nothing but that song. I smiled through tears, hidden in the dim light. A warm breeze from the riverbed carried animal scents, caressed my shoulders as his hands used to do. He was here now, conducting a concert. Right now. I could have saved him a place at the table. But he no longer required it.

I breathed out. He breathed me. I invited him to use my body. Borrow my lungs. Possess me. Remember the power of breath. Be restricted. Borrow my legs and walk, my ears, and teach me to hear you. My voice, and laugh. *Borrow it, my leg. I am yours.*

Suddenly the grazing gazelles and giraffes scattered. A male lion bellowed. Lalesho turned his square head to me, instantly. "The only animals that don't fear this drought. They have no need to hunt. They eat what dies, and there is much dying."

And I thought, *Then the night air is alight with the glow of God.*

The following morning, I woke early to bathe; I walked alone down the river bed out of sight. I could still remember my lover's body bulldozing the sand, creating a hollow where water filled in. I dug my hole and waited. And waited. It took much longer in this drought, but a couple of fistfuls was all I needed. As I splashed the cool water onto my skin, a large shadow circled overhead. I looked up to see three eagles, spiraling against a pale blue sky and thought, *Maybe one day you'll drop a feather for me?*

I turned to the bush that held my clothes and discovered, teetering in a branch, the largest wing feather I had ever seen. I swept the dark-brown tip across my eyelashes, soft as a breeze, and walked under their syncopated shadows, feeling so beloved by the sky, the eagles, and my sweet man.

Lalesho, it seemed, took *Ngang nabo* to heart. On our drive back, he relived the months my lover lay in the hospital, fighting the infection. Losing.

"Natiyon told Lintan to find you in America. She said, 'Tell Micah he is sick. She will come.' Even he told me that you might come looking for him—"

"I did. I came with my sister, we searched Ukunda. I believe it may have been the year he died," I said, hoping he might try harder to remember an exact date. But no. I also gathered I would never know a precise diagnosis. Africans called all illness by three names: malaria, cancer, or AIDS. What I had learned from these people was that almost everything I thought I had to know, I didn't.

Lalesho rested his eyes and drove blind for the time it took a thicket of sandalwood to pass into dust. "He told me to take care of you and treat you like his family." And then he tainted the whole *one family* concept by adding, "I will be looking for a second wife. You could stay here with Lintan and her shildrens. Maybe you also want a baby."

I let silence speak for me.

He understood, but I knew Lalesho's tenacity hovered, biding time.

"He was not fearing to die, Micah. He told me that his sick leg was too strong for him. The next morning, he was dead."

We descended together into his memory of the hospital, the bindings of the flesh. "Who was with him when he died?"

"I was in Lamba, but not with him. His brother was with me, also. Maybe he died in the night while he was sleeping," he said, incapable of giving me the bad news directly, a characteristic so African. Be gentle and meandering with bad news.

"I am sorry to ask, but what did the hospital do with his body?"

"If he died in the village, we would put his body out for wild animals. This you know. The lions would have taken him. But he died in hospital, so they buried him." Lalesho broke left to avoid a gaping crater in the road. He looked up and said, "Do you need to see that place?"

"No, it's okay. He is not there." I would have loved to have one of his bones, maybe a femur. Why is that wish considered so morbid for everyone but archaeologists?

"I am happy you know that," he said.

*Know which*, I thought, *that spirit is no longer confined to body or that bones make good keepsakes?* My sense of humor had rounded a corner, lay within sight.

Lalesho looked right at me, letting on he *heard* me.

I felt the pressure of one knee on my chest and the whistle of an eagle in my throat.

Every day, I walked to see Lintan and the children. We ate and sang together, mostly the warrior songs. Lintan passed me the baby, and this time he let me hold him. She said, as she salted the cabbage, their next child would be called Micah. After lunch, I wandered outside and found *Apaya* resting under an acacia beyond the compound. No one knew he had come. A threadbare sheet with blue flowers wrapped his bony shoulders and chest. He sat motionless, watching the clouds move. I ran to this man who had spent more time outside than inside. A lifetime full of breeze tickle, sun, and desert nip.

*"Apaya?"* I called out. His response was delayed, literally re-membering himself, calling his mind and eyes back to this place.

*"Ditai!"* he sang out thinly. I sat with him. It was so wonderful, sitting. Lintan and her *shildrens* came to be with us. They all gathered for grandpa's stories and gentle teasing. That afternoon, when Lalesho returned from a meeting, we brought *Apaya* to Erayy for a beer and a meal. In a rare moment, away from the kids, Lintan held her father's arm and helped him into the booth. She sat beside him on fire with love, with pride. Her earrings jangled as she eased away the strangeness of forks and spoons, and joined him, eating with their hands. She winked at me, and I put down my silverware.

*Apaya* asked Lalesho to translate.

"I was in the back of a truck, and the trees were moving fast by me. The smell of fuel was less in the back so I wanted to ride there. When the vehicle stopped, the trees stopped but my body thought it was still moving and I fell down."

He had motion sickness even as I found him under the tree.

He continued, "Then I remembered how far *Micahai* has traveled to see us and I got up. *N'kai* has brought her to see us. You must get up, I told myself. When I see her, I see my son. And I remember him.

I have come to see her where she stays while in our care and to send her back with blessings for her and her family. I believe that my son has helped Micah find her way to us."

My heart leapt at his words, but his concentration broke. Sammy, the bar manager, turned on the small overhead TV in the corner. It played a nature video of the African savanna. A large elephant crossed the screen. *Apaya* asked in earnest astonishment, "How did they get that huge elephant into that small box?" His eyes widened in disbelief.

Lintan looked at her father with such understanding. And the future pushed toward us all.

Over the remaining weeks, I sought *Apaya's* company. A few minutes under a tree, giving him tobacco, sharing laughter, listening to the quiet. He was my fire born father and I was his daughter, strange as a phoenix passing time with a baby sparrow.

I treated his arthritic knees with homeopathy—*dawa ya miti* or medicine from trees. He asked for arnica. I held the tiny pellet in the cap and gestured for him to open his mouth. He tipped his head back, turned his face to the sky, and sucked the sugary pill in. The amber beads in his earlobes tilted, too, and I memorized the stubble on his narrow chin. My father told others, tribesmen who lived in Lamaresh, so I often woke to a line of suffering, smiling elders at my *banda*.

That line is all of humanity. Those who remain and those who have passed.

*Apaya* knew his ways were dying—his generation of nomads, the last keepers of The Story. They lived with nature, with spirit, with balance, in harmony. They lived without shame. The Earth knowledge that honored and guarded our sacred origins comprised stories, links told and retold. The elders kept that knowledge ablaze. That same fire fueled my lover's dancing. The chanting, the dancing, the dance like stars that told of humanity's well-traveled path to creation. *Apaya* kept it fresh by refusing to possess the words. He shared them—he shares them, elders gather around a fire, whisper the last Story, and vaporize like smoke.

Those of us left, when the keepers are gone, will sort the ashes, ragged with remorse. But ashes do not speak of the trees before them. Ashes return in silence to the Earth and wind.

We still flirt, my lover and me, nudging our worlds back and forth, back and forth across the thin veil. He sends foxes and hawks. He hands me auspicious synchronicities, some silly, some sacred. When I laugh, he nods in consort. When I pray in my half-nomad way, my beloved's face is God's face—one luminous facet of the infinite. He keeps one last, renewing surprise: he offers me my very own creation story to tell. Still today, my love for him colors the world in Goddess hues, a shining incandescence, where even the sordid has a certain beauty.

I now see God in the sparkle of dew, eagles and stars, cracked Earth and honeybees, every feather. Your eyes.

This planet, my temple.

Her ground, my pew.

Each vista, an altar.

Perhaps our fire circle, whether the stories are written or spoken, consists more of iron than of ash.

# Epilogue

I am a teacher. The first drafts of this book read like a prescription, full of medicine. I even employed the ever-motivating aspects of fear. I wanted everyone to know what humanity risked losing with the disappearance of nomadic peoples; I wanted the nomadic youth to realize that abandoning tradition, in the quest for modernization and shiny gadgets, had consequences. Today, I recognize my place in the circle of young elders, gathered around the council fire, picking up the threads of the Story and weaving it anew, into our current version of humanity and planet.

It still causes me sadness that a way of life, a beautiful version of the collective Story, so exquisite and balanced, must end, and it brings me joy to know this same way forged my character. This book is an attempt to cast it into eternity, not as an ancient artifact, but in rich vision and melody, requiring the reader's own experience, a personal alchemical remembrance, so this wandering way in us, this freedom of being, can never cease to exist. Now we are all the Keepers of The Story. May we use it to rebuild the fellowship of human beings on Earth in order to return to nature, to one another—the circle complete.

I still visit my family. Climate change and political turmoil continue to devastate Africa, especially nomadic lands. I send money every month. They give me courage and laughter. A reiki master asked recently, after our session ended, "Do you know you have an African warrior protecting you?"

I thank God for the nomads, and Goddess for the ecstatic poets. I cannot imagine life without either and it is their Story I wish to keep telling.

# Gratitude

For the Earth and all who dwell here on sky, sea, and soil. How true my community of support is; how far it stretches. I wish to thank you. To Kasia Martin for her friendship and her "why not?" To my mom Jolie Springer, because her trust in the rightness of things is stronger than a mother's fear, and her inability to criticize me propelled me naïvely forward. To Paul Batchelder for our secret conversations. To Lee Eldridge, my "laugh pardner," who is brilliant and belly-holding funny and whose devotion gave this story a cover and recycled paper pages. *I love you.* To my sister, Desi, for her insight and heart, and my other sister, Lintan, for hers. I am grateful to live life with you both. To Duane Springer for choosing sobriety and becoming a traveling companion, a wonderful father, and a friend. To Michael Pines and Apaya for teaching me to be a loving daughter. To James Gardner, whose love is as true as the sun. To Stephen Richards and Mark Collen for teaching me, each of you, about love and fallibility. To my first readers, Denisa, Fabian, Rada, Jane, Doug, Seth, and Gina. You helped me through doubt. To my champion of an editor, Barb Richardson, who cherishes trees and birds as much as one can, and who simply said "No" sometimes. To Deepak Chopra, who likes the title and taught me about non-local correlation. To Jalaluddin Rumi, Coleman Barks, and silence, for urging me toward ecstasy. To Eli Gottlieb for the brief, yet unforgettable handholding. To my Kenyan family, who called me "daughter" and stayed steady and loved me through time and miles. To Desi and John Friend's Bowspring inspiration. All writers should be required to practice it and remove the chair from the derrière. To CRMS for the view of humanity. To my Vital community who kept asking "when?" And finally, to my cats, Tigre (26) and Seva (11), for insisting, at times, I stop writing and do something useful, like play string-mouse.

I remained true to actual events, only changing names and places and one other tiny detail: Although in a year she should have, Kas never farted. I never heard a soft hiss.

*Currently, sourcing 100% post-consumer recycled fiber for publication is uncommon, and therefore challenging. A wonderful collaboration has been born between Micah's vision and Thomson-Shore's expertise, and this book as well as future books from Vital Plume will demonstrate our commitment to the trees, the Earth, and one another.*